DEMOCRACY AND CLASSICAL GREECE

DEMOCRACY AND CLASSICAL GREECE

SECOND EDITION

J. K. DAVIES

Harvard University Press
Cambridge, Massachusetts

Library of Congress Cataloging-in-Publication Data

Davies, John Kenyon.
　Democracy and classical Greece / by J.K. Davies. — 2nd ed.
　　p.　cm.
　Includes bibliographical references and index.
　ISBN 0-674-19607-4 (paper)
　1. Greece—History—To 146 B.C.　I. Title.
　DF214.D37　1993　　　　　　　93-795
　938—dc20　　　　　　　　　　CIP

Contents

List of Illustrations

Preface

TWENTY-FIVE YEARS ago Arnaldo Momigliano wrote: 'All students of ancient history know in their heart that Greek history is passing through a crisis.' The observation still holds. Some difficulties are technical – those of establishing a chronology, restoring the text of documents written on stones now broken, or integrating events which take place in different areas. Others have to do with sources, such as the challenges to emancipate ourselves from politico-military history and from the leisure-class bias of our literary sources, or to link archaeological finds with the record from narrative sources. Most fundamental of all is the problem of deciding what counts as a satisfactory interpretative understanding of events and social structures. In this book I have tried to illustrate such problems and to meet such challenges, while not losing sight of the plain unrolling of events which for most of us most of the time counts as 'history'. I am scarcely the best judge of whether that balance has been kept.

As to practicalities: the *maps* are meant to serve merely as guides to the places and areas named in the text. The political boundaries indicated on them are often only approximate. For the *abbreviations* and *conventions* used in the citations of sources see the section on Primary Sources (p. 269). The *translations* are sometimes my own, sometimes taken with or without amendment from Loeb, Penguin, or Everyman editions, and from publications in the LACTOR Series. For permission to use such published translations I am grateful to Messrs William Heinemann Ltd, Penguin Books Ltd, Messrs J. M. Dent and Sons Ltd, and the London Association of Classical Teachers.

For help during the writing of this book I owe thanks to many persons and institutions. It was first planned during a period at the Foundation Hardt in April 1973, and a substantial portion of it was written on leave of absence in Michaelmas term 1975: for these breathers I am most grateful to the Foundation and its Director, Professor Reverdin, and to the Provost and Fellows of Oriel College, Oxford. The publishers, in the persons successively of Michael Turnbull, R. B. Woodings, Colin Murray, and Helen Fraser, bore with forbearance and encouragement the delayed birth of a manuscript which was much longer, and arrived much later, than they had bargained for. Oswyn Murray as general editor, Russell Meiggs, John Ferguson, and Martin Ostwald all read some or all of the draft chapters. Their criticisms, suggestions and amendments saved the final version from many blunders and inclarities: their time, knowledge and helpfulness are most generous gifts of busy men. My chief debt is to my father, Harold Davies, whose thorough-going but constructive criticism of eight chapters amended innumerable points of substance and presentation, altered emphases and focuses, and made the whole thing more readable and less pretentious. To him and to all my warmest thanks.

Liverpool
December 1977

Preface to the Second Edition

ARISTOTLE'S SUCCESSOR at the Lykaion, that archetypal don Theophrastos, once remarked in a letter, 'Readings of one's works make for corrections. To postpone everything and to be uncaring is something which the younger generations no longer tolerate' (D.L. v 37): and if he really did have up to 2000 students at his lectures, as Diogenes reports, his problems and ours are not far apart. Feedback from colleagues and students suggests that this book found its niche not so much as a novice's first introduction to classical Greece but rather as a guide for a second round, when a more reflective and analytical eye can be cast on the political and social landscape. The two changes I have made are therefore meant to help such readers. First, the notes on Primary Sources and especially Further Reading have been considerably expanded, so as to flag a great proportion of significant recent work in English and thereby to bring self-tuition within closer reach. Secondly, because of the dramatic increase in work on Athens since 1978, a new chapter (XII) on fourth-century Athens has been inserted. The other chapters remain unchanged, apart from a few typogaphical corrections and the updating of references to some inscriptions.

Liverpool
July 1992

The Spelling of Greek Names

THE TRADITIONAL spelling of Greek names follows Latin rather than Greek practice; recently some scholars and translators have tried with more or less consistency to render Greek names according to their original spelling. In the interests of clarity we have adopted a compromise: generally geographical places and names of extant authors appear in their conventional Latinized form, other names in Greek spelling; but where this would lead to confusion we have not hesitated to be inconsistent. Apart from variations in the endings of names, the main equivalences are that Latin *C* represents Greek *K*, and in diphthongs Latin *æ* represents Greek *ai*. Where the difference in spelling is substantial, both forms are given in the index.

I

The Sources and their Limitations

GREEK HISTORY before 480, intricate, energetic, but largely self-contained, unfolded on or near the barbarian frontiers of Mesopotamian and Eastern Mediterranean civilization: for all the colonizing movement, its influence outside the areas of long-standing Greek culture was politically intermittent and geographically marginal. Greek history after 480 has entered the mainstream. With 478 marking the collapse of Persian expansion on the western border of their empire and 336 marking the start of the violent takeover of that empire by Greeks or quasi-Greeks, the limiting dates of this volume are not just Greek dates but are also, and even primarily, Eastern Mediterranean dates. In between, moreover, lies that period of Greek history wherein the long-term possibilities and limitations of Greek material, political and intellectual culture revealed themselves in full clarity – when much that was best in Greek art and literature was created, and when the Greek states and their inhabitants were at their most powerful, ambitious and quarrelsome.

It is also, of all periods of Greek history, the best documented – using 'document' in its widest sense. The non-verbal witness is itself substantial. Both in terms of sites – shrines, temples, fortifications, public buildings, houses, graves or the whole pattern of city and country settlement – and in terms of artefacts – sculpture, decorated or plain pottery, weaponry and other metalwork, coins, domestic objects, agricultural or craftsman's tools, jewellery – the bulk and quality of the tangible material alone reveal a rich and creative civilization, wherein at least *some* individuals and communities had moved far beyond subsistence level to command the human and natural resources of a wide area.

If we had no written material at all, it would still be right to speak of a major culture. Moreover, extant written sources allow us to create a political and social context for it with some precision. They fall into some six categories. Individual authors or sets of documents will need more detailed evaluation later, but it will be as well to begin by describing what we have in each category and by noticing some of the limitations of the written evidence. First, inscriptions – nearly all on stone, a few on bronze or lead tablets. Sparse before c. 460, they proliferate thereafter (above all in Athens) to yield hundreds of documents of varying importance, ranging from treaties, decrees of state, and accounts of public administrative committees to lists of names from public and private contexts, records of dedications to the gods, grave monuments and magical curses. They will be quoted extensively in this book, partly because translations are not easy to come by and new documents or additional fragments are emerging all the time, but mainly because their format and phraseology reveal more clearly than any other source how Greek public life was conducted and what it was thought important to record.

Second, the narrative historians (all readily available, as are nearly all the literary sources, in various translations in Loeb, Everyman, or Penguin editions or elsewhere). Those whose work survives in whole or in part give us an outline of political and military events, sometimes in remorseless detail, sometimes only as a basic minimum. The most detailed of them all is Thucydides' History of the Peloponnesian War, which gives a very full coverage from the late 430s until it breaks off in mid-sentence in late 411. His narrative was continued by Xenophon, in his extant *Hellenika*, down to the battle of Mantinea in 362. For the period between late 479, when Herodotus' narrative ended, and the late 430s, we depend mainly on a summary survey inserted by Thucydides as a digression, but for the whole period covered by this book we also have a very summary narrative compiled from earlier sources by Diodorus of Sicily in the 40s and 30s. What we have of him is books 11–20 of his *Historical Library*, covering the years 480–302 BC. Since his source for Greek mainland history in the years 479–31 was ultimately Thucydides, he is of little value there, but after 411 he was using historical sources otherwise lost save for fragments. We can now mostly identify them and be confident that he was using the best standard accounts, but he was not always very good at summarizing them.

These historical writers share certain characteristics. History as an art-form hovered uneasily between rhetoric and moral philosophy, and just as they all had strong views about the morality of this or that action, so too at critical moments they all gave their leading characters elaborate speeches which may or may not record what was actually said. Again, they concentrate above all on political and military affairs, leaving aside the wider ethnographic or cultural interests which Herodotus had inherited from the Ionian geographers of the sixth century. Thirdly, they are writing about Greek affairs in general, leaving local history and antiquities to become a separate genre (which we know of in this period only from fragments), and concentrate inevitably on the interrelations of the leading states. Lastly, they all faced the problem of narrating events in several centres, or theatres of war, at once, and devised various solutions such as strict sequence (so Thucydides) or grouping events in one area together until a natural break occurred (so Xenophon after 403 and some of Diodorus' sources). In consequence the exact dating of events is a perennial problem, not helped by the lack of any universally intelligible system of chronology. Since each city had a different calendar and a different New Year's Day, Thucydides had to date the start of the Peloponnesian War (431 BC in our terms) 'in the fifteenth year of the Thirty Years' Peace, when Chrysis had been priestess at Argos for forty-eight years, when Ainesias was ephor at Sparta and Pythodoros had two months to go as archon at Athens, in the sixth month after the battle at Potidaea and at the start of spring'. (2. 2. 1) Admittedly, matters became simpler once Hippias of Elis had constructed a list of winners since 776 in the original event at the Olympic Games, the *stadion* or 200-metre race. Thus for example Diodorus identifies the year 380–79: 'When the previous year had gone by Pytheas was archon at Athens. At Rome instead of consuls six tribunes were elected . . . The 100th Olympiad was celebrated by the Eleans, at which Dionysodoros of Tarentum won the stadion.' (15. 23. 1) It was still a very rough system, especially when used carelessly (as by Diodorus), to equate years which began in January, March, July and September. Hence we are often not sure in which of two or three years a given event took place, or even sometimes in which decade an anecdote or a document should be put.

A third category of evidence is Athenian speechwriting and pamphleteering. The boundary between speech and pamphlet is not easy to draw, for speeches survive only because copies were preserved by the author or written up for publication as a manifesto, and the first man who did this, the Athenian Antiphon in the 420s, also wrote speeches for imaginary occasions as samples of argument. About 145 speeches or speech-style pamphlets survive, distributed over the century from the 420s to the 320s, and we are fortunate in having the work of many different writers represented. They range from the great orators and stylists Lysias and Demosthenes through minor public figures such as Andocides or Apollodorus to speeches and pamphlets inserted in the 'collected works' of this or that author but certainly not by him. One of the most valuable of these anonymous works is a pamphlet of the 420s, ascribed (wrongly) to Xenophon in the tradition which has come down to us, describing Athenian society of the time from so jaundiced and reactionary a viewpoint that it is often called 'the Old Oligarch' (and will be so cited in this book). Apart from such pamphlets, speeches were written for delivery either in lawcourts, before mass juries of citizens, or in the assembly of the citizen population. Those in the latter group naturally concern public policy, and so may the former if they are part of the prosecution or defence of a public figure on charges arising from his political activity (and such charges came to be frequent, at least in Athens). Other lawcourt speeches concerned inheritance disputes, titles to citizenship, and so forth, and in that way tell us much about private law.

Biography is a fourth category. This genre seems to have developed out of late fifth-century pamphleteering, through the praise and blame of famous men: the earliest extant examples, by Xenophon and Isokrates, are decidedly hagiographic. Later writers in Greek and Latin picked up anecdotes about generals and politicians from earlier historians, and the most valuable contribution here was made by Plutarch, writing from c. AD 70–120. He read endless sources now lost to us, and combined an enviable (though sometimes uncritical) recall of them with his training and temperament as a stoic moral philosopher to produce, in his *Lives*, character sketches which are splendid vignettes of historical re-creation and psychological acuteness.

So far, all the sources mentioned have been in prose, but no historian dare ignore the poetry of the fifth century. Lyric poetry did not survive 450 as a major art-form, but, as we shall see, the context and contents of the extant choral odes of Pindar and Bacchylides tell us a great deal about the values and preoccupations of the upper class. So, too, though the Athenian tragedians of the fifth century dealt nearly always with mythological themes set in some remote past time, they treated these myths in terms of contemporary language and values, modes of argument, obsessions, and occasionally even political preoccupations. In consequence, their reworking of myth provides valuable historical evidence. Even more is this true for the extant plays of Aristophanes and for the fragments of the 'Old Comedy' of the fifth century. This genre was a weird compound of farcical contest, ritual obscenity, mythological burlesque, animal impersonation, escapist fantasy, and lyric poetry, and to this mixture was added political satire, caricature and comment from about 450 onwards. Unfortunately, we have no extant comedies after 388 till the plays of Menander, which were written from the 320s onwards and therefore lie outside the chronological limits of this book. However, it is worth adding that though the manic fantasy of Old Comedy has vanished, and the overt political content of Menander's plays is *nil*, yet their themes and obsessions – concerned above all with status, citizenship, wealth enough to be comfortable, and the strains imposed by romantic love – reveal all the more about contemporary wish-fulfilments by being expressed in quasi-realistic form.

The last category, philosophical writing and its congeners, is the most miscellaneous, for to the extant works of Plato and Aristotle can be added many monographs by other writers of a recognizably scholarly or scientific kind. They have in common the systematic collection and analysis of data and of recommended patterns of action in many fields, ranging from local history, oratory, political systems and military techniques to household and estate management, medicine, botany and mineralogy. For the historian – operating here as the sociologist of science – what matters most is the need to explain why this intellectual activity was being carried on as and when it was, but for the moment we need note only the bulk and quality of the information made available.

Yet the quality, quantity, and immediacy of this evidence is dangerously seductive. First, we have only a tiny fraction of what was once available. The philosophical and scientific writing of the fifth century is all but totally lost. The writings of many major historians, such as Ephoros and Timaios, or of local historians and antiquarians are lost except in brief citations or through Diodorus. Of the 158 *Constitutions of Greek States*, compiled by Aristotle or under his auspices, only one – that of Athens – survives, mutilated, on a papyrus copy first published in 1891. Against some 145 speeches or speech-style pamphlets preserved more or less intact we can set at least 440 known only by title or fragments. In any case what we have may not be the best, or most typical, of what there once was. For example, in 1908 and 1949 there were published some papyrus fragments of a first-rate, unidentifiable, and hitherto utterly unknown historian who continued Thucydides. We can now see that his account is the basis of Diodorus' narrative after 411, and we can tentatively name him. Yet were this book being written before 1908, we should have not the faintest idea of his existence, let alone his quality. Secondly, our sources for these two centuries concentrate overwhelmingly on Athens. Of Plutarch's fourteen extant *Lives* covering the period, eight are of Athenians. Of extant speeches, all but two were written for delivery at Athens. Surviving tragedy and comedy come almost exclusively from Athens, as does most philosophical writing and treatise-compila-tion. Against nearly 200 preserved Athenian decrees from the years 478–336, and several hundred other administrative documents, we can set no more than a trickle of epigraphic evidence from elsewhere (mainly from the great sanctuary-sites such as Olympia and Delphi). Only two documents illustrate the Peloponnesian War from the Spartan side, and many areas – Sicily, Southern Italy, Thessaly, Corinth – are epigraphic deserts. Thirdly, even apart from the preoccupation with Athens, there are other, more subtle biasses, visible only if we set the spectrum of what we *are* given in the sources against the spectrum of activities and preoccupations which can be predicated of Greek society in general. A specific instance: building accounts (e.g. for the Parthenon or the Erechtheion in Athens: for the shrine of Asklepios at Epidaurus; for the post-370 temple at Delphi) tell us a lot about major temple-building under public auspices, but nothing about public works constructed under private auspices, about minor or private cult-buildings, about private house-building, about the planning and construction of new settlements such as Thurii or Amphipolis, or about the new quarters at Piraeus, Olynthus, and Miletus. Or again, we have documents about cults and festivals, in the form of dedications, calendars of sacrifices, or lists of victors in cult-linked athletic or musical contests. Yet such documents inevitably reflect the formalized public act, just as religious poetry and mythography reflect the creative but intellectualizing search for the origins, and thereby for an explanation and validation, of traditional rituals. The ecstatic or spectacular or magico-sympathetic sides of Greek religion are far less well reflected, and the most fundamental of all, which has to do with symbolizing, and easing passage through, the main crises of life (birth, puberty, marriage, childbirth, bereavement, and death), more poorly still. More generally, we learn about wars, politics, and lawsuits in some detail, but precious little about the everyday business of getting a living in the fields or the vineyards, on the mountain pastures, in the craftsman workshops, down the mines, on board ship, or in the household. Women and slaves scarcely exist, whether as individuals or as groups; we are always being directed, willy-nilly, towards the activities and preoccupations of the upper or leisure class. Lastly, and perhaps most important of all, the Homeric traditions of formulaic utterance died hard. A 'document' is something formulated in terms of a relatively restricted number of clear-cut genres, and its existence and survival derive from what the writer and his society thought had value and from the influence which form had on expression. We have no one's 'private papers'. If we exclude the collections of letters which are either political or later forgeries, or both, we have just two private letters written in Greek before the 320s. There are scarcely any graffiti of the sort which make the study of Pompeii so entertaining. Even the potsherds inscribed with the names of Athenian politicians, and used as votes in the process of exile by ostracism, are mostly taciturn and eschew what would be, for us, usefully rude language. So outwardly personal an expression, on a curse-tablet from Athens, as '(I curse) Kittos the branded slave net-weaver and his handwork and his workshop, Euphrosyne the net-weaver and her handwork and the workshop, Philomelos of Melite and Phileas of Melite (and) Eugeiton son of Eugeiton of Acharnai' (E. Ziebarth, *SBAkad. Berlin* 1934, 1032 No. 5), is deeply formulaic, as its congeners show. Granted, new forms and genres were always emerging and crystallizing, but throughout our documentation we shall always have to cope with a deep-seated elusiveness of shaped and formalized expression.

Our documentation, then, is less straightforward than it seems. We must indeed start with it, and stay with it and with the problems it poses in its own terms, but we must also try to fill its gaps and to free ourselves from its biasses. We can best do so by searching for interpretative themes and patterns and by moving as directly as possible towards a general reconstruction of Greek history and society. Fortunately, one helpful fact will emerge. Even for oligarchies or monarchies it would be rash to speak of politics and power as an autonomous area, effectively confined to a small, clearly defined élite. Rather, whatever form it took, there tended to be a high degree of inter-penetration between the 'political' area and the economic foundations of life (especially the ownership of land), social values as a whole, and the content of artistic expression. The source material does reflect the relationship, however obliquely, so that though this book inevitably leans towards political and social affairs at the expense of the figurative arts, imaginative literature, or philosophical thinking, we shall be dealing with a cultural continuum. The extent to which it was to move towards political unification will preoccupy us throughout: to see what was favouring, and what was hindering, this movement in the circumstances of 478 is a good starting-point.

II

The Greek World in 478

WHEN WE SPEAK of 'Greece' in 478, we mean both more and less than present-day Greece. It included a large portion of what is now Libya, most of Cyprus, a more or less continuous strip of land up the western coast of Turkey from Rhodes to the Hellespont, scattered settlements all around the Black Sea, the Gallipoli peninsula, a strip along the North Aegean coast, scattered settlements up the east coast of the Adriatic as far as Albania, most of the toe of Italy and most of Sicily. Conversely some areas of present-day Greece either were not Greek (Thrace) or were not normally felt to be (Macedonia) (see map 1). This geographical delineation is well enough assured, from historians and later antiquarians, from finds of inscriptions written in Greek, and from the archaeological evidence of temples, houses and public buildings of recognizably Greek style. It is less simple to define what made the Greek world Greek. One way is to accept that we are observers from outside, and to identify some of the ways in which it differed from ours, even though concepts such as 'politics' and 'democracy', 'ethics', 'rhetoric', 'logic', or 'geometry' are our inheritance from it, and even though so many of the patterns of public and private life (written laws, coined money, deliberative decision-making) are superficially or deep-rootedly similar to our own. Some differences are salient: religious practices based on polytheism and linked closely with fertility and the seasonal year; widespread slavery, appearing as chattel slavery or as serfdom according to local circumstances; full literacy only for a minority, but semi-literacy probably extending well down the social scale of free men; and political units so small that present-day Luxembourg would count as one of the larger states.

The implications of such differences are clear. Others, though equally revealing of the gulf between Greek society and our own, need more subtle handling. I mention two only. First, we can be virtually certain, by analogy with other pre-industrial societies, that well over half, perhaps even 90 per cent, of the adult population (slave or free, man or woman) will have been engaged in agriculture. Communities were therefore above all aggregations of peasant households. They might become towns, if craftsmen and the political élite moved in as well. There was a tendency to move towards places which had been Mycenaean castles (e.g. Thebes, Athens, or Orchomenus) or had a defensible Acropolis habitable in an emergency. However, it seems to have been only in the sixth century that towns grew large enough to need specifically urban facilities such as walls, drains, and fountains, and, as we shall see, in many areas urbanization had yet to begin in 478. In consequence, since many cult-spots such as the major oracles at Delphi and Dodona had become important before urbanization gathered pace, many precincts and temples such as those of Hera outside Argos or of Apollo at Bassae in Arcadia lay in open country. The power-relationships between temple and local communities were therefore sometimes tense and complicated.

The second major difference was the virtual absence of fossil fuels. True, iron and bronze were available and were used for weaponry, ploughshares, and so on. However, they were smelted with charcoal, and were scarce enough for most household or agricultural utensils to be made of wood or reeds or pottery. (This is why, since the other fabrics have perished, the various shapes and sizes of pottery containers, each with its particular use, take so prominent a place in any museum.) So too charcoal or wood were the fuels for cooking, and even they may have become scarce. We hear of erosion and deforestation: timber for Athenian ships had to be imported from Thrace or Macedon: and even the structural timbers of Athenian houses were removed if the house had to be abandoned. Transport by sea depended on sail or oars, by land largely on panniers carried by men or mules. Roads were too bad, and harness too inefficient, to allow much use of wheeled vehicles. An army marched, or went by sea: for one state to communicate with another meant sending a herald or an envoy and awaiting his return. Clothes were mostly made at home, this being work common to women of all ages and statuses. Artificial light came only from vegetable oils, which provided a minimum indoors and nothing outside. Moon and stars therefore matttered enormously, all the more because they also provided the only reliable signals of the seasons for sailors and farmers. Lastly and not trivially, Greeks lived in a world entirely without clocks.

Much of all this could of course be said about all Mediterranean or European communities of the period. Yet Greeks rightly thought that compared with many others they were notably civilized and enjoyed a distinctive culture. We have therefore to define in what senses Greece was, and was felt to be, a unit, in the absence of any administrative capital or cultural centre. We shall have to distinguish between, on the one hand, the factors common to all Greek communities and, on the other, those which impinged on particular areas and cities. This distinction will also help us to understand why different areas went on to follow very divergent political and cultural paths. The most illuminating single source will be the *Histories* of Herodotus. The main thread of his narrative ends with the military campaigns of 479, but his anecdotes and discursive descriptions illuminate the values and attitudes of a man born in the 480s and writing in the 440s and 430s.

The first and fundamental factor common to all Greek communities was of course the Greek language – or rather the Greek languages, for there seem to have been as many 'dialects' as there were communities. Herodotus describes the extreme case in saying that the Ionians

do not all speak the same language, but have four types of divergences. To the south their first city is Miletus, and then Myus and Priene. All these three are settlements in Caria and have the same dialect. Their cities in Lydia are Ephesus, Colophon, Lebedos, Teos, Clazomenae, Phocaea. Those cities do not agree at all in speech with the forementioned, but share a common dialect with each other. There are three other Ionian cities, of which two are islands, Samos and Chios, and one, Erythrae, on the mainland. Chios and Erythrae share the same

dialect, but the Samians have one to themselves. These are the
four varieties of speech. (Herodotus 1. 142. 3–4)

Again, the 'Old Oligarch' noted how the Athenians 'from hearing
every dialect have adopted this from one dialect and that from
another. Each Greek community tends to have its own speech
and habits of life and dress, but the Athenians have theirs blended
with elements from all the Greeks and barbarians' (*Old Oligarch*
2. 8). It is a measure of our ignorance that from the available
literary and inscriptional evidence we cannot identify the distinctions Herodotus referred to, which may have been apparent
only in the spoken language. However, we can at least identify
the major dialect-groups (Ionic/Attic: Doric: Aeolic: Arcado-
Cypriote: NW Greek) and see that none of them counted as
'standard' Greek. There was no such thing. We can see, too, that
though Athenians, for example, found the Doric speech of
Megara or Sparta comic, ears were attuned to other dialects well
enough to understand them, while Greeks never seem to have
found difficulty in understanding documents or literary works
written in another dialect. This continuum of speech and
literature is fundamental. It formed the basis of the division
between Greek and 'barbarian'. It created an equation between
'Greek', 'Greek-speaker', and 'civilized' so strong that even the
Roman conquest of the Eastern Mediterranean barely broke it.
Conversely it made possible, by cultural-linguistic assimilation on
the part of outsiders, the near-infinite extension of the field of
reference of 'Greek' which followed in the wake of Alexander's
conquests.

In close association with a common language and literature
come, as a second unifying factor, certain common institutions,
above all those of cult and religion. The Apollo worshipped at
Delos, the Apollo Pythios of Delphi, and the Apollo Karneios of
Sparta may well once have been separate gods, but the perceived
similarities had long since led to their assimilation in the guise of
god of all Greece. The same had happened for all the other major
gods, and their interrelationships had been expressed as a 'divine
family' long enough ago for the poetry of Homer and Hesiod to
reflect them and to serve as the main point of departure for Greek
theology. Similarly, myths about gods and heroes were widely

known, through epic, lyric, and (in its infancy) tragic poetry, through sculptural representations on temples, paintings on vases, and so on, though some myths were linked to certain cities and cult-spots and were therefore mainly commemorated locally for chauvinistic reasons. The spectrum of forms of worship and ritual was the same everywhere: prayer direct to the god, sacrifice of foodstuffs (animal or vegetable, burned at the altar or not), dancing, singing, and the dedication of votive offerings. So were sacred enclosures, altars, shrines, and (from the ninth century onwards) roofed temples. Belief in pollution and the possibility of purification, in various forms of oracular utterance and prophecy, or in the protection given by Zeus to beggars and suppliants, were common to all. Moreover, though of course most religious expression took place within the local context of household, village, or city-state, there were shrines, cult-acts, and festivals of pan-Greek appeal and importance, which would be frequented sooner or later by people from all Greek states.

A third common element which we can single out and see reflected in the sources is that political societies, by and large, had similar organizations and senses of community. Herodotus makes a character say to King Xerxes of Persia in 480: 'When the Spartans fight individually, they are second to none, but when they fight in a body they are the best of all. The reason is that though they are free, they are not completely so, because they have a master over them – the law – which they fear more than your subjects fear you' (Herodotus 7. 164. 4). Ironically the speaker was the deposed Spartan King Demaratos, in exile at the Persian court, but his point holds good. Such authoritarian or non-accountable governments as had existed had by now been generally repudiated in favour of constitutional forms, however rudimentary and oligarchic (as in Sparta itself); of fixed (but not yet necessarily written) codes of laws; and of a sovereign governmental unit, the 'city-state', which can be given a basic definition. This definition consisted *not* in terms of an area or a set of peoples unified simply by being ruled over by a monarch through dynastic inheritance or amalgamation or force of arms, but in terms partly of geographical unity and partly of the participation of all the citizens in some real or fictional kinship- or descent-group structure. It is fair to call this the predominant pattern, true of most of the states which played a significant role in the cultural history and the power-politics of the fifth and fourth centuries. At the same time there were major and significant exceptions. Non-accountable monarchy or something much like it survived, notably on the geographical periphery in Cyprus, Sicily, and the as yet scarcely urbanized mountain areas of North-West Greece. Another form of monarchy survived in Sparta herself. For reasons which remain totally undiscoverable, she had two kings, one each from two quite independent royal houses. Their powers had been attenuated with time, but they remained hereditary commanders-in-chief of the army and, if they had the ability, they could use their position, continually at the centre of affairs, to become major politicians on a national and international scale. In other areas, such as Arcadia and Achaea, networks of small cantonal communities were slowly becoming federal organizations which would prove to have a better capacity for survival and adaptation than the big unitary nation-states. However, the attraction of the city-state as administrative unit, cultural unit, and political unit was so strong that other forms of political organization were increasingly assimilated by it. The documentation of Delphi, for example, shows how the settlement round the shrine gradually took on more and more of the administrative characteristics of a miniature city-state.

Of the two defining criteria of a city-state, geographical unity and kinship structure, the second mattered more. The sentiment of unity-by-kinship and common descent could survive geographical fragmentation, the physical transplantation of the community, or its forcible suppression for years or even generations. It was reinforced both by the tribal nature of the segments which comprized every Greek polity we know of (even when, as in Athens, new and 'artificial' ones were created), and by the way in which citizenship was a purely hereditary status. In Athens,

those born of citizen father and mother have citizenship. They are enrolled among their fellow-demesmen at the age of 18. When they are being enrolled, the demesmen take a vote on oath about them, first to decide if they seem to be of legal age.

If they are not, they are demoted to being 'boys' again. They then decide if they are free and were born according to the laws. (*Athenian Constitution* 42. 1)

Similarly, the questions asked of a magistrate-elect before he was entitled to hold office were

Who is your father and of which deme? Who is your father's father? Who is your mother? And who is your mother's father and of what deme? After this they ask if the candidate has an Ancestral Apollo and a Zeus of the Courtyard, and where their shrines are. Then they ask whether he has family tombs and where they are, and then whether he treats his parents well and performs his civic duties and has served on the due number of military campaigns. (*Athenian Constitution* 55. 3)

One sees how secondary the last three questions were to considerations of proper status in the descent-group. If possible, status-considerations mattered even more in Sparta, with consequences in the form of tensions and contradictions which we shall explore in Chapter Eight. They could be felt strongly even at the ethnic level: just before the invasion of 480, Xerxes, King of Persia, hoped to secure Argive neutrality by sending this message:

Men of Argos, King Xerxes speaks thus to you. We Persians deem that the Perses from whom we descend was the child of Perseus the son of Danae, and of Andromeda the daughter of Kepheus. Hereby it would seem that we come of your stock and lineage. So then it neither befits us to make war upon those from whom we spring; nor can it be right for you to fight, on behalf of others, against us. (Herodotus 7. 150. 2)

Whether his claim, which the Argives accepted, counted for them as a reason or as a rationalization is immaterial. What mattered and matters is that it was suitable and effective.

The fourth common factor we can single out is a generally comparable level of technology and resources. In itself it hardly serves to distinguish Greek culture crisply from those of the rest of the Mediterranean, the Balkans, or the Near East (any more than does the city-state, prevalent in contemporary Etruria and on the Phoenician coast). Yet some uniformities inside the Greek linguistic area can be seen to have been felt as defining characteristics, while others are visible to the observer through literary texts or material remains. It may be helpful to illustrate the latter category first, in respect of the three most fundamental activities of any Greek community, farming, building and fighting. Unfortunately the most basic, farming, is also the worst documented and the least explored by modern scholars, so that what follows here can only be a preliminary and tentative sketch. The evidence is unhelpful. There are a few representations, on vases or sculptural reliefs, of agricultural implements and processes (see Plate 1). There has been some aerial photography, but enough rather to be frustrating than to show the ancient cultivation pattern or the distribution of rural settlement. A few large farmsteads of the classical periods have been excavated in Attica and on the island of Chios, and a few metal implements have survived from the town-site of Olynthus in Chalcidice, destroyed by Philip of Macedon in 348. Lastly, there is a certain amount of literary material, which shows all too clearly how silk purses have to be made out of sows' ears. For example, the only indication of seasonal migration, or 'transhumance', as still practised by the Vlachs between Mt Pindus and the Gulf of Arta, comes from a scene in Sophocles. A messenger recognizes an old slave of Oedipus' father Laius, and explains why:

I know well that he recognizes the time when he frequented the Cithaeron area with two flocks, and I with one flock was this man's neighbour for three whole six-month periods, from Spring till the rising of Arcturus. Once winter came I drove my flocks to my folds, and he drove his to the stables of Laius. (Sophocles, *Oedipus the King* 1133–9)

We have no means of telling how common transhumance was, whether in Old Greece or Sicily or Asia Minor. Again, though there grew up a voluminous technical literature about farming (the Roman writer Varro says he has read over fifty Greek writers), all that survives to us, apart from Theophrastus' two lengthy treatises on plants and Hesiod's eighth-century epic *The Works and Days*, is Xenophon's short treatise *Oikonomikos*, about half of which concerns estate management. Creations such as market-gardens or ornamental parks emerge merely from casual references in an Athenian speech or inscription. Knowledge of the practices of the seasonal year has to come from Hesiod, or from the agricultural associations of dated cults and festivals, or even from the assumption of continuity of practice until recent times. It is quite by chance that Pliny the Elder transmits the remarkable information that 'Lucerne grass is foreign even to Greece, having been imported from Media during the Persian invasions under Darius' (*Natural History* 18. 144). Even so fundamental a thing as the balance, in various areas and periods, between tenant-farming, slave-worked estates, and peasant freeholding is totally beyond us. Nonetheless, some uniformities can be perceived, albeit at a fairly elementary level. First, dry farming was universal, with a heavy concentration on corn staples (barley or wheat according to the soil). Again, whatever soil could be tilled was tilled: pasture was a matter only for marginal land, and animals were kept far more for dairy products, hides, and wool, than for meat. Thirdly, the interculture of crops with olive trees may have been as common as it is today in the same areas. Lastly, vines, olives, and figs were so universal and fundamental a source of food as to be defining characteristics of Greek culture. Beer-drinkers such as Thracians and Egyptians were distinguishable on that very account, and it has long been seen that the northern limit of Greek penetration in the North Aegean and in the Black Sea corresponded closely to the northern limit of the cultivation of the olive.

Of building we know rather more, mainly of course because some of the actual fabric of so many buildings survives or can be disinterred, but also because again there developed an extensive technical literature from the sixth century BC onwards, dimly reflected in Roman writing. The trouble is that most of the source material, whether tangible or in the literary tradition, concerns temples and other public buildings. Houses in city or country were made of less durable materials, seem to have been fairly unpretentious, at least until the later fourth century in Athens, and aroused virtually no artistic interest. Yet even these facts already tell us something important about classical Greek society, and point a sharp contrast to the key social roles of the large house, roles which can be imputed to the Mycenaean palace or Homeric *megaron* and which still survive in part for us from feudal and Renaissance Europe. Moreover, though such house-plans as we now have show endless variations, they also reveal a strong family likeness. The basic principle, of building round a small courtyard which incorporated a south-facing portico or peristyle and served as the focus of the rooms, is universal, whether in city or country, in large houses or small (see Plate 2). Xenophon formulated general Greek practice in making Sokrates say:

> In those houses, then, that look toward the south, the winter sun shines down into the porticoes, while in summer, passing high over our heads and over our roofs, it throws them in shadow. To obtain this result, therefore, the part of the house facing south must be built higher in order that the winter sun should not be excluded, whereas the part facing north should be built lower so that the cold winds do not strike it. (*Memorabilia* 3. 8. 9)

Even more appropriately can the term 'family likeness' be applied to temples and public buildings. True, there were variations: the 'orders' of architecture (Doric, Ionic, Aeolic) had originally been real regional styles, while the Western Greek colonies developed certain architectural traits of their own. However, by now the regional styles had so inter-penetrated geographically and stylistically that one can properly speak only of continual experiment and innovation inside a common tradition of genres of buildings and of structural and decorative components. Architects copied each other, emulated each other, and might execute commissions in more than one city or region. Iktinos, for example, worked on the Parthenon at Athens and on the remote temple of Apollo at Bassae in Arcadia, and a century later Pytheos worked on the mausoleum at Halicarnassus, the temple of Athene at Priene and probably also the temple of Zeus at Labraunda. As these examples show, the unity of the tradition was further reinforced by the fact that the buildings which they were asked to design had to fulfil the same sort of cultic or civic or military function in each locality.

Of the three activities of farming, building and fighting, fighting is the one we know most about, for various reasons. Some weaponry survives, in physical form or in representations, but this evidence helps less than it might because Greeks were now ceasing to bury weapons with the dead and because vase-painters lost interest after about 450 in showing scenes of arming or fighting by land. Rather, our information comes from the extant historians, who spent much of their time in describing war in greater or less detail, from the technical treatises of Xenophon and Aeneas which survive from the fourth century, and, more indirectly but pervasively, from the whole literary tradition. Fighting by now involved so high a proportion of the free adult male population of each state, and was so embedded in the exemplary exploits of myth and history, from the *Iliad* through the labours of Herakles to the heroes of Marathon and Salamis and Plataea, that it provided a common ideal of manly action and the framework for a substantial part of the moral code. True, war and fighting lost this central position, and the search for a less combative base of moral action yielded contradictory solutions, but for the moment what matters is the evidence for common military practice rather than for a common moral framework. First, naval warfare did indeed show much uniformity. The 200-man fighting galley, the trireme (see Plate 3), had become the standard warship of all major Greek fleets in the previous generation, and was to remain so till the 330s, vulnerable, unseaworthy, and ludicrously expensive to man and to maintain though it was. However, this uniformity was not so much specifically Greek as a part of a naval tradition common to all the major maritime powers of the Mediterranean – Greeks, Phoenicians, Carthaginians, and Etruscans. The variations and innovations in design and tactics which we hear of are mainly Greek, but that reflects our Greek-centred source-material rather than historical facts. Indeed, the one major new departure we do hear of, the invention of the *tetreres* in order to put the pulling power of four men (two men on each of two oars) in the room within which the trireme allowed only three, was not Greek but Carthaginian, as we learn from a fragment of Aristotle (F 600) preserved in the Elder Pliny. Again, Diodorus says that in 399 Dionysios I of Syracuse took the idea a step further and 'had decided . . . to build ships of *tetreres* and *penteres* types, no ship of the latter size having ever been built at that time' (14. 41. 3), but the sources say nothing about the spread of the new types until 18 *tetrereis* suddenly emerge in the Athenian dockyard accounts of 330–29. However, more specifically tending towards the creation of a common Greek tradition was the fact that manning the major fleets of the fifth and fourth centuries was always a problem beyond the resources of the single states. Rowers had to be hired from other areas (especially the Aegean islands), and experienced men could and did go where the money was. In this way there came to exist a mercenary pool of common skills, available to states or even individuals. In 434, for example, 'Corinth, exasperated by the war with the Corcyraeans, spent the whole of the year after the engagement and that succeeding it in building ships, and in straining every nerve to form an efficient fleet; rowers being drawn from Peloponnese and the rest of Greece by the inducement of large bounties.' (Thucydides I. 31. 1)

Again, in 361 the commander of an Athenian warship at the Hellespont found that his tour of duty was being prolonged and that:

> many of my crew became disheartened and deserted the ship, some to take up military service on the mainland, others to the ships of Thasos and Maronea, attracted by high wages and having received a lot of money in advance . . . I suffered more desertions than the other trierarchs, . . . since their men had come on board as conscripts and stayed on board so as to get back home safely, while mine, who trusted in their abilities as rowers, went off wherever they reckoned to get most money . . . So I sent my assistant officer Euktemon to Lampsacus with some money and letters to my father's guest-friends, and told him to hire the best sailors he could, while I stayed at Sestos, gave what money I had to the previous sailors who stayed on, . . . and hired others at full rates. (Demosthenes 50. 14–18)

We shall see how pervasive such mercenary service later becomes, on both land and sea.

Common practice in land warfare is even easier to discern, for the standard fighting man throughout Greece in 478 – as for the previous two centuries or so – was the hoplite, the citizen foot-soldier heavily armed with metal helmet, corselet, greaves, sword, and spear, providing his own armour and weaponry, brigaded in tribal or local regiments and trained for murderous, set-piece, close-formation fighting on level ground. True, as befitted a living tradition, there was variation and innovation. For example, the chain-mail corselet was a recent development, as was the slashing sword (see Plate 4), while the shape and design of helmets had always varied regionally, but these were variations inside a narrow range as substantially uniform in Greece as it was unique to Greece in the whole European-Mediterranean zone. There was good historical reason for such uniformity. Greek states had fought each other so much in the previous two centuries that a rough comparability of weaponry, tactics, and skills had become a prerequisite of survival, while the relative unimportance of archery, cavalry, or light-armed infantry had its roots in the geographical position of the leading and most combative states of the previous century. Sparta, Corinth, Argos, Athens or the Aegean island-states occupied areas where horse-breeding sterilized too much valuable land for it to be tolerable on a militarily significant scale and where battles were not about passes or upland pastures but about the possession of the agriculturally fertile plains. Nonetheless, good historical reasons were gradually to become bad historical reasons, and the partial erosion of the classical hoplite tradition is a recurrent theme of the military history of the fifth and fourth centuries. It came about partly because of innovation inside the hoplite tradition, partly because Athens' wealth and connexions allowed her to employ mercenaries of different military traditions (Cretan, Scythian and Thracian archers, slingers, and light-armed men), but mainly because powers whose military resources lay in other directions came to impinge much more directly than hitherto on Greek affairs. There will be a close and complex link between the erosion of the central military role of the hoplite, the erosion of his central political role, and the erosion of the value-system which he symbolized.

Beyond the uniformities of farming, building, and fighting, and helping to mould the forms they took, there lay, as a fifth common factor, the most salient uniformity of Greek resources – their scarcity or absence. As Herodotus made Demaratos say, 'Poverty has always been Greece's foster-sister, while our valour is an acquisition laboriously created from practical intelligence and strict law.' (7. 102. 1) His emphasis on law may well be his own (see p. 13), but it merely makes more complex and striking a formulation which was a cliché in Euripides ('Poverty espoused practical intelligence because of their close kinship' (F 641)). Yet thoughts become clichés precisely because they encapsulate continuing facts, and poverty was indeed a primary fact. True, the occasional city was lucky enough to possess a surplus of agricultural or mineral resources whose exploitation changed the picture. Herodotus records how about 525 'The Siphnians . . . were at the height of their greatness, no islanders having so much wealth as they. There were mines of gold and silver in their country, and of so rich a yield, that from a tithe of the mines the Siphnians furnished out a treasury at Delphi which was on a par with the grandest there. What the mines yielded was divided year by year among the citizens' (3. 57. 2). Likewise, Diodorus tells us that just before its capture and sack by the Carthaginians in 406:

> both the city and the territory of Acragas enjoyed great prosperity . . . Their vineyards excelled in their great extent and beauty, and the greater part of their territory was planted in olive-trees from which they gathered an abundant harvest and sold it to Carthage; for since Libya at that time was not yet planted in fruit-trees, the inhabitants of the territory of Acragas took in exchange for their products the wealth of Libya and accumulated fortunes of unbelievable size. Of this wealth there remain among them many evidences. (13. 8. 4–5)

The temples which he goes on to describe still confirm his point (see Plate 5a). The same explanation probably accounts for the even more spectacular complex of temples at Selinus, further west – and closer to Carthage – along the Sicilian coast.

However, exceptions should not mislead. Rarely, in any areas of Greece, was the margin of available food-supply over

population, or of other resources over needs, enough to extend
even the elegancies of life, not to speak of leisure or luxuries, to
more than a tiny fraction of the population. Admittedly, our only
approach to quantitative evidence comes from Athens and even so
is sketchy in the extreme, but it is probably fair to say of fifth- and
fourth-century Athens that fewer than 1000 men out of a total
population which may have reached 250,000 could be called 'rich'
in normal Greek parlance. In 300 Demosthenes could say
seriously of his law of 340, which transferred the responsibility
for financing warships from the richest 1200 men to the richest
300, that

> I could see, men of Athens, that your navy was going to rack
> and ruin and that the rich were getting tax exemptions in return
> for small outlays, while citizens who had small or moderate
> properties were losing their substance and the city was missing
> her opportunities in consequence. I passed a law by which I
> compelled the rich to do what was equitable, and stopped
> injustice being done to the poor. (18. 102)

'Rich' in this context means owning an estate worth 3–4 talents or
more, and consistently a contemporary speaker could tell a jury
that 'My father left property worth only 4500 drachmai (¾ of a
talent) each to my brother and myself, and it is not easy to live off
that' (Demosthenes 42. 22). Twenty years earlier Demosthenes
had described as 'a poor man, uninvolved in public affairs, but
not a villain' the man of full hoplite status who had acted as
arbitrator between Demosthenes and his opponent (21. 83 and
95). Much the same use of language is attested, spasmodically but
consistently, from all over Greece. One assumes, cautiously, that
it reflects a similar economic reality.

Moreover, the evidence of language is not simply economic. In
the 420s the Old Oligarch contrasted, on the one side, 'the
knavish', 'the poor', 'the mass', 'the plebians', 'the men of the
people', 'the worse people', and 'the raving men', and on the other
'the virtuous', 'the noble', 'the rich', 'the powerful', 'the best', 'the
most able', 'the most good', 'the few', 'the fortunate', and 'the
farmers'. Nearly a century later, in his *Politics*, Aristotle
contrasted 'the few', 'the wealthy', 'the better', 'the best', 'the

notables', 'the reasonable and fair', 'the men who are reasonable and fair and able to enjoy leisure', 'the unequal in property', 'those distinguished by virtue' and 'the well-born with ancestral virtue and wealth', with 'the populace', 'the masses', 'the mob', 'the poor', 'the manual labourers', 'the workers for hire', 'the mechanics' and 'the unleisured'. For both authors, concepts at once numerical, economic, educational, moral, behavioural, and occupational are not separated out but form a single, deeply complex polarization. The problem is, again, whether such language accurately mirrors society. The language of opposites – word/deed, hot/cold, wet/dry, left/right, mind/body, and so on – had come to obsess Greek thought and expression as the fifth century developed and to form an intellectual inheritance from which Plato and Aristotle could not wholly escape, while Aristotle himself took up and warmly commended the tradition which saw a middle class as the ideal and as the foundation of social stability. Yet the polarization is far more than word play, and the invocation of the 'middle part' was always more a projection of fantasy than an appeal to reality. Aristotle recognized that:

> the middle class is in most states generally small; and the result is that as soon as one or the other of the two main classes, the owners of property and the masses, gains the advantage, it oversteps the mean, and drawing the constitution in its own direction it institutes, as the case may be, either a democracy or an oligarchy. (*Politics* 1295^b 23 ff.)

It is very hard indeed to isolate any context in classical Greek history where a 'middle class' in any sense (most plausibly small landed proprietors, never in a professional or entrepreneurial sense) exercised a specific interest and pressure of its own rather than being assimilated to the value-system either of 'the few' or of 'the many'.

From poverty and social polarization came tensions and expedients which had themselves become defining aspects of Greek experience. Three in particular deserve mention. First, one could move men to where the resources were. Colonization, by now a traditional way out, continued intermittently in the fifth century and after, while the argument that overseas expansion at the expense of Persia was a morally acceptable and socially preferable alternative to revolution was repeatedly formulated by Isokrates in the fourth century. Secondly, one could import the resources and materials which were lacking – metals, wood, fibres and above all corn. That this was done on a large scale in classical Greece is unquestionable, even though we still do not know where many metals came from and can often not trace the nature of the goods which were exchanged for the raw materials. It is often still harder to see the link (if any) between such acitivity and public policy. Diodorus' description of Acragas (see p. 22) does not go on to describe how the relationship was seen, either in Acragas or Carthage, and it is only with Athens (likely enough untypical) that we can see how the need to ensure an imported corn supply and to protect the route helped to form public policy. The third, and perhaps the most salient, of the consequences of poverty in Greek society was the continuous pressure either to conserve, or to dismantle, the position of privilege enjoyed in each community by those whose control of the ownership of land (however gained, justified, and legalized) had allowed them to concentrate resources and to create an aristocratic life-style, a literature, and a set of institutionalized values. Here, one notable fact deserves attention. Only rarely in the fifth and fourth centuries did the pressure to dismantle take directly economic or redistributive form. Calls for the 'abolition of debts and the redistribution of land' were more commonly feared than made. Rather, it took the form of pressure to abolish or to render more widely accessible formal political or cultic privileges and to extend downwards, to the rest of the descent-group, the applicability and appropriateness of aristocratic life-styles and values. The form of government which such pressure created when successful was being called 'democracy' by the 440s if not earlier, while its converse, the preservation or re-establishment of control of the state by an aristocratic or wealthy minority, came to be called 'rule by the few', 'oligarchy'. Both labels had become canonical by the time Aristotle was writing his *Politics* in the 330s, but it is important to remember that the two concepts were not diametrically opposed. Participants in a democracy never extended beyond the descent-group to include slaves, foreigners, or women, while oligarchies often recognized in some way the status of those who were free and of the descent-group though not among the politically enfranchized. We shall see in Chapter Four that though Athens in the 460s and 450s is the best attested and perhaps most extreme example of such successful pressure from below, the idea-structure behind the pressure was deeply conservative.

Why pressure took such a form is a major problem of historical interpretation. One answer is suggested by Herodotus' account of events in Argos after her defeat by King Kleomenes of Sparta c. 494.

> Argos was left so bare of men, that the slaves managed the state, filled the offices, and administered everything until the sons of those who were slain by Kleomenes grew up. Then these latter cast out the slaves, and got the city back under their own control, while the slaves who had been driven out fought a battle and captured Tiryns. After this for a time there was peace between the two; but a certain soothsayer, named Kleandros, who was by origin a Phigalean from Arcadia, joined himself to the slaves, and stirred them up to make a fresh attack upon their masters. Then they were at war with one another for many years; but at length the Argives with much trouble gained the upper hand. (Herodotus 6. 83)

Historians find it one of his most intractable chapters, for events are only vaguely dated and it is barely conceivable that by 'slaves' he means actual chattel slaves rather than poor people or half-citizens, the unenfranchized. Still, it does suggest what some other evidence confirms, that status-improvement and access to power may have been more realistic targets. A second answer may be that this pressure was largely negative, directed either towards destroying a power-structure which was felt to be anachronistic or adventitious, or towards securing protection from an overbearing oligarchy. Some evidence suggests the former for Athens (as we shall see), while Thucydides suggests that the latter may have been felt strongly in the cities of the Athenian Empire. He makes the Athenian oligarch Phrynichos say, in 412:

> the allied cities thought that the Athenian so-called 'noble and

good' would give them just as much trouble as the Athenian popular government. The former were those who made possible and sponsored, and for the most part themselves benefited from, those acts of the Athenian people which damaged the allies. Indeed if it depended on them the allies would actually be being executed without trial and more brutally, while the Athenian people were their refuge and kept the Athenian 'noble and good' under control. (Thucydides 8. 48. 6)

Fitly enough for so highly intelligent an oligarch, the analysis which Thucydides gives to Phrynichos also illustrates the contrary pressure, the determination on the part of the 'haves' to retain and enhance their position of privilege. His example shows one form, wherein active political initiatives on the part of the Athenian 'noble and good' were stimulated by self-interest as well as by 'Athenian' interest, and he may well have had in mind the paradigm case of such mutually reinforcing motivations, the career of Alkibiades (see p. 127ff). Another technique was the coagulation of like-minded members of the leisure class into clubs, associations, or 'conspiracies'. They are best attested at Athens in 411 and 404, when the activities of the 'clubs already existing in the city for help in lawsuits and elections' (Thucydides 8. 54. 4) were unified and redirected towards successful coups d'état, but their existence can be documented in Athens both earlier and later. Their central role in leisure-class social life can be gauged from the institutions which reflected them. These ranged from the banquet scenes so frequent on Athenian red-figure vases, to the very size and shape of the men's dining rooms in the larger private houses where such banquets and symposia took place, to the gymnasia and wrestling-schools which provide the setting for many of Plato's earlier dialogues. But the most striking example comes from outside Athens, in the form of the Freemason-like elect societies, founded under the inspiration of the philosopher Pythagoras, which seem to have effectively controlled the political life of Croton and several other South Italian towns in the first half of the fifth century. It is probably not chance that these societies, the earliest known Greek examples of oligarchy based on election and theory rather than tradition and family membership, should have formed in colonial cities where ties of kinship, descent and locality may have been weaker.

A third form which conservationist pressure took transcended local loyalties, indeed might well conflict with them. Ties of guest-friendship and intermarriage between the noble families of different areas had been part of Greek myth and legend since Homer, and from the late seventh century onwards other evidence confirms that they were social realities. By the 570s, too, the contests in athletics, music and the ritualized arts of war at the great international festivals at Olympia, Delphi, the Isthmus and Nemea had largely taken the form and scale they still had a century later, and though theoretically any free Greek man could compete, in fact wealth, leisure and professional training were essential. The Games had long become a forum for contact, display and competition among the members of what has well been called the 'international aristocracy', and it is our good fortune that the extant victory odes commissioned from Pindar and Bacchylides in just these decades from 490–460 allow us to see, in rich and elaborate formulation, the common code of competitive excellence, pride in ancestry and sense of kinship with the gods which unified this broader society. Here, for example, is Pindar commemorating the victory of Alkimidas of Aegina, perhaps in the 460s, in words which firmly link the world of athletic striving with the highest human values:

One is the race of men and of gods; we both draw breath from the same mother. Yet a total difference of power divides us, so that the one is nothing, while for the other the brazen heaven remains as a sure dwelling-place forever. But in some measure, we have some likeness to the immortals, either in great mind or at least in our nature, even though we do not know, either in waking or in the night-time, towards which goal fate has prescribed that we should run.

And now Alkimidas sets forth visibly his inherited quality like fruitful fields, which at one season bring forth abundant crops for mankind from their soil, and at another lie fallow and recover their strength. So the athlete-boy has come from the lovely contests of Nemea and, pursuing this dispensation of fate from Zeus, has shown himself no empty-handed hunter in the wrestling ring.

Setting his own foot in the kinsman-footsteps of his father's father Praxidamas. For he, being conqueror at Olympia, was the first to bring the garland of victory to the descendants of Aiakos from the river Alpheus, and having crowned himself five times at the Isthmus and three times at Nemea, has redeemed Sokleidas from oblivion, who has become the most notable of the sons of Hagesimachos.

For Hagesimachos' three contest-enduring sons, who experienced the hardships, reached the summit of goodness. By the help of the good fortune of God no other house has been ordained by the art of boxing to be the steward of more crowns in the recesses of all Greece. (Pindar, *Nemean* 6. 1–25)

The common code could slide into becoming a mere basis for partisan action by an embattled upper class, but it was far more than that. It also formed part of a shared mode of thinking about social and political relationships, which extended well beyond the upper class and constituted a sixth and last unifying factor on its own. Demaratos' insistence on freedom under law (see p. 13) is another part of it, as was the growing awareness, focused by the Persian Wars, that Greek customs and values were relatively uniform in comparison with the non-Greek world. This uniformity did not derive from an explicitly formulated and theologically backed moral code, for there was none. There were moral maxims, of course, not just the three famous ones inscribed on or by the temple of Apollo at Delphi ('Know thyself', 'Nothing in excess' and 'Go bail and destruction is at hand'), or the epigram on the propylaia of the temple of Leto at Delos,

Most noble is that which is justest, and best is health;
But pleasantest is it to win what we desire,

which Aristotle twice quoted but strongly disagreed with (*Nicomachean Ethics* 1099ᵃ 25 ff; *Eudemian Ethics* 1214ᵃ 1 ff). There were many others, whether anonymous or attributed to the Seven Wise Men or formulated by a poet. Yet that was just the point: unsystematic, sometimes mutually contradictory, formulations might be given approval by this or that shrine of god, but were of only limited authority. As Pindar's first stanza (see p. 28) suggests, gods were differentiated from mortals by their power and their immortaility rather than by being morally perfect or by being guarantors of a morally ordered universe. The gods oversaw, and, if roused and propitiated by prayer and sacrifice, might protect certain areas of activity, such as the sanctity of oaths (Zeus Herkeios), marriage (Hera) or craftsmanship (Athene and Hephaistos). They might protect certain especially vulnerable conditions such as suppliants and beggars (Zeus Hikesios), mariners (the Dioskouroi) or women in childbirth (Artemis). They might protect certain essential preconditions of life, especially the fertility of the land, of animals, and of humans. Such concepts of their activity gave their presumed existence an undeniable moral component, but one which often sat in uneasy company with their primary aspect of power and remained fragmented and unsystematic.

In part, the uniformity of customs and values simply reflected a common language and culture. Greek speakers inevitably shared a moral vocabulary, in such a way that Eteokles' praise of Amphiaraos as a 'self-restrained, just, valiant (*agathos*), and godfearing man' (Aeschylus, *Seven* 610) would convey much the same denotations of behaviour, and express the same attitudes of approval, anywhere in Greece. Of course, matters were more complicated than that. A decision to use these words rather than others to commend a person's behaviour might well be helped, but would not be determined, by the existing configuration of uses in a given semantic field, any more than the shift and development in the use of certain complex words is a purely linguistic fact. Aeschylus here used the Greek word conventionally translated 'good', *agathos*, with what must be its traditional, mainly military nuance, but a philosopher of the next generation, Demokritos, used it to say that 'a noble word does not dim a mean act, nor is a good (*agathe*) action injured by defamation in speech' (DK 68 B 177). Such a shift is as much an enlargement of moral horizons as is the jump from Pindar's use of the corresponding abstract noun, *arete*, in a context of competitive athletics (see p. 29) to Thucydides' use of it in describing behaviour during the plague at Athens in 430:

If they were afraid to visit each other, they perished from neglect; indeed many houses were emptied of their inmates for want of a nurse. On the other hand, if they ventured to do so, death was the consequence. This was especially the case with such as made any pretensions to goodness (*aretē*). Honour made them unsparing of themselves in their attendance in their friends' houses. (2. 51. 5)

Yet what matters most here is that such decisions and developments do seem to be autonomous in Greek and confined to Greek, in contrast, say, to the way in which new words and new uses nowadays spread simultaneously in all Western European languages, closely reflecting a largely uniform culture.

However, shared modes of thinking, or the effect of a common vocabulary, are elusive just because they are taken for granted. We are on easier ground in exploring those aspects of cultural uniformity of which Greeks themselves were or became aware. Our chief witness here is Herodotus, a good half of whose *Histories* describes the customs of non-Greek nations, and in whom we can see such awareness taking various forms. In part he is continuing an ethnographic tradition which stemmed from earlier Greek expansion and is already visible in the *Odyssey*. Yet the arrangement of his narrative, and his choice of regions to describe, is so clearly made in terms of the sequence of areas which the Persians conquered or attacked that the predominant pattern has clearly become historical in the true sense. Still, much that is purely ethnographic remains. A notable example is his description of Egypt, where among many other respects in which 'the people, in most of their manners and customs, exactly reverse the common practice of mankind', he notes that 'sons are not obliged to support their parents unless they choose to, but daughters must, whether they are willing or not. When they write or calculate, instead of going, like the Greeks, from left to right, they move their hands from right to left; and they insist, notwithstanding, that it is they who go to the right and the Greeks who go to the left' (2. 35. 2 and 36. 4). Again, he retails an anecdote about King Darius of Persia:

After he had become King, Darius summoned certain Greeks

who were present, and asked them for what price they would be willing to eat the bodies of their fathers when they died? They said they would not do that at any price. He then sent for certain Indians, called Callatians, men who eat their fathers. In the presence of the Greeks, who understood through an interpreter what was being said, he asked them for what price they would consent to burn the bodies of their fathers at their deaths. The Indians exclaimed aloud, and asked him not to utter impiety. Such then are men's customs, and Pindar was right, in my judgement, when he said that 'custom was king over all'. (3. 38. 3–4)

A second response was to perceive that if indeed 'different people have different customs, and each praises his own view of what is right' (Pindar, F 215), then *either* different customs were indeed of equal value as systems of living, or a ranking order had to be created. In the former case, the problem of choosing a system was open and unavoidable. It could be resolved only by appealing to superior force, or to nature, or by constructing new systems based on rational premises (and this was what much of Greek moral and political philosophy came to be about). The other, far more analytical response, of creating a ranking order, is best illustrated in the late fifth-century essay *On Airs Waters Places,* which may well be by Hippocrates himself and in any case stands among the first surviving Western writing on medicine. The first part describes the differences in health and physique due to living in places facing hot or cold winds, or to having soft or hard water or rainwater, or to suffering abnormal weather at certain times of the year. Then, after characterizing the peoples of Asia Minor in these respects, the author moves to generalization:

With regard to the lack of spirit and of courage among the inhabitants, the chief reason why Asiatics are less warlike and more gentle in character than Europeans is the uniformity of the seasons, which show no violent changes either towards heat or towards cold, but are equable. For there occur no mental shocks nor violent physical change, which are more likely to steel the temper and impart to it a fierce passion than is a monotonous sameness. For it is changes of all things that rouse the temper of man and prevent its stagnation. For these reasons, I think, Asiatics are feeble. Their institutions are a contributory cause, the greater part of Asia being governed by kings. Now where men are not their own masters and independent, but are ruled by despots, they are not keen on military efficiency but on not appearing warlike . . . All their worthy brave deeds merely serve to aggrandize and raise up their lords, while the harvest they themselves reap is danger and death . . . Even if a naturally brave and spirited man is born, his temper is changed by their institutions. Whereof I can give a clear proof. All the inhabitants of Asia, whether Greek or non-Greek, who are not ruled by despots, but are independent, toiling for their own advantage, are the most warlike of all men. For it is for their own sakes that they run their risks, and in their own persons do they receive the prizes of their valour as likewise the penalty of their cowardice. You will find that Asiatics also differ from one another, some being superior, others inferior. The reasons for this, as I have said above, is the changes of the seasons. (*Airs Waters Places* 16)

Here, in contrast, observations have been sorted into a system derived from environmental and institutional differences, and a moral ranking order has been imposed, couched inevitably in Greek terms of the criteria of bravery and freedom in a way which again recalls Demaratos (see p. 13). If we now return to Herodotus, we can see a third response, wherein such perceptions become a basis of political action. He records that in winter 480–79 King Alexander Philhellen of Macedonia tried to persuade the Athenians to make a separate peace with Persia. They replied:

. . . Not all the gold that the whole earth contains – not the fairest and most fertiles of all lands – could bribe us to take part with the Persians and help them to enslave our countrymen. Even could we anyhow have brought ourselves to such a thing, there are many very powerful motives which would now make it impossible. The first and chief of these is the burning and destruction of our temples and images of our gods, which forces us to make no terms with their destroyer, but rather to pursue

him with our resentment to the uttermost. Again, there is our
common brotherhood with the Greeks: our common language,
the altars and the sacrifices of which we all partake, the
common character which we bear – did the Athenians betray all
these, of a truth it would not be well. Know then now, if you
have not known it before, that while one Athenian remains
alive, we will never join alliance with Xerxes. (Herodotus
7. 144, 1–3)

We cannot tell if the speech is historical or not, but what matters
is that for Herodotus, writing in the 440s or 430s, it was meant to
be true. It encapsulated, for Greek (and especially for Athenian)
opinion, the twin notions of Greek unity of speech, religion, and
customs, and that of permanent enmity towards the Persians.
These notions were to have a long and influential descendance. As
a political programme they underlaid and legitimated the
Athenian military expansion which began in earnest in 478. They
survived the realistic but messy compromises and treaties made
with Persia in the later fifth and early fourth centuries to be taken
up by Philip of Macedon and his apologists as a means of
legitimating *his* power over Greece. As a formula for often very
soft-minded and unrealistic oratorical elaboration, they served to
define the nature and frontiers of Greekness and to divert hard-
headed attention away from the divisions and contradictions in
Greek society.

For contradictions there were. The most basic were naturally
those that stemmed from owning and working the land. Aristotle
could say:

The first and best kind of populace is one of farmers; and there
is thus no difficulty in constructing a democracy where the bulk
of the people live by arable or pastoral farming. Such people,
not having any great amount of property, are busily occupied,
and they thus have no time for attending the assembly. Not
possessing the necessities of life, they stick to their work, and
do not covet what does not belong to them. (*Politics* 1318ᵇ
9–14)

He also says:

Upon these principles it clearly follows that a state with an ideal constitution, i.e. a state which has for its members men who are absolutely just, and not men who are merely just in relation to some particular standard, cannot have its citizens living the life of mechanics or shopkeepers, which is ignoble and inimical to goodness (*aretē*). Nor can it have them engaged in farming; leisure is a necessity, both for growth in goodness and for the pursuit of political activities. (*Politics* 1328ᵇ37–1329ᵃ2)

The criterion of leisure as a necessary condition of active political life conflicts with the moral superiority of farming over all other gainful activities. Again, the frequently made equations between 'being an owner of landed property' and 'being a full citizen' could be as deeply conservative a formula, if the first element were taken to be primary, as it could be dangerously radical if it were applied in terms of an existing citizen body.

Three further contradictions involved the role and definition of the city-state even more directly. Firstly, its definition in terms of descent in the male line, kinship, and participation in common cults and sacrifices was vulnerable to challenge both from above, by minorities who claimed exclusivist superiorities, and from below, by those whose legal status conflicted sharply with their functional status. A rationale is given to the former by Aristotle's statement. 'Those who are pre-eminent in merit would be the most justified in attempting sedition, though they are the last to make the attempt; for they, and only they, can reasonably be regarded as enjoying an absolute superiority' (*Politics* 1310ᵃ39–1301ᵇ1). The latter comprised those 'outside' the community in varying senses (women, resident aliens, serfs, slaves). Secondly, though the city-state had largely come to be, and largely went on being, a viable and satisfying unit of culture and administration, the Persian Wars in Greece and the Punic War in Sicily had exposed its weakness as a power unit. Fifth- and fourth-century power-politics at the level that mattered were in fact to be matters no longer of individual city-states but of groups of states, united more or less willingly and stably either under a personal regime (e.g. the Syracusan dynasts) or more usually in some sort of institutional framework of leagues or alliances. Yet the prevailing idea-structure went on being articulated in terms of the autonomy of the city-state. It was not until the full Hellenistic period that Greek political society found in federalism a way of coping with the tensions and resentments which this contradiction between ideals and reality aroused. Thirdly, over against the vague Panhellenism which Herodotus illustrates (see p. 34) stood both the chauvinist particularism of the stronger powers and a wide diversity of local geographical, social, and political influences and pressures. Since it was from such diversity and from other tensions and contradictions that the interactions which we call Greek history stemmed, it may be best at this point to look at them regionally.

III

Regional Ambitions

VERY BROADLY, Greek affairs throughout the fifth and fourth
centuries are the affairs of five regions: the Aegean, Peloponnese,
Sicily and South Italy, Central Greece, and the outliers. Of course
interaction among them all was continuous and influential.
Throughout, we know most about the Aegean, both because
Athenian ambitions, and the presence of Persian power in Asia
Minor and the Levant, generated more military activity there than
elsewhere and because the sources say so much more about Athens.
This is true, not just of the epigraphic material and of imaginative
or philosophical literature, but also of the narrative sources.
Thucydides' skeleton narrative of Greek history from 478–31
(1. 89–118) is very largely, and intentionally, a sketch of the
growth of Athenian power. His fully detailed narrative of the
Peloponnesian War from 431 till he breaks off in 411 is inevitably
Athenocentric, for all his efforts to be impartial. Similarly,
Xenophon's *Hellenika*, narrating events in Greece from 411 till
362, concentrates mainly on Athens and Sparta, not least because
he clearly disliked Thebes intensely. The only corrective comes
from Diodorus. He provides us with most of what little we know
about the Greeks in the West during the fifth and fourth centuries,
and for the period after 411 his use of traditions independent of
Xenophon and with different regional and political biasses and
interests mades him indispensable. The sources therefore present
us throughout with the methodological problem of eliciting
information equitably for all regions and communities, while not
sacrificing the depth of analysis which our heavily weighted
material allows for one region in particular.

Yet to some degree the bias is a true reflection of differences in activity and experience, and at no time was the contrast between the Aegean and the other regions sharper than in the generation after 480. Crudely put in terms of power, in the Aegean a new power-unit emerged and consolidated its position: power-units elsewhere stagnated, disintegrated, or failed to emerge at all. In Sicily, for example, the tyrant dynasty of Syracuse, for all its successful leadership against Carthaginians and Etruscans, collapsed in 466. The manpower resources which had sustained it were dissipated, and city after city emancipated itself from Syracusan control to re-create a patchwork of independent states vulnerable to local quarrels, to pressure from the active population of the interior, and to Athenian finesse. So too, in South Italy, whatever cohesion or imposed hegemony the cities of Croton and Tarentum had created by 480 had vanished by the 440s, leaving the field open for Athenian diplomacy and even Athenian settlement. Boeotia and Thessaly, morally dis-advantaged by having taken the Persian side in 480–79, lost the sense of political direction which they had once had to become by 457 the objects respectively of Athenian control and Athenian alliance. Macedon barely emerges at all until the 430s.

Much the same seems to be true of the outliers of Greek culture, though our ignorance of their affairs is often near-total. For example, virtually all we know of the Molossian monarchy in Epirus, in the fifth century or much later, comes from an anecdote in Thucydides which reveals how Homeric public life still was there in the 460s. Further south, as we learn from Thucydides' report of an Athenian campaign in 426, the Aetolian nation, although numerous and warlike, 'yet dwelt in unwalled villages scattered far apart, and had nothing but light armour', while inland 'the Eurytanians, who are the largest tribe in Aetolia, speak, as is said, a language exceedingly difficult to understand, and eat their meat raw. These once subdued, the rest would easily come in' (Thucydides 3. 94. 4–5). One could hardly find a more pointed correlation of archaic custom with disunity and military vulnerability.

Similarly, we know very little of the Greeks in North Africa in the fifth and fourth centuries. Three odes of Pindar reveal that the monarchy at Cyrene lasted till after 460. Aristotle in the *Politics* refers to measures taken to establish a democracy there at an unknown date. Thucydides and an honorary decree from Athens record Cyrenean help to both sides during and after the Athenian invasion of Sicily in 415–13. Diodorus recounts a brief tyranny and a bitter civil war in 401. One series of documents from Cyrene records tithes of agricultural produce, another the names of soldiers and commanders. Apart from the record of monuments and artefacts, which indicate considerable prosperity, that is virtually all we know. It is enough to suggest that the city deliberately stayed out of Greek affairs, for all her affinity with Sparta, just as the total lack of Egyptian influence on Cyrenean art may show how the pull of political geography was being resisted.

Much the same seems to be true of Crete. Though invited by the Greeks, the island took no part in the Persian Wars and remained aloof throughout our period. The evidence of Cretan coinage, some allusions in Plato and in the later geographer Strabo, and a few inscriptions suggest that by and after c. 450 the islanders were choosing to take increasingly seriously the old tradition that Crete owed her Dorian dialect and institutions to having been colonized from Argos. Hence, Argos' own policy of non-involvement in Greek power-politics may have been influential on the island, complementing the intense activity in the codification of customary law which the surviving law-codes on stone from Gortyn and elsewhere (see Plate 5b) allow us to see in part. True, other outlying islands were less lucky. Cyprus, as we shall see below, was too strategically important in the East Mediterranean, and her copper too essential for what was still largely a Bronze Age, for her not to be a focus of military and political attention. As for Corcyra, we can see from Thucydides' narrative of the 430s in Book I how reluctantly and how late in the day the island, neutral in 480 and detached ever since, was dragged into the Great Power politics of Greece.

Corcyra brings us back, via her estranged mother-city of Corinth, to the Peloponnese, whose affairs need and allow more detailed description. By now it was not just a geographical expression, but was virtually under the control of Sparta. Her conquest of Messene by c. 716 had allowed Spartan citizens to live as absentee rentiers at the expense of an oppressed serf population (the so-called 'helots'), and had compelled the

Spartans to become professional soldiers, unequalled in Greece or outside. Her alliances with Tegea, by *c.* 551, and with Corinth, by 525 at latest and probably much earlier, had allowed her to box in Argos, her one serious rival for the leadership of the region. Most recently, the creation of a league of her allies in or by 503 comprising many, if not most, of the Peloponnesian states had both made relationships more formal and equitable and provided a model for joint organization and action by the anti-Persian states in 481. So much is clear from Herodotus. What is not clear is why Sparta did not exploit her distinguished performance in the Persian Wars to consolidate and extend her influence, but relapsed into what seems at first sight to have been inert sluggishness. The missed opportunity affected the entire subsequent history of independent Greece. The trouble is that the evidence is both desperately scrappy and chronologically opaque. One basic signpost has to be Herodotus' account of the soothsayer Teisamenos of Elis, who had managed to blackmail the Spartans into making his brother and himself full Spartan citizens:

> Afterwards as a seer he helped to bring the Spartans five very great victories . . . These five battles were, first, this one of Platea, the second that at Tegea, against the Tegeans and the Argives, the third that at Dipaea against all the Arcadians except the Mantineans, then that over the Messenians at Ithome, and lastly that at Tanagra against the Athenians and the Argives. (Herodotus 9. 35. 1–2)

We therefore have two major battles to fit in, between Platea in 479 and Ithome in (probably) 459, against Arcadian and Argive enemies. Other evidence makes things clearer. Herodotus tells us that the Mantinean and Elean contingents turned up late for Platea. There is evidence of fighting between cantons in Arcadia but also of a coinage inscribed *Ark(adikon)*, which probably reflects a federal structure. In 471–70 'the Eleans, who dwelt in many small cities, united to form one state which is known as Elis' (Diodorus 11. 54. 1), and 'other places in Peloponnese . . . each consisted of a collocation of many villages, from which the recognized cities were later brought together into a unity. For example, Mantinea in Arcadia was united

from five villages under Argive influence, and Tegea from nine'
(Strabo 8. 3. 2), almost certainly in this period. It looks, then, as if
between 480 and 460 several cantons in northern Peloponnese
(perhaps, as Strabo goes on to suggest, in Achaea as well as Elis and
Arcadia) were each concentrating their resources and populations
into cohesive units in opposition to Sparta. It was an inherently
radical process, with democratic overtones. That Argos encouraged
it is clear. This is easily understandable in the light of her hostility to
Sparta and of the evidence, from Herodotus (see p. 26) and from
Aeschylus' *Suppliants* of 464–3, that she counted as a democracy
herself. Moreover, our other main evidence for the area and period
comes from Thucydides' digressions at the end of Book I on the
careers of the Athenian Themistokles and the Spartan Regent
Pausanias after their triumphs in the Persian Wars. He tells us that
Themistokles 'had, as it happened, been exiled by ostracism
[probably in 471] and, with a residence in Argos, was in the habit of
visiting other parts of Peloponnese' (1. 135. 3). They were
presumably not just social visits.

Here, then, in the near-disintegration of the Peloponnesian
League, lay one strong reason for Spartan lack of initiative, but
there were others too. In 478, indeed, she did take the lead. The
combined force which subdued most of Cyprus in that year and
went on to besiege Byzantion was led by Pausanias with 20 ships
from Peloponnese. However, Thucydides goes on to say, his
behaviour caused such offence that the Spartans recalled him and
tried him (but acquitted him) on a charge of treasonable dealings
with Persia. Meanwhile:

> the hatred which he had inspired had induced the allies to
> desert him . . . and to range themselves by the side of the
> Athenians . . . (In his stead) the Spartans . . . sent out Dorkis
> and certain others with a small force. They found the allies no
> longer inclined to concede them the supremacy. Perceiving this
> they departed and the Spartans did not send out any to succeed
> them. They feared for those who went out a deterioration
> similar to that observable in Pausanias: besides, they desired to
> be rid of the Persian War, and were satisfied of the competence
> of the Athenians for the position and of their friendship at the
> time towards themselves. (Thucydides 1. 95. 3–7)

This passage, though describing one of the most crucial shifts of power in Greek history, raises more problems than it solves. The reception given to Dorkis suggests that Pausanias' behaviour was not the only obstacle; the accusation of treason comes from nowhere; and Herodotus is less certain than Thucydides that the transfer was agreeable to Sparta. However, what matters here is the position of Pausanias himself. Thucydides later records in detail (1. 128–134) how his treasonable dealings both with the Persian King and with the helots in Messenia were ultimately discovered and gave the authorities the chance to let him starve to death in a temple. Not all of his account is trustworthy and the chronology presents acute problems, but it does look very much as if for ten years or even more from 478 Sparta may have been saddled with a major politician, ambitious, of royal blood, and in an entrenched position as Regent, whom she could neither trust not get rid of, while his ward Pleistarchos was not of age till the late 460s. Worse, the other royal house of Sparta (see p. 14) was in the same state. King Leotychidas, Herodotus tells us, had let himself be bribed to call off a punitive expedition against Thessaly and had been exiled in 476. Hence, till he died (in 469) and his grandson Archidamos came of age (perhaps even later), neither royal house could provide the political or military leadership which was their traditional role and responsibility, and Spartan society was not geared, either then or later, to deal with such a crisis.

There were two further reasons for Spartan inertia. One was adventitious. Unrest among the helots in Messenia, which had erupted in 491–90 and was allegedly being encouraged by Pausanias, broke out in earnest in 464, after an earthquake had destroyed the city of Sparta and killed so many of her citizens that she had to call for assistance from her remaining allies. The other reason was built into the state. Diodorus records under the year 476–5 that the Spartans,

> now that for no good reason they had lost the command of the sea, were resentful; consequently they were incensed at the Greeks who had fallen away from them . . . When a meeting of the Council of Elders was convened, they considered making war upon the Athenians . . . Likewise, when the general

Assembly was convened, the younger men and the majority of the others were eager to recover the leadership, believing that, if they could secure it, they would enjoy great wealth, Sparta in general would be made greater and more powerful, and the estates of her private citizens would receive a great increase of prosperity.

However,

a member of the Gerousia, Hetoimaridas by name, who was a direct descendant of Herakles and enjoyed favour among the citizens by reason of his character, undertook to advise that they leave the Athenians with their leadership, since it was not to Sparta's interest, he declared, to lay claim to the sea. (Diodorus 11. 50. 1–6)

His view prevailed. Scholars suspect that Diodorus' account is based on fourth-century modes of thought, when Sparta had briefly become a major seapower with damaging consequences, but there should be an underlay of fact, and one can create for Hetoimaridas some powerful arguments. To lead Greece now entailed being a seapower, which in turn entailed major expense on building, equipping, manning and training a fleet. Such a policy was in direct conflict with the Spartan tradition of self-financing fighters by land, a tradition which had so far allowed Sparta to avoid using coined money and suffering its attendant corruptions. To have a fleet involved major problems of supply (where would the money come from? where would sails, pitch, cordage, etc., come from?). It also involved yielding political power to those concerned with a navy, in a way thoroughly subversive both to traditional leadership patterns and to the key military role of the Spartiates which had so far legitimated their political and economic predominance.

At Athens, in contrast, all the pressures pointed one way. Some can be seen directly from Thucydides' narrative of the growth of Athenian power or from Plutarch's biographies of Kimon, Themistokles, and Aristeides. Others must be disentangled from later or less direct evidence, but in all they amounted to an explosion of energy which seems to have taken the rest of the

Greek world by surprise. It was directed towards firm long-term Athenian domination of the Aegean and of its northern and eastern seaboards (see map 2). The course of events in the region down to 454 is clear enough in outline from Thucydides 1. 94–111 and some ancillary evidence, though it is rarely possible to date events precisely. The Aegean states in revolt from Persia invited and accepted Athenian leadership of a Confederacy, usually referred to as the Delian League because it was created in the winter of 478–7 by a conference at Delos. Its main known activities till 463 were the extrusion of Persians from their remaining strongholds in the Aegean; the defeat, at Eurymedon River in Pamphylia at some date between 469 and 466, of a strong Persian counter-attack on the Aegean by land and sea; and the forcible subjection of two islands which revolted from the League, Naxos c. 470 and Thasos in 465–3. The next ten years saw major accretions to the League (Aegina in 457) and to Athens herself, either by separate alliance (Argos and Thessaly c. 461; Megara c. 460) or by conquest (Boeotia and Phocis in 457), but the main League activity was the diversion in 459 of an enormous fleet of 200 ships from Cyprus to Egypt, in order to support a revolt in the Delta against Persian control. The revolt began with considerable success, dragged on for six years, and ended in late summer 454 in a major disaster involving, it seems (though Thucydides is not as explicit as he might be) the loss of nearly the whole League fleet and of many thousands of men. The disaster more or less ended aggressive League action against Persia.

In his narrative Thucydides does no more than hint at Athenian drives and attitudes. He notes how, when 'the violence of Pausanias had already begun to be disagreeable to the Greeks, particularly to the Ionians and the newly liberated populations, they resorted to the Athenians and requested them as their kinsmen to become their leaders' (1. 95. 1). He records that the Athenians 'fixed which cities were to contribute money against the barbarian, which ships; their professed object being to retaliate for their sufferings by ravaging the Persian King's country' (1. 96. 1). He also reports that the Thasian revolt began because they 'were in conflict (with the Athenians) about the trading-posts on the coast of Thrace opposite Thasos and about the silver-mine which they possessed' (1. 100. 2), and ended with the Thasians 'razing their walls, surrendering their ships, and arranging to pay the moneys demanded at once, and to pay tribute in future, giving up their possessions on the mainland together with the silver-mine' (1. 101. 3). Such hints can be expanded. The notion of special kinship between Athenians and Ionians, already well-established in attitudes and in some sense clearly based on fact, remained a major ingredient in Aegean relations throughout, but is not enough by itself to explain Athenian action. Thucydides made a later Athenian speaker say that once the Spartans had left the war to them, 'we were at first compelled by the force of events to advance our Empire to its present position, primarily by fear, secondly by considerations of honour too, and later on by self-interest as well' (1. 75. 3). Even this is too simple, indeed disingenuous. Each item needs comment.

Fear of a Persian counter-attack, which the battle at Eurymedon River had proved well-founded, pressed harder on the islands and on vulnerable Asia Minor than on Athens. Thucydides comments, in the context of the revolt of Naxos, that:

> of all the causes of defection, that connected with arrears of tribute and vessels, and with failure of service, was the chief; for the Athenians were very severe and exacting, and made themselves offensive by applying the screw of necessity to men who were not used to and in fact not disposed for any continuous labour. In some other respects the Athenians were not the old popular rulers they had been at first; and if they had more than their fair share of service, it was correspondingly easy for them to reduce any that tried to leave the confederacy. For this the allies had themseves to blame; the wish to get off service making most of them arrange to pay their share of the expense in money instead of in ships, and so to avoid having to leave their homes. Thus while Athens was increasing her navy with the funds which they contributed, a revolt always found them without resources or experience for war. (1. 99)

To judge from this passage, or from the way recalcitrants were dealt with, Athenian politicians exploited fear rather than felt it.

Honour, too, is only superficially straightforward. Service abroad did come to give status and perquisites to many Athenian citizens, but, as both foreign poets such as Pindar and Athenian politicians themselves recognized, what gave the city at large her prestige was not so much her League leadership as her heroic role in the wars of 480–79 against Persian invasion. It may not be too cynical to say that the chief recipients of 'honour' were the members of the Athenian upper class. By virtue of commanding League fleets, serving as League treasurers (an Athenian office from the start), or commanding League ships (increasingly Athenian, as the above quotation shows), they could hope not just to recoup their position in Athens, which had been badly battered in the political agitations of the 480s, but also to gain a level of power and prestige unattainable in a purely Athenian context.

Here we touch one aspect of self-interest. Events at Thasos illustrated another aspect, the forcible transfer of the key natural resources of the Aegean into Athenian hands, which is documentable throughout. There was yet a third, where self-interest merged with necessity. By the late fifth century, and even more in the fourth century, the sources are explicit that 'we Athenians use more imported corn than anybody else' (Demosthenes 20. 31), and that half of Athens' imports came from the Crimea region. No source tells us when this pattern developed, but Athenian overseas involvement before 480 is revealing. A failed colony at Sigeum c. 610, the capture of Chersonese c. 544, the interest which the Peisistratid dynasty showed in Sigeum and Lampsacus before 510, the installation of Athenian settlers on Lemnos and Imbros c. 499, and perhaps also the seizure of land at Chalcis c. 506, all yield a consistent pattern, that of appropriating the key staging posts to and from the Black Sea. The pattern was extended by the siege and capture of Byzantium in 478 and the capture and colonization of Scyros in 476, and completed by the near-total takeover of Chersonese by Athenian citizen colonists in 449–7. Bluntly and summarily, large tracts of Athenian history in the fifth and fourth centuries (and indeed down till the Roman period) can be written round her absolute need to control, or to prevent other major powers controlling, the sea-route from the Crimea through the Hellespont across the Aegean to Piraeus which brought her the corn without which her population would starve. Either she controlled the Dardanelles, or she had to be subservient to the power which did.

To accumulate motives in this way is of course to over-determine action, but it also serves to explain why we can detect no Athenian opposition to expansion as such. The argument, it seems, was not whether to expand but how. The League as created was formal, even parliamentary:

> At this time the office of Hellenotamiai ('Treasurers of Greece') was first established by the Athenians. These officers received the tribute, as the money collected was called. The tribute was first fixed at 460 talents. The common treasury was at Delos, and the Congresses were held in the Temple. At first those whom the Athenians led were independent allies who acted on the resolutions of common Congresses. (Thucydides 1. 96. 2–97, 1)

The balance between archaic and modern was delicate. The choice of Delos, Apollo's sacred island where Aegean gatherings had taken place for centuries, looked back to the cultic Amphiktyonies. These were regional assemblies, based on major shrines and meeting during seasonal festivals, and they had been the main form of interstate common action in archaic Greece. In contrast, the officials and the assessment of contributions reveal modernization and secularization. The whole seems meant to balance leaders and led and to incorporate the need for consultation and agreement. Yet against the two Athenian politicians most closely linked with the League in the 470s and 460s, Kimon as commander of expedition after expedition and Aristeides as the equitable assessor of contributions, stood Themistokles, in 478 the leading Greek politician. We know enough about him from Plutarch and Thucydides for it to be significant that he is never associated with League affairs. Indeed, anecdotes about him suggest that he thought Athenian leadership of the Aegean should be much less parliamentary and soft-footed. Herodotus (8. 111–112) records in detail his bullying exactions of money from the islanders in the wake of the victory at Salamis, and Plutarch quotes a poem of Timokreon of Rhodes:

Come, if you praise Pausanias, or you Xanthippos, or you
Leotychidas, I praise Aristeides, the one best man of all
who came from holy Athens; for the goddess Leto loathes
Themistokles, the liar, cheat, and traitor, who, though
Timokreon was his guest-friend, was induced by crappy money
not to restore him from exile to his native Ialysos, but took
three talents of silver and went sailing off to perdition,
restoring some exiles unjustly, chasing some away, killing
others – and rolling in money. (*Themistokles* 21. 2–3)

Other evidence suggests that Themistokles saw Sparta as a
greater danger to Athens than Persia. We can see his insistence,
against Spartan pressure, on rebuilding the walls of Athens in the
winter of 479–8 (described in detail in Thucydides 1. 89–93): his
successful opposition to a Spartan proposal to expel those who
had fought for Persia from the Amphiktyony of Delphi: his very
probably anti-Spartan activities in Argos *c.* 471–67: and his
ultimate willingness to accept the protection of the Persian King
from *c.*465 till his death *c.* 459. However, neither this view nor
his line in the Aegean stood much chance against Kimon's
phenomenally successful formula of combining aristocratic
patronage of the populace with close partnership with Sparta,
while taking every available opportunity in the Aegean under
cover of a constitutional League. Plutarch's life of Kimon, lively,
full of anecdotes, and chronologically chaotic, gives us the
material to judge. We see him as the honest curly-haired war
hero, as the military leader, as the aristocrat with friends and
connexions all over Greece, as the patron of poets and artists, as
the local squire, as the improver and beautifier of Athens, as the
womanizer, and as the selfless patriot but resolute friend of
Sparta.

He was also of no mean presence, as Ion the poet says, but tall
with an abundant and curly head of hair. Since he displayed
brilliant and heroic conduct in the actual battle at Salamis, he
quickly acquired reputation and goodwill in the City. Many
thronged to him and exhorted him to conceive and carry out
exploits worthy of Marathon. So when he entered politics the
people gladly welcomed him, and since they were tired of

Themistokles they promoted him to the highest honours and offices in the city, for he was engaging and attractive to the masses because of his gentleness and artlessness (*Kimon* 5. 3–5)

However, it is perfectly apparent that Kimon was given to the love of women. Asteria, of a family from Salamis, and a certain Mnestra are mentioned by the poet Melanthios, in a playful elegy addressed to Kimon, as having been the objects of his affections. Clearly, too, he was passionately attached to his lawful wife Isodike, the daughter of Euryptolemos son of Megakles, and was deeply afflicted at her death, if we may judge from the elegy addressed to him for the mitigation of his grief. Panaitios the philosopher thinks the physicist Archelaos wrote it, which is chronologically possible. (4. 9–10)

Since he was already wealthy, he lavished the revenues from his campaigns, which he was thought to have won with honour from the enemy, on his fellow citizens – to his even greater honour. He took away the fences from his fields, so that foreigners and needy citizens could help themselves to the crop without fear: and every day he gave a dinner at his house – simple, but enough for many – to which any poor man who wished could come in . . . But Aristotle says that it was not for all Athenians, but only for his own demesmen of Lakiadai, that he provided a free dinner. (10. 1–2)

By the sale of the captured spoils (from Eurymedon) the people were able to do various things with the money. In particular they built the southern wall of the Akropolis with the resources from that expedition . . . Kimon was the first to beautify the city with the so-called 'liberal' and elegant resorts, which were so extraordinarly popular a little later, by planting the Agora with plane trees and by converting the Academy from an arid and waterless spot into a well-watered grove, which he provided with clear running-tracks and shady groves. (13. 5 and 7)

(After the earthquake of 464) the Spartans sent Perikleidas to

Athens to ask for help. Aristophanes portrays him in a comedy as 'sitting at the altars, pale of face, in purple cloak, soliciting an army'. But Ephialtes opposed the project, and besought the Athenians not to help or restore a city which was a rival to Athens, but rather to let the pride of Sparta lie fallen and be trampled on. Whereupon, as Kritias says, Kimon placed the benefit to his own country in second place to the interest of Sparta, and persuaded the people to go and help with many hoplites. Ion records the actual phrase by which Kimon especially moved the Athenians: he begged them not to let Greece become crippled or their city be robbed of its yoke-fellow.(16. 8–10)

There has clearly been an element of hagiography right from the start, and many details, one suspects, have been 'improved' in the 550-year process of retelling before Plutarch, but the whole rings true as a portrait of traditional leadership. Yet Kimon's formula broke down in 461, and Themistokles' views came to prevail and to be powerful and lasting elements of Athenian foreign policy. How and why that came to be so needs more detailed and more indirect explanation.

IV

The Athenian Revolution

FROM THE LATE eight century onwards there is a trickle of documents from Athens written on stone, bronze or pottery, but till the 460s only about ten of them are public documents, decrees or dedications, set up by the state or its officials. From about 460 onwards there is a flood of documentation. About 300 public documents survive from the period from then till the end of the century, and a similar spate continued till the Macedonian occupation of Athens in 317 temporarily cut short independent political activity. These documents allow us to follow Athenian affairs in far greater detail than is possible elsewhere, but they also present a major problem of interpretation. Why did this explosion of documentation take place?

Part of the answer comes from the specific evidence of a major political upheaval in Athens about 460. The only connected account comes from the *Athenian Constitution* attributed to Aristotle, and mainly concerns the Areiopagos, the Council comprising all those men who as 'archon' (literally 'ruler') had held one of the nine traditional annual magistracies. This account tells us that:

The supremacy of the Areiopagos lasted for about seventeen years after the Persian Wars although gradually declining. But as the strength of the masses increased Ephialtes son of Sophonides, a man with a reputation for incorruptibility and public virtue, who had become leader of the people, made an attack upon that Council. First of all he ruined many of its members by bringing actions against them with reference to their administration. Then in the archonship of Konon (462–1) he stripped the Council of all its acquired prerogatives from which it derived its guardianship of the Constitution, and assigned some of them to the (annually elected and locally representative) Council of Five Hundred and others to the Assembly and Lawcourts. (*Athenian Constitution* 25. 1–2)

A little later we are told that:

After this Perikles became one of the leaders of the people, first becoming famous when as a young man he prosecuted Kimon at the investigation of his conduct at the end of his term of office as general. With Perikles the state became still more democratic; he deprived the Areiopagos of some of its powers and turned the state particularly towards naval power, with the result that the masses had the courage to take more into their own hands in all fields of government . . . Perikles introduced pay for those serving in the law-courts as a political move to counter the effects of Kimon's wealth . . . Damonides of Oe, who was thought to have suggested most of Perikles' measures and was later ostracized for this very reason, suggested to him that since he could not match Kimon in private resources, he should give the people what was their own. Perikles accepted his advice, and introduced pay for the jurymen (*ibid* 27. 1 and 3–4)

Yet, though we are in no position to ignore this account, it is dismally unsatisfactory. We are not told why Ephialtes or Perikles prosecuted, nor why the members of the Areiopagos were convicted; we are not told what the 'acquired prerogatives' were; the introduction of pay for jurymen is made a matter of purely tactical personal rivalry; and the motivations imputed are naive and simplistic. To give it flesh and plausibility we need more evidence, and this is probably one of the cases where it may be wiser to look at the general picture first, in the hope that what the documents concentrate on may reveal the preoccupations of the men who created them, and the political system they reflect.

The documents fall into four main groups. One concerns foreign affairs in the most general sense – treaties, decrees honouring foreigners, decrees regulating affairs in cities of the

Empire or throughout the Empire as a whole. It forms by far the largest group of assembly decrees from the fifth century, gives us much of our information about the Empire and suggests, not surprisingly, that foreign affairs and running the Empire bulked large in Assembly preoccupations. A second enormous group consists of accounts, set up by administrative boards to record transactions during their year of office. The Tribute Lists, set up by the Hellenotamiai (see p. 47) from 454–3 on, are the first securely dated series, but the document from which the following comes may refer to an earlier date. It records the expenses of the committee in charge of erecting the statue of Athene Promachos and exemplifies a type of which many more were soon to follow:

[(Sum lost) When K]a[list]ratos of A [– –]i [was secretary], the over[seers receive]d fr[om the state treas]ur[ers];

[(Sum lost) Receipts left ov]er [from the p]re[vious year];

[(Sum lost) Sacred expenses from th]is sum;

[(Sum lost) – talents of copper; price of this];

[(Sum lost) – talents of tin; price of this];

[(Sum lost) – for the j]ob [– and constr]uction [of furnaces];

[(Sum lost) Charcoal and wood f]or burning;

[(Sum lost) –];

[(Sum lost) Wages by day, wa]ges by [prytany, wages] by piece rates;

[(Sum lost) Earth and hair];

[(Sum lost) Wages for the overseers a]nd secreta[ry and assistant];

[(Sum lost) Uncoined silver for] decoration [of the statue];

[(Sum lost) Total];

[(Sum lost) was left over from the rece]ipts [to the subsequent year];

(*IG* i³ 435, lines 24–48; the restorations are less arbitrary than they look, being made by analogy from entries for other years).

Accounts were also set up by other committees of public works by the superintendents of various major sanctuaries, by the Public Accountants, intermittently by the Public Auctioneers, and by the treasurers of temple funds both at national level and at

local level. A third large group of documents are the public gravestones, set up from *c.* 465 onwards to commemorate those who
died in battle for the city; a fourth group comprises decrees and
specifications concerning cults, festivals, and rituals, while a few
lists of officials, boundary stones and public dedications complete
the picture.

This explosion of documentation tells us various things.
Firstly, it illuminates the wealth and resources at Athens'
disposal, and their deployment on building the temples and
creating the works of art which have defined Athens ever since.
Secondly, the fact that these documents were all put up in public
places, especially the Akropolis and the Agora, means that they
were meant to be read. The records of government have become
ostentatiously public, for the first time in Mediterranean or
European history, in contrast with the Linear B tablets – records
of government, certainly, but kept by and for a palace administration – or with the self-advertising records of achievement set up
by innumerable Near Eastern kings and princes. A fourth-
century historian indeed believed that 'Ephialtes removed the
axones and the *kyrbeis* (the physical objects on which was written
the text of Solon's legislation) from the Akropolis down to the
Council-Chamber and the Agora' (Anaximenes, *Philippika, FGH*
72 F 13). If this is true the symbolism of linking the laws with
democratic institutions could hardly be clearer. Thirdly, and
most important of all, the documents reveal the importance of
the Assembly as *the* effective sovereign governing body; the
importance which the Council of 500 came to have as the main
executive organ of government; the way in which amendments to
proposals could be and were made from the floor of the
Assembly; and the devolution of power to the citizenry, via the
proliferation of committees all reporting to, and dependent on,
Council and Assembly. By good fortune we have one document,
of about 450, which well exemplifies the whole picture, even
though earlier lines are missing.

(Part A) [. . . the] festival-organizers and t[he . . .] and spend
[–] of the same; and let the steering committee of Council bring
the [–] forward to the Council whenever they require.

(Part B) Thespieus moved: in other respects in accordance with the Council's motion, but choose five men from Athenians; they are to receive four obols each (per day) from the city-treasurers, and one of them is to serve as secretary in accordance with a vote. These men are to be in charge of the moneys of the Two Goddesses, in the same way as those in charge of the building-works on the Akropolis were in charge of the temple and the statue. Refusal of office on oath is not to be allowed. Those selected are to approach the Council and inform it if they find any debts due to the Two Goddesses, and are to try to recover them. They are to hold office for a year, after swearing an oath between the altars at Eleusis, and in future the men are to be selected every year in the same manner. They are also to take care of the yearly offerings which are received (as tithes) for the Two Goddesses, and if they discover that anything has been lost they are to recover it. The public accountants are to reckon up (i) at Eleusis what moneys have been spent at Eleusis, and (ii) in the City what have been spent in the City, summoning the architect Koroibos and Lysanias in the Eleusinion, and (iii) at Phaleron in the shrine what has been spent at Phaleron. In future they are to spend what is most necessary in consultation with the priests and the Council. After their term of office they are to summon from the magistracy [–] the moneys (the meaning of this sentence is not clear). Inscribe the decree on a stele at Eleusis and [in the City and at Ph]aleron in the Eleusin[ion].

(Part C) [Lysanias move]d; in other respects in accordance [with Thespieus' motion; but the reckon]ing [of the moneys which the trea]surers handed over is to be made by [the five men selected and] the archi[tect –] (the rest is broken off). (*IG* i³ 32)

The immediate context is clear enough. It looks as if there has been some spectacular scandal of financial maladministration at the sanctuaries of Demeter and Kore in Eleusis, in the City of Athens, and at Phaleron, probably the embezzlement of funds for building. The Council had proposed certain measures (Part A) which Thespieus thought, and persuaded the Assembly so, were inadequate. Proposing an amendment from the floor of the Assembly, he secured nothing more nor less than the creation from scratch of an entirely new five-man administration board to deal both with the present scandal and with finance in future, together with a specification of how they were to be paid. Lysanias' supplementary amendment, also from the floor, seems to be defining their powers even more uncompromisingly. The Assembly's power and freedom of action are palpable.

But Thespieus' amendment also illustrates four other aspects of the Athenian revolution. Firstly, we notice his and Lysanias' freedom to speak, though they are not known to be, and need not be, current or past office-holders or even members of Council. It is disputed when free access for any citizen to speak and to propose motions became either a legal right or an everyday reality, but the contrast with the Assemblies of contemporary Sparta or of Rome at any period is real enough. Secondly, we can see in action the principle of access to office. The five men are to be selected 'from Athenians', without restriction of birth or wealth, and the same was true, or came to be true, of nearly all magistrates and official posts. The treasurerships alone remained confined to the wealthy, for there was then something to distrain up on in case of embezzlement. Indeed, a few years previously, 'in the sixth year after the death of Ephialtes [i.e. in 458–7] they decided to admit *Zeugitai* to the preliminary selection of those from whom the nine archons would be selected by lot' (*Athenian Constitution* 26. 2). Thereby they admitted all but the lowest property-class and made even the highest office of state open to well over half the citizen population. Thirdly, and closely related to this opening of offices, came the principle of pay for office. That the new board of 'superintendents from Eleusis', as they came to be called, received a daily wage from public funds put the five men concerned, during their year of office, in the same position as already were (or came to be: we are badly informed about dates) the 500 men on the Council each year, the archons and certain other administrative officials, and the 6000 members of the panel of jurymen, who received payment for the days they spent in court. As Aristotle's narrative (see p. 52) shows, pay of this sort was new, and our (uniformly conservative) sources both disapprove and misunderstand. That is to say, there may have been some reason to ascribe the introduction of pay to tactical manoeuvring on the part of Perikles, but such an explanation ignores the question of function and effect. Pay allowed all citizens, even the poorest, to perform time-consuming public tasks which they would otherwise not have had the leisure to fulfil, and thereby gave them a share in executive power. Not for nothing was pay for office ever afterwards a political symbol: abolished by oligarchs, reinstated by democrats, it lasted into the third century BC in Athens (and was copied elsewhere).

Fourthly, and most far-reachingly of all, we can see that an administrative default has provoked the creation of a new entity of government with stated powers. It is not clear who has been at fault, though the architect hardly emerges with credit. However, one begins to envisage the sort of situation which may have lain behind Ephialtes' prosecutions ten or fifteen years previously 'with reference to their administration'.

The picture becomes clearer still in the light of another document of the 450s.

[Resolved by] Council [and People: – was the tribe in prytany, –] was Secre[tary, – was presiding officer, – moved]: Concerning the requests made by [the Praxiergidai, the prophecy of the] god and the (privileges) which were prev[iously voted to them are to be writ]ten up on a [stone] stele [and deposited on the Akropolis behi]nd the Old Temple: [the Public Auctioneers are to] let the contract. The money [for the inscribing is to come from the funds] of the Goddess (Athene) in accordance with ancestral custom. [The treasurers of the Goddess and the] City Treasurers are to give [them the money].
Apollo gave oracular response that the following are c[ustomary usages for the Praxiergidai: to] drape the sacred robe round the (statue of the) [goddess and make preliminary sacrifice to the Fa]tes, to Zeus the leader of Fate, to E[arth –.] The following are ancestral customs for the Prax[iergidai: –.]
(break in the stone)
[– to] provide [– for the Praxiergi]dai [–; but] the Fleece [–] give in accordance with [ancestral custom –] provide [–:] the

Archon is to seal the Temple (during the month of) Thargelion [until the] 28th and to give [the keys] in accordance with ancestral custom to the Praxiergi[dai. The] Praxier[gidai] are to drape [the image] (of the goddess) with a tu[nic] costing two *minai* or pay a [fine of one *mna*]. (*IG* i³)

The document is badly broken, but much detective work has made its contents and date clear. It deals with an aristocratic family who had a prominent hereditary position in the cult of Athene at one or more of her festivals. It looks as if there had been a major disagreement between the family and the City over its place in the ritual. It was ultimately resolved by referring the dispute to the oracle of Apollo (presumably at Delphi), and by doing so in such a way as to have Apollo sanctify and state explicitly what was 'ancestral custom' – and, by implication, to prohibit what was not. To say that what was not 'ancestral custom' was 'acquired prerogative' is a short, indeed unavoidable step, for the two words are often used as formal contraries in Greek. We are being given a parallel, at the level of cult, to what is said to have happened to the powers of the Areiopagos.

With these developments in mind we can look again at the narrative of surface events. There is undeniably an external, even accidental, element. After the earthquake of 464 Sparta had appealed for help against the helots in revolt, and Kimon prevailed upon the Athenian Assembly, against Ephialtes' opposition, to send such help (see p. 50). Yet the rug was pulled from under Kimon's feet when the Spartans,

apprehensive of the enterprising and revolutionary character of the Athenians, and further looking upon them as of alien extraction, began to fear that if they remained, they might be tempted by the besieged in Ithome to attempt some political changes. They accordingly dismissed them alone of the allies, without declaring their suspicions, but merely saying that they had now no need of them. But the Athenians, aware that their dismissal did not proceed from the more honourable reason of the two, but from suspicions which had been conceived, went away deeply offended, and conscious of having done nothing to merit such treatment from the Spartans, and the instant that they returned home they broke off the alliance which had been made against the Persians and allied themselves with Sparta's enemy Argos; each of the contracting parties taking the same oaths and making the same alliance with the Thessalians. (Thucydides 1. 102. 3–4)

Plutarch adds what Thucydides omits, that they 'proceeded to take public revenge upon the friends of Sparta in general and Kimon in particular. They seized upon some trifling pretext to ostracize him and condemned him to exile for ten years, which is the period laid down for all those who are banished by ostracism' (*Kimon* 17. 3).

However, as the evidence has shown, there is much more to it than a débâcle in foreign politics and a purge of the men responsible. What Thucydides says of the mood of the Athenian soldiers on the Ithome campaign is revealing. Their sympathies were clearly with the Messenians, who were after all Greeks and whose bid for emancipation from Spartan domination and exploitation closely resembled that of the Asian Greeks after 478 for freedom from Persia. To assist the latter, as they had been doing for 17 years, mostly under Kimon's leadership, and now to help keep the Messenians in subjection was a manifest contradiction which reflected very badly on Kimon: at least on this occasion the Athenians had been quite literally misled. This consideration links up with Ephialtes' prosecutions, with the drastic curtailment of the powers of the Areiopagos, and even with the negotiations between the City and the Praxiergidai, to suggest that what came to be at issue was the style, openness, and accountability of political leadership to the people at large. What is more, the issue is plainly visible in contemporary tragedy. Whatever Aeschylus' own views and dramatic intentions may have been, it can hardly be chance that the language which he gives in 464–3 to the Argive king, faced with a request from the 50 daughters of Egyptian Danaos for asylum and protection, could serve as a programme for much that was done in the next ten years:

You are not suppliants at my own hearth;
If the city in common incurs pollution,
In common let the people work a cure.

But I would make no promises until
I share with all the citizens.

Or again:

Judgement is not easy to give; choose me not as judge.
I said it previously too, that without the people
I should not take this step, even if I have the power, lest
The people say
'You honoured strangers and destroyed the city'.
(*Suppliants* 365–9 and 397–401)

So, too, it is probably no accident that the motif of 'account-ability' is frequent in his poetry.

Some of the innovations of this period can certainly be seen simply as the much needed creation of a modern administrative apparatus adequate for Athens' new responsibilities at home and in the Aegean. However, the larger part comprises a firm subordinaation of that apparatus to the organs of popular government, in a way which involved older magistracies and institutions in major trauma. The process helped, and was probably intended, to bring under control an aristocracy which was clearly as ambitious as it may have been untrustworthy or incompetent. Major internal violence was indeed avoided, though Ephialtes himself was murdered in 462–1 and Thucydides records that in 458 a Spartan army entered and stayed in Boeotia partly because 'secret encouragement had been given them by a party in Athens, who hoped to put an end to the reign of democracy and the building of the Long Walls' (1. 107. 4). Yet these were, in effect, ten deeply revolutionary years which permanently changed the political landscape of Greece. On the international scale there stemmed from them, as the quotations from Thucydides' narrative are already enough to make clear, the hostility between Athens and Sparta, and the increasing polarization of Greece between them, which were to mould Greek experience for nearly a century. On the Aegean scale it became so much more valuable to have Athenian citizenship that in 451–0 Perikles' citizenship law (see quotation, p. 92) made the Athenian citizen body into a closed group, inaccessible from

outside, which it remained until the late third century BC. On the
national, Athenian, scale the old aristocratic governing class,
largely dispossessed of its hereditary power, fought for survival in
various ways. In part it adopted the appropriate new techniques
and attitudes without necessarily believing in them. As the Old
Oligarch (2. 20) remarked, sourly but not entirely unjustly:
'. . . a man who is not of the common people and chooses to live in
a city that is ruled by a democracy rather than one with an
oligarchy is preparing to do wrong, and realizes that it is easier to
get away with being wicked under a democracy than under an
oligarchy.' In part it retreated, regrouped, and sought for new
weapons with which to fight back. It is not too much to say that
the search for such weapons goes far to explain why Greek
political theory as we see it in Plato, Isokrates, and Aristotle,
developed as it did.

Yet, and this is the central and formidable difficulty which the
source-material forces on to our attention, such hints as we have
of what the 'revolutionaries' thought they were doing (e.g. in the
Athenian Constitution or in the decree for the Praxiergidai) do *not*
talk the language of revolution. They speak rather of the abolition
of accretions and of the return to ancestral custom. The paradox
has parallels. One might recall how the sixteenth-century
Reformation in Europe was thought of as a return to the practices
and values of primitive Christianity, or how the seventeenth-
century English Levellers advocated lifting the 'Norman Yoke'
and returning to the freer society of Saxon and pre-Conquest
England. The latter parallel, indeed, is suggestive and helpful,
for it introduces a motif, that of political myth, which is clearly
recognizable in the material from Athens. Precisely in this period,
in Aeschylus' *Eumenides* of 458, we have what can only be called
the 'charter myth' of the institution which was at the centre of the
tensions of these years. On Apollo's advice Orestes has come
to Athens to submit himself to trial for his matricide of
Clytaemnestra before a special court set up by Athene. Towards
the end of the hearing she says:

Now hear my ordinance, people of Athens,
As you sit in judgement at this first trial for bloodshed.
Hereafter too there shall be for the folk of Aigeus (*sc.* Athenians)

For all this time this tribunal of jurymen.
This Hill of Ares – once the site of
The tents of Amazons, when in jealousy of Theseus they
    came
On armed expedition, and at that time raised up
This high-walled counter-citadel in opposition,
And sacrificed to Ares, from whence is named
The crag and Hill of Ares – here Reverence
Of the citizens, and her kinsman Fear, shall restrain
Wrong-doing both by day and even by night,
If the citizens for their part do not innovate laws:
By polluting clear water with bad new liquids
And with mud, you will never find drinking water.
The rule 'neither ungoverned nor governed despotically'
I advise the citizens to maintain and revere,
And not to banish Fear entirely from the city;
For what mortal man who fears nothing is righteous?
But if you dread righteously an ordinance such as this,
You might have a bulwark of the land and salvation of the
    city
Such as none of mankind has,
Neither among the Scythians nor in the land of Pelops.
This tribunal, untouched by corruption,
Reverend, quick to anger, on behalf of those who sleep
Ever awake, I establish as the bastion of the land.
(Aeschylus, *Eumenides* 681–706)

At first sight no charter could be more explicit. The court is set
up by divine authority, it is placed in the timeless past, and the
crime it was set up to consider, homicide, is precisely that which
was left with it, as 'ancestral custom' by Ephialtes' reforms. Yet
the import of the warning (if it is that) in lines 693–5 is
far from clear, and the phrases 'bulwark of the land' and 'bastion
of the land' could go far beyond the simple responsibility of
adjudicating homicide, to suggest a role uncommonly like
Aristotle's 'guardianship of the constitution' (see p. 52).
However, though the problem of what precisely Aeschylus was
commending is real and important, and its resolution is endlessly
debated by modern scholars, it is more a problem about

Aeschylus than one about Athenian politics. Whatever he thought 'ancestral custom' sanctioned, that was the sanction used, both by him and others: if this is a revolution, it is a revolution couched in deeply conservative terms.

V

The Athenian Empire

WE SAW IN Chapter Four how Kimon's formula for Athens broke down, at home in favour of a régime based on participation and accountability, abroad in the form of war with Sparta and her Peloponnesian allies. In the 450s and 440s the war was a desultory affair, formally ended in the winter of 446–5 in a Thirty Years' Peace between Athens and Sparta, but in 431 it broke out again, far more intensely, in what posterity knows as *the* Peloponnesian War. In part both sides saw it as a struggle to survive, but in part too it was meant to decide whether Greece would continue to be a politically pluralistic geographical expression or whether it would be united under Athenian hegemony, in much the same way as Italy was to be united under Roman hegemony a century later. It is therefore natural to derive this conflict (and the earlier one) from the growth and consolidation of the Athenian Empire in the Aegean, but there are two difficulties. To begin with, there is a good case for thinking that, for the Spartans, the Empire did play the positive role of keeping the Persians out of Greece. Their acceptance of the Athenian takeover suggests as much for 477, whatever counter-currents of resentment there came to be. Twenty years later 'The Persian King sent Megabazus, a Persian, to Sparta with money to bribe the Peloponnesians to invade Attica and so draw off the Athenians from Egypt. Finding that the matter made no progress, and that the money was being spent to no effect, he recalled Megabazus to Asia Minor with the remainder of the money' (Thucydides 1. 109. 2–3).

Secondly, Sparta did intervene against Athens or in her area of influence as opportunity offered: in 465, by a promise to the Thasians to invade Attica; in 457, by covert links with a planned coup d'état in Athens; and in 446, by an actual invasion of Attica. Yet she does largely seem to have accepted the *fait accompli* in the Aegean and to have recognized it diplomatically in terms of the peace-treaties of 446–5 and 421. The conflicts, then, may not have been primarily about the Athenian Empire as such. Rather, as Thucydides' detailed analysis in Book I of the tensions and crises of the 430s makes clear, they concerned the threatened extension of Athenian influence and techniques of control from one region of Greece (the Aegean) to a second (Central Greece) and, though only marginally at first, to a third (Sicily and Western Greece in general). The Corinthians made the point explicitly in their speech to the Spartans and their allies at Sparta in July 432:

> Time after time we warned you how we were about to be damaged by Athens. Each time, instead of taking the trouble to ascertain the value of what we told you, you were more inclined to suspect the speakers of being inspired by private interest. And so, instead of calling these allies together before the blow fell, you have delayed doing so till we are smarting under it. Among these allies we have the best right to speak, since we have the most serious complaints to make, complaints of Athenian outrage and Lacedaemonian neglect. Now if these assaults on the rights of Greece had been made in the dark you might be unacquainted with the facts, and it would be our duty to enlighten you. As it is, long speeches are not needed where you see servitude accomplished for some of us, meditated for others – in particular for our allies – and prolonged preparations by the aggressor against the hour of war. Why else should they have taken over Corcyra by fraud, and held it against us by force, or have beseiged Potidaea? The latter is a most convenient place for any action against the Thracian towns, while the former would have contributed a very large navy to the Peloponnesians. (Thucydides 1. 68. 2–4)

We have here not just a confirmation of Spartan reluctance to move against Athens but also an additional reason for it. The fact that the Spartans suspected 'private interests' sounds sour but makes sense both in the 450s and the 430s, in that any extension

Athenian influence outside the Aegean into Central Greece or towards the West affected Corinthian interests very directly but Spartan interests hardly at all. There are, then, three powers involved, not two: three regions of Greece are involved, not just the Aegean. Yet the logistical basis of action always remained the Aegean, so to begin with that region, and with the developing Athenian techniques of control over it, is to follow the logic of resources, even at the cost of some violence to chronological sequence. It is also to follow political logic, by tracing how Athens changed her techniques as she intervened in new regions, and to go with the sources, for to move from the Aegean outwards is to go from the better documented to the less well-documented.

There are five main sources for studying the Athenian Empire in its heyday. Thucydides' narrative is primary. Sketchy till the 430s but full thereafter, it gives us the basic sequence of political and military events, much factual detail, and a formidable and wide-ranging interpretation of action, scattered through the work in editorial asides or in the speeches which he gives to participants. Second come the records of tribute paid by the allied cities, inscribed from 454–3 onwards on large pillars, or *Stelai*, set up on the Akropolis. The preamble to List I records that : '[The following quotas] were all [severally] received [for the Goddess (Athene)] from the Hellenotamiai for whom [– was secretary] and were the first to be declared for audit [to the] Thirty (public accountants), [out of tribute which the allies brought] to the Athenians in the archonship of Aris[ton] [454–3] [at the rate of] one mna in [the talent]' (*IG* i³ 259). What was recorded, therefore, was the one-sixtieth which was officially paid as a quota to Athene, though in fact the rest came (by means which mostly remain very obscure) into Athene's treasury too and could be made available for general purposes. Since cities might pay the same amount for many years, the historical value of the lists lies in absences (indicating revolt or enemy occupation), in general changes in tribute levels, in specific changes affecting a particular city or region, and in indicating the scale of income available to Athens each year over and above her own resources. Third come those decrees of the Athenian assembly which were concerned with Aegean affairs.

They might be of general application throughout the member states of the League, or might concern the affairs of a particular city and its relationship to Athens and the League, or might concern the status of one particular person or group of persons from one city. Fourth come references, mostly casual, in literary sources. Some are contemporary or nearly so, such as Aristophanes from 425 onwards, the fragments of the other comic poets, the 'Old Oligarch', or the speech-writers from *c.* 420 onwards. Others are of the fourth century or much later, Plutarch's *Life of Perikles* being especially valuable. Lastly, there are a few documents emanating from the allied states themselves.

Such sources yield a picture of interaction in the Aegean. The narrative is clear enough, as are the techniques of Athenian control, but interpretation is inevitably deeply controversial. We must therefore start with what is clear. The main Athenian effort in the Aegean and the Near East in the 450s had been the expedition sent to help Egypt regain her independence from Persia (see p. 44). It is not clear from Thucydides just how many ships and men were lost when the expeditionary force was surrounded, besieged and captured at Prosopitis in the summer of 454, but if we include a relief fleet of 50 ships which was also captured, the figure may be as high as 250 ships, and Thucydides describes the disaster in much the same terms as he describes the end of the Sicilian expedition in 413. It is generally supposed that the disaster had three major consequences in the Aegean. Firstly, the Treasury of the League was moved from Delos to the Athenian Akropolis (whether genuinely for safety, or merely ostensibly so, we cannot tell). That is a certain inference from the start of the Tribute Lists (see quotation p. 66). Secondly, it is probable that offensive operations largely ceased, both against Persia and in Central Greece. Thirdly, there was widespread revolt in the communities of mainland Asia Minor which were most vulnerable to Persian counter-attack by land. We can infer this from surviving Athenian decrees which concern post-revolt settlements in Erythrae, Miletus and Colophon; from entries, absences and irregularities in the Tribute Lists which suggest trouble in Caria and elsewhere; and from the warmth of an Athenian decree of 451–50:

Sig[eians]. Resolved by the [council and the People] : Oineis [was the tribe in prytany, –]s was secreta[ry, – presided, An[tidotos was archon, – o]chides moved: [Praise the] Sigeians [as being] good [men] towards [the people of the Athenians –, and the secretary is to inscribe this decree on a pillar of] stone at the e[xpense of the S]igeians, and is to deposit it on the Akropolis, as they themselves request, so that there is to be a written record, and let them not be injured by any of those on the mainland (of Asia Minor). (*IG* i³ 17)

However, probably also in 451, a major League expedition to Cyprus, commanded by Kimon on his return from exile, seems to have re-established the security of the Aegean at the cost of Kimon's own death on the island. Thereafter hostilities between the League and Persia simply ceased. For the next 37 years the predominant activities in the Aegean came to be, firstly, the widespread takeover, by and for Athenian citizens, of fertile land in strategic places within the Aegean region or on its borders, and secondly the anticipation or suppression of major revolts, whether or not backed by Sparta or Persia. Instances are those of the cities of Euboea in 446, of Samos and Byzantium in 441–39, of Chalcidice from 433 onwards, of Lesbos in 427, and of the cities of the Thracian coast in the wake of a Spartan expedition in summer 424. During these years, until Athenian weakness after the collapse in 413 of her invasion of Sicily allowed Sparta and Persia jointly to move into an Aegean power vacuum, the membership and extent of the League remained extremely stable, comprising some 150 tribute-paying communities largely within the Aegean area bounded by Byzantium to the north and Phaselis to the east. All the communities ever involved (with the trivial exceptions, in the 430s, of a handful of Hellenizing Carian princelings) were Greek in their language and culture, at least in their citizen class. The fact stemmed directly from the original programme and profoundly influenced the control and cohesion which Athens could wield or expect.

First and foremost, it allowed the League to be based upon kinship among Ionians. At the start the cities involved were mostly Ionic in speech. Athens' claim to be 'the eldest land of Ionia', attested long since in Solon (F 4a West), seems to have been generally accepted in the fifth century as true and as implying a metropolis-colony relationship. Use of the link may at first have been unsystematic and indirect. The ruling class of one city (Miletus) claimed descent from Athenian kings; two islands show cults of 'Athene the ruler of Athens'; various authors developed the legends of the foundation of the Ionian cities from Athens; and Kimon called a son of his 'Oulios' after a cult-title of Apollo current in Delos and Asia Minor. However, two Athenian decrees of the mid-century point a different way. One, moved by Kleinias *c.* 447 and laying down tighter rules for tribute collection, specifies that 'If anyone commits an offence over the bringing of the cow or [of the panopl]y (of shield and helmet), he shall be prosecuted' (ML 46, lines 41–2). Another, of *c.* 445, which concerns the despatch of Athenian colonists to a city called Brea somewhere in Thrace, lays down that colonists '[are to br]ing a cow and a p[anoply] to the Great Panathenaia [and] a phallos [to the Dionysi]a' (ML 49, lines 11–13). Both clearly reflect the imposition, which we cannot date, of a uniform practice on all the communities in the League, even though by now many were not Ionian and could claim no kinship with Athens. Fortunately, we can see its re-enactment in 425: '[The ci]ties [assessed] for tribute . . . are all [to bring to] the G]reat Panath]enaia a co]w and a panop]l[y]. They are to take part in the procession [in the same manner as colo]n[ists]' (ML 69, lines 55–8).

This looks peremptory and insensitive. Yet, 'the Athenians took under their rule very many Greek cities not founded by themselves, which had been hard hit by the Persians but were still in existence, and nevertheless maintained their rule over them for over seventy years, because they had men who were their friends in each of the cities' (Plato, *Seventh Letter* 332b–c). Document after document shows the truth in this claim. It revolved above all round the institution of *Proxenia*, whereby a prominent citizen of state A residing in state A was selected by state B to give hospitality to B's citizens, to represent them in court and to protect B's interests in general. It was by now an old-established institution, deriving from the *xenia*-relationship between persons and families which we can see in Homer, but Athenian predominance altered, indeed re-institutionalized it. In Corcyra in 427 'Peithias was self-appointed proxenos of the Athenians and was the leader of the people; he was brought to trial on a charge of enslaving Corcyra to the Athenians' (Thucydides 3. 70. 3). The next stage would be formal recognition by Athens:

> Resolved by the Council and [the Peop]le; Antiochis was the tribe in prytan[y, Kle]ophrades was secretary, [–]ades presided, Charia[s was archon, K]allisthenes moved; since Ana[ximene]s with his sons [does benef]it to the city and to Ath[enians], inscribe him as proxenos [and benefa]ctor of Athenians on [a sto]ne [stele at his own] ex[pense –]. (*IG* i³ 95, of 415–14)

Such honours could be dangerous. Peithias was acquitted in court but lynched soon afterwards, and twenty years earlier the assembly had decided that

> [– Acheloion is to be proxenos and b]enefact[or of the Athenians: and if] Acheloion [is wrong]ed [by anyone, he can prosecute] them at A[thens in the court of the pol]emarch, [and he is not to pay] court[-fees] except for five drachmai [–]. If anyone kil[ls Acheloion or] one of his sons [in one of the cities wh]ich the Athenians [rule, the city is to owe a fine of] five talents, [as if] one of the [Athenia]ns were to die, [and vengeance] is to be taken again th[is person as if an Athenian had] died. (*IG* i³ 19; *c.* 450)

One can see too why proxenoi were vulnerable and needed protection. Overtly or covertly they might attempt to swing their state to a pro-Athenian stance, as Peithias was trying to do. They might act as informers, as when in 428:

> the Tenedians (who were at variance with the Mytileneans), the Methymnians, and for private reasons individuals from Mytilene itself who were proxenoi of the Athenians turned informers to the Athenians that the Mytileneans were forcibly uniting the island of Lesbos under Mytilene and were pushing ahead with all preparations for revolt in collaboration with the Spartans and their kinsmen the Boeotians. (Thucydides 3. 2. 2)

They might stage-manage a coup d'état, as when in the summer of 429 an Athenian fleet on its way round Peloponnese was diverted to Crete on the instigation of Nikias of Gortyn, who 'was a proxenos of the Athenians and had persuaded them to sail against Cydonia, promising to bring that town (which was hostile) over to them; his real impulse being to do a favour to the men of Polichna, neighbours of Cydonia' (Thucydides 2. 85. 5). In this way the transformed institution became an instrument of government. The proxenoi got protection, status and power: the Athenians got a means of keeping allies in line which was cheap (proxeny decrees cost nothing), indirect and therefore diplomatically acceptable.

Analogously, some key communities might receive favoured treatment in status or finance. All the allied states had been 'autonomous', but the term came to denote providing ships rather than money to League resources, which was impossible without internal self-government. By 446 only three states remained thus autonomous. Samos lost the status in 439, Lesbos in 427, but Chios remained autonomous, and oligarchic, right down to her revolt in 412. Her special position, recognized in Athenian decrees and even in prayers, had perhaps become a precarious privilege by 412, but it had also given Athens the active co-operation of the Aegean's most viable alternative power centre. Again, though tribute was exacted fairly uncompromisingly, exemptions were made, and we can often guess why. For example, surviving fragments of the Tribute Lists tell us that Ainos on the eastern coast of Thrace paid twelve talents till 449–8, ten talents from 444–3 till 439–8, four talents in 435–4, and nothing in 434–3, 431–30 and 429–8. It may be that money was being diverted to pay for a garrison, but more likely Athens had been persuaded that the Thracian tribes under two successive able and ambitious kings exerted pressure which needed compensation. Even more revealing is the evidence about Methone in southern Macedonia, since we have a dossier of Athenian decrees concerning her, inscribed en bloc in 424–3. She apparently entered the League in 434–3, when relations between Athens and the Macedonian king Perdikkas were fluid, unpredictable and bad. In 430–29, the first decree said,

The people are to vote at once on the question of the Methoneans, whether it is right for the people to assess tribute at once or whether it is sufficient for them to pay the quota of one-sixtieth for the Goddess out of the tribute which was assessed at the previous Panathenaia for them to pay, but otherwise to be tribute-free. As for the debts which they are inscribed in the public treasury of the Athenians as owing, if they are loyal to the Athenians as they are now or even better, the Athenians shall allow them to be classified separately in respect of these arrears, and if a [general] decree is passed concerning the debts posted on the [public notice boards] let no demand be made on the Methoneans [unless] a separate decree is passed about Methoneans. Three [envoys] over fifty years of age are to be sent to Perdikkas, and are to tell him that it is just that he should let them use the sea and not restrict their movements, that he should allow imports into the country as before, that neither side should harm the other, and that he should not lead an army through the Methoneans' territory without their consent . . . (ML 65, lines 5–23)

Again, in 426–5:

The Methoneans are to be allowed to export corn from Byzantium up to [(several thousand)] medimnoi every year. The guardians of the Hellespont are not themselves to stop these exports or to let anyone else stop them, or else they are each to face a fine of 10,000 drachmai on leaving office . . . Any general decree which the Athenians may pass concerning the allies, demanding military assistance or any other service from the cities, whether concerning the Athenians themselves or the cities, is to apply to the Methoneans if the decree mentions the city of Methone by name, but otherwise not; they should play their proper part by defending their own territory . . . (ML 65, lines 34–47)

How far Methone was genuinely being squeezed between the sea power and the hinterland power, or how far she was cleverly playing Athens and Perdikkas off against each other, is not clear, but seaboard states, though more vulnerable, could play that game more confidently than the islands could.

There were other techniques, too, besides the use of naked force. The decree for Acheloion shows how cases involving some privileged individuals could be brought before Athenian courts, and the privilege could be extended. If the restorations are right, a decree of 425–4 reads:

> [K]l[eo]nuymos moved [: in other respects according to the Council, but] it is not permitted to fine Ach[— without] the people of the Athenia[ns: if anyone transgresses any of the] pledges, the penalty [for him is to be to be death and his proper]ty is to be confiscated a[nd a tithe of it is to go to the goddess] . . . (*IG* i³ 70, lines 5–9)

Similarly some, perhaps all, cases involving certain specified penalties were transferred to Athens. The decree settling the affairs of Chalcis in Euboea after her revolt in 446 lays down, among much else, that:

> legal suits for Chalcidians against their own fellow-citizens are to be held in Chalcis, just as those for Athenians in Athens, except for cases involving exile, death and loss of civic rights: in these cases there is to be a right of appeal to the lawcourt of the *thesmothetai* at Athens in accordance with the decree of the people. (ML 52, lines 71–6)

About 415 the speech-writer Antiphon could make a Mytilenean client of his, accused of murder, say in an Athenian court that his prosecutors, in allegedly killing the principal witness, had done something 'which is not permitted even for a city to do, namely to sentence someone to death without the permission of the people of the Athenians' (5. 47). He may be exaggerating, but the statement had to be at least plausible. Again, the need for complaisant régimes in the allied cities might require not just collaborationist 'friends' and proxenoi but also a change of constitution. Fourth-century sources asserted that 'the Athenians destroyed oligarchies everywhere' (Aristotle, *Politics* 1307ᵇ 23) and that:

we came to the aid of the masses, and made war on despotism. We thought it monstrous that the many should be subjected to the few, or that poor but decent men should be excluded from office, or that some should lord it over what should be a commonwealth of citizens while others who were citizens by birth should be resident aliens, deprived by law of civic status. These and worse criticisms of oligarchy led us to establish among others the same constitution as we had ourselves. (Isokrates 4. 105–6)

Yet the specific contemporary evidence mostly stems from past or imminent revolts, and hardly suggests a moral crusade. When Miletus quarrelled with Samos in 441, and 'private citizens from Samos herself, who wished to change the constitution, added their weight to the Milesian complaints, the Athenians sailed to Samos with 40 ships, set up a democracy, took 50 Samian boys as hostages, and as many adult men, deposited them on Lemnos, installed a garrison, and returned home' (Thucydides 1. 115. 2–3). Twelve years earlier, in 453–2, a decreee dealing with Erythrae after her revolt laid down that:

there is to be a Council, selected by lot, of 120 men; the [–] in the Council; a non-citizen, or a man less than thirty years old, is not to serve on Council . . . No one shall serve on the Council twice within four years. The first Council shall be set up, through the drawing of lots, by the [inspec]tors and the garrison commander; future Councils shall be set up by the Council and the [garrison] commander not less than 30 days before [the Cou]ncil goes out of office. (ML 40, lines 8–16)

It is usually inferred that democratic Council implies democratic Assembly, and that it is here an innovation. Yet other settlement documents leave it unclear whether a democratic régime is being established or restored; some oligarchies were certainly left in peace; documents from late on in the Peloponnesian War give a free choice of constitution to cities returning into alliance; and it could be said that democracy was fashionable anyway. It does look as if most Aegean communities were democracies by the 420s, but this was the product of many separate situations and decisions (not all of them Athenian) rather than of an imposed regularity.

However, the will and the ability to impose regularity were there. We have some examples of what the second decree for Methone (see p. 72) called 'general decrees which the Athenians may pass concerning the allies, demanding military assistance or any other service from the cities'. Some were concerned with tribute. A decree of 425, providing for a general reassessment and for heavy increases in tribute, is the only one extant from what must have been a long series. Again, Kleinias' decree of *c*. 447 (see p. 69) is uncompromising:

Resolved by the Coun[cil and the] people; the tribe Oineis was in pry[tany, Sp]oudias was secretary, [–]on was chairman of the assembly, Kleini[as moved]: The Council and the *arch*[*ontes* in] the cities and the [inspect]ors are to ensure that the tribute is collected each year and is brought to Athens. They are to arrange with the cities for identification-seals, so that it shall not be possible for those who bring the tribute to defraud. Each city is to record on a tablet the tribute which it is sending, seal it with the seal, and send it to Athens. Those who bring it are to hand over the tablet in the Council when they pay the tribute . . . The Athenians are to choose four men [and send them to] the cities to give a receipt for th[e tribute which has been paid and] to demand the [unpaid] tribute [from those who are in defa]ult . . . if any Ath[enian or ally commits an offence in respect of the] tribute which [the cities] ought [to send to Athens, after recording it on a tab]let for those who bring it, [any Atheni]an or all[y who] wishes [may pr]osecute [him] before [the prytaneis] . . . The [Hellenotamiai are to record on] a whitened notice board [and are to display both the assessmen]t of the tribute and [the cities which have paid up in full, and] are to record [–] . . . (ML 46)

Other general decrees, however, went well beyond tribute or military matters. We have already seen reason (see p. 69) to infer the existence of a general decree requiring the cities to participate with offerings at the Panathenaia and Dionysia. Another, extant in several copies but even so very fragmentary, provided for the withdrawal of all allied coinages in favour of Athenian. The most explicit clauses are:

[(8) And if anyo]ne proposes a mo[tion on these matters] or puts a motion to the vote, [that it should be allowed] to use or lend [foreign currency, he is to be indicted at once] before the Eleven (prison-commissioners): and the [Eleven] shall p[unish him with de]ath [: but] if he disputes (the sentence), let them br[ing him before the] court . . . (12) The Secretary of the [Council] is to add the following clause to the Councillor's Oath [for the future]: If anyone mints silver coinage in the cities and does not use [Athenian currency] and weights and mea[sures, but uses foreign currency] and weights and measures, [I shall punish him an]d [fine him according to the for]mer decree which Klearcho[s moved]. (13) [Any person may hand ov]er foreign currency [which he possesses and exchange it] whenever he wishes [in accordance with these same principles]. The city [is to repay him with our own coinage], and each individual is to [bring] his own [to Athens and deposit it at the m]int. (ML 45)

The date, purpose and effectivenes of this decree are all disputed, for it has proved difficult to date breaks in the coinage issues of the Aegean states or even sometimes to perceive them. No Greek coins, now or till much later, carried dates; stylistic criteria help little as between 440s, 430s, or 420s; and coinage issues seem to have been spasmodic anyway, unless (like Athens) the state concern had a steady supply of bullion under its own control.

The major value of this and the other general decrees lies partly in revealing the assumptions which Athenians were making, namely that their decrees could be enforced throughout the Aegean, and that they could go beyond tribute and war. Partly they show us how enforcement involved, or relied on, the invasion of the Aegean states by Athenians on a temporary or permanent basis. At one level we hear of 'inspectors', who seem to have been civilians sent out to supervise a delicate post-revolt situation (as at Erythrae: see p. 74), or 'to review the situation in the various cities', as a later lexicographer put it (Harpocration s.v. *Episkopos*). At a second level come Athenians whose presence in a city was evidently intended to be long-term. They seem to have become so widespread that the Coinage Decree entrusted the enforcement of its provisions primarily to them, and only secondarily to local magistrates of the cities 'in cases where there are no *archontes* from the Athenians' (ML 45, para. 4). Some of them were garrison-commanders. Garrisons were expensive and far from common till the Peloponnesian War erupted, being used, it seems, only to control a potential or subdued rebel city (Samos: Erythrae) or to protect a city against external threat. Far more important, pervasive and effective were the Athenians installed abroad in permanent settlements and given land enough for economic independence. Some went as colonists, either becoming citizens of existing towns or participating with others from the Aegean in new foundations, while others went as 'allotment holders' (kleruchs), remaining Athenian citizens apart from the local community. We know of some 24 settlements in all (there may well have been more), and we cannot always tell from the sources which settlement fell into which category. Nor, unfortunately, do we know how many men altogether left Athens in this way, but a guess of at least 10,000 would be of the right order. The problem is to understand why they were sent where they were, for motives seem to have been mixed and changing. One pattern is clear: the chain Chersonese–Lemnos–Imbros–Scyros, all under Athenian occupation by 447, protected the corn-route from the Black Sea to Athens and must have been so intended. But Plutarch knew of other motives:

> In addition Perikles sent 1000 kleruchs to Cheronese, 500 to Naxos, half of that figure to Andros, and 1000 to Thrace to live among the Bisaltai, and others to Italy when Sybaris, which they re-named Thourioi, was being refounded. By doing this he was relieving Athens of a lazy rabble which was meddlesome because of its idleness, was providing a remedy for the poverty of the people, and was installing fear and surveillance as neighbours for the allies to guard against any revolutions. (*Perikles* 11. 5–6)

His language is loaded and his source untraceable, but his interpretation does fit other evidence. Many kleruchies were settled on the land of cities which had revolted and were precautionary as well as punitive. The decree of *c.* 445 founding the colony of Brea had an amendment added to it, from the floor of the Assembly, providing that 'the colonists going to Brea are to be drawn from thetes and zeugitai' (ML 49, lines 39–42). Here the two poorest property-classes were being given explicit preference. However, neither strategic garrisoning nor the actual movement of men from Athens was always primary. In describing the aftermath of the revolt of Lesbos, Thucydides says that in 427:

> tribute was not imposed upon the Lesbians; but all their land, except that of the Methymnians (who had remained loyal), was divided into 3000 allotments, 300 of which were reserved as sacred for the gods, and the rest assigned by lot to Athenian kleruchs, who were sent out to the islands. The Lesbians took upon themselves the obligation to pay them a rent of two *mnai* a year for each allotment while they themselves cultivated the land. (Thucydides 3. 50. 2)

Whether the men concerned went out to stay is unclear, but the important aspect is that they had become rentiers, appropriating some of the surplus value of the Lesbians' labour. The more we suspect such kleruchs were likely to be poor citizens, the more such action illustrates the populist programme 'to make all the landless citizens into hoplites' which Antiphon (F 61) referred to a few years later. Kleruchies and colonies emerge not just as garrisons or strategic points, but as land. Since we know too that Athenians came to own much land privately in the allied states, the Athenian presence in the Aegean amounts more and more to a tremendous land-grab, carried out and protected by Athenian naval power for the benefit of Athenian citizens of all classes.

Of course, underlying all these phenomena and techniques lay force or the threat of it. The Persian sack of Miletus in 494 had left Athens the biggest community in the Aegean, with the population and revenues to sustain so large a navy that its control of the Aegean could be effectively stopped only by the combination of Persian resources with those of at least part of Greece. Even in 322–1 her final naval defeat was at the hands of

Macedonians who had taken over Persian resources. Yet, for so important a politico-military phenomenon, we know infuriatingly little about the fifth-century navy. Herodotus says that Athens had 180 ships in 480, Thucydides that she had 300 in 431. There was clearly growth, but we do not know when. Emergencies in 458, 454, 430 and 428 probably saw more than 200 in commission, and in any case the aim must have been to have so many hulls available that even a major disaster would not leave the dockyards empty. Equally important was the availability of trained rowers and of adequate finance. In the 428 emergency:

> the Athenians became aware that the Spartans were making preparations for an expedition because of their perception of Athenian weakness. They wished to make it clear to the Spartans that they were mistaken, and that they themselves were well able to repel the force attacking them from Peloponnese without moving the fleet at Lesbos. They manned 100 ships by embarking the citizens of Athens, except for those of the two richest property-classes, and the resident aliens, put out to the Isthmos, displayed their power, and made descents on Peloponnese wherever they pleased. (Thucydides 3. 16. 1)

Two facts emerge. Firstly, every man in Athens (except, perhaps, the two top property-classes) had had the basic training; indeed Thucydides' accounts of several naval engagments make clear how the levels of skill they reached allowed small Athenian squadrons to run rings round far larger enemy forces. Secondly, however, by now ships manned exclusively by Athenian residents were exceptional. Thucydides makes the Corinthians say in August 432 that 'by borrowing the moneys from Olympia and Delphi we shall be able to take over their foreign rowers by offering higher pay. Their strength comes from mercenaries rather than citizens, while our own strength lies more in men than money and is less exposed to the same risk' (1. 121. 3). He then gives Perikles a rebuttal, with the words 'we have more and better citizen helmsmen and petty officers than all the rest of Greece: and to say nothing of the danger of such a step, none of our foreign sailors would consent to become an outlaw from his country, and to take service with them and their hopes, for the sake of a few days' high pay' (1. 143. 1–2). This turned out to be largely justified. Granted, naval warfare was expensive. Even aside from the capital cost of the hulls, it cost at least 3000 drachmai to pay a crew's wages for a month, and it has been suspected that many tribute-assessments of the allied states were fractions or multiples of three talents because that was the average cost of keeping a trireme in commission for the campaign season. But, even apart from Athens' own revenues, the reserve fund of the League had grown from nothing in 478 to 9700 talents at the time of its transfer from Delos to Athens in 454. Built up from the booty of successful campaigns, and kept up by tribute contributions, it allowed the navy to be deployed at the discretion of the Athenian assembly without danger of veto from the allies or from the Athenian upper class.

Thus far, then, matters are clear enough, but the Empire also sets interpretative problems which remain intractable. One is that after Kimon's death hostilities with Persia ceased for a generation. Writers from about 350 onwards, with a few pre-echoes in the 380s, maintain that there was a formal peace. The fullest version, taken by Diodorus from the fourth-century historian Ephoros, is that in 449–8:

> the Athenians and their allies concluded with the Persians a treaty of peace, the principal terms of which run as follows: All the Greek cities of Asia are to live under laws of their own making; the satraps of the Persians are not to come nearer to the sea than a three days' journey, and no Persian warship is to sail between Phaselis and the Cyanean rocks (at the mouth of the Black Sea); and if these terms are observed by the King and his generals, the Athenians are not to send troops into the territory over which the King is ruler. (Diodorus 12. 4. 5)

Since other references reflect much the same terms, the problem is to decide whether Diodorus was transmitting an authentic document or not. Those who think he was argue that the tradition is not seriously vulnerable to charges of anachronism or of inconsistency and vagueness of context or content (and that is as far as one can go when vindicating a document transmitted via literary tradition); that some turns of phrase in the sources seem to reflect an Ionic documentary style; and that, in general, if we did not have the tradition about the Peace, it would be necessary to invent it in much the same terms in order to account for the fifth-century facts. Hostilities *did* cease. Since there was almost certainly no Tribute List for 449–8, something very peculiar, probably a complete suspension of payments, *did* happen to League tribute in that year. Phaselis and Byzantium *were* the easternmost and northernmost extremities of the League for a generation. The Ionian cities *did* stay securely within the League orbit until Persia moved in after 413. Doubters object, on various grounds. Fifth-century sources, notably Thucydides, are silent about any Peace in 449. The first reference to the Peace, by Isokrates in 380, is a version at variance with that which later became canonical. One fourth-century historian roundly labelled the Peace a forgery, on the ground that the copy which could evidently then be read in Athens was written not in the Attic alphabet which Athens used publicly till 403 but in the Ionic alphabet which she used from then on (Theopompos, *FGH* 115 F 153–4). Most disquieting of all, there is a very substantial case for regarding as forgeries, or at best as imaginative re-creations, a whole series (over a dozen) of documents or decisions which have reached us through the literary tradition or later copies on stone. These begin to be referred to about 350, all purport to be Athenian decrees or documents emanating from about 490–40, and all place Athenian patriotism, generosity, and military success in a very favourable light. In this way the Peace of Kallias, so named after the Athenian politician said to have been the Athenian negotiator, has become a classic historical problem. The arguments pro and con elicited from the source-material suggest that both views must be partly right, but no solution has yet found general assent. Yet, until one does, no history of the Aegean in the mid-century can be written which is other than frustratingly provisional and tentative.

A second controversy emerges from the same context. The years after 454 yield a series of a dozen or so documents in which many see a hardening of Athenian attitudes and an intensification of control over the Aegean. Sometimes the impression is direct, as with Kleinias' decree or the decree about coinage (see p. 76). Sometimes it is indirect, as when in 453–2 members of the new

Council at Erythrae are required to swear to act 'in the interest of the massed people (*plethos*) of Erythrae and the massed people of Athens and her allies' and exiles 'shall be exiled from the whole Athenian alliance' (ML 40, lines 21f. and 31). Yet in 446–5 the alliance has vanished, all Chalcidians swear 'not to revolt from the people of Athens in any way or by any means whatever, in word or in deed . . .' (ML 52, line 21f.) And Acheloion is given protection 'in all cities which the Athenians rule' (see p. 70). However, not all the evidence points the same way. The allies recur in the oath to be taken by the Samians in 439 after the end of their revolt. We have hardly any document before 454 to serve as a control. Athens' conduct towards Thasos in 465–3 (see p. 44) is quite as ruthlessly self-interested as any later episode. Though Thucydides does acknowledge that a hardening took place, he sets it in the early 460s and blames it on allied laziness rather than Athenian usurpation (see p. 45). His obsession with the roots, forms and rat onalization of power may have given him too pro-Athenian a view, but the ensemble of the evidence does suggest that we have to do more with a steady drift of power to Athens than with a brief intense spasm in mid-century.

In these ways, then, one Greek region, the Aegean, became an Athenian lake, and what resistance there was came more from the communities affected than from Sparta or Corinth or even Persia. Central Greece was another matter. Virtually all we know of Athenian penetration there between 462 and 446 comes from Thucydides' survey, of telegraphic brevity, in 1. 102–15. There clearly was resistance, but since Thucydides gives no analysis whatever (or dates: those which follow are scholars' approximations), the interpretative responsibility is wholly ours. He tells us of the following: an alliance with Argos and Thessaly in 462–1; the settlement of Messenian exiles in the new Athenian possession of Naupactus c. 460; an alliance with Megara c. 460; naval battles at Halieis and Cecryphalea against Corinthian and Peloponnesian ships respectively c. 459; a land battle against Corinthians at Megara c. 458; a sea-battle, blockade and capture of Aegina in 459–7; two land battles in 457, one against Spartans and Boeotians at Tanagra, the other, against Boeotians only, at Oenophyta which gave Athens control of Boeotia, Phokis and

East Locris; a naval expedition which destroyed the Spartan dockyard at Gytheum and assaulted the territory of Corinth and Sicyon in 456–5; an unsuccessful Athenian-Boeotian attempt to impose a pro-Athenian king at Pharsalus in Thessaly c. 453; an expedition to Delphi c. 449–8; an expedition to regain control of Western Boeotia in 447 which was cut to pieces at Coronea and led to the Athenians abandoning Boeotia; and a revolt by Megara and Euboea in 446 which provoked a Peloponnesian invasion of Attica and a formal Peace in the winter of 446–5 by which Athens abandoned her remaining land possessions in Central Greece.

It is a major challenge, still not fully met, to make political sense of so disjointed a series of episodes. One can begin by isolating some patterns. For example, Athenian long-term gains were limited and were noticeably confined to areas which could be held by seapower alone. Again, Spartan activity was very spasmodic, perhaps through her losses from the earthquake and the helot revolt (see p. 42). Till 446 it concerned Doris and Delphi rather than other allies or pressure-points, and Thucydides' account suggests that Sparta was sucked into the Tanagra campaign rather than consciously sought it. More important, the initiatives were largely Athenian, so that one asks whether any one objective was consistently in view. As so often, to plot the points of conflict on a map (see Map 3) suggests an answer, for the epicentres of activity are plainly Corinth and Boeotia. It is a guess, but a plausible one, that the aim was two-fold: first, to create a solid block of Athenian-held territory north of the Isthmus, which would both give Athens direct access to the Corinthine Gulf and prevent the forces of the Peloponnesian League (see p. 40) from moving north with any ease or security; secondly, to render Corinth's position as the most northerly member of that League so exposed and vulnerable on all sides that she would bow to geostrategic logic, abandon Sparta, and join Athens or Argos. At that point the basically bipolar Peloponnesian League, shorn of its second pole, would collapse and leave Sparta isolated.

To move so rapidly to so wide-ranging an interpretation may seem irresponsible. Yet, as so often in Greek history, the choice is between the risky creation of an interpretation and the stultifying regurgitation of what the surviving sources happen to say.

This particular interpretation can be supported in the short, the long and the medium term. Short-term support comes from Thucydides: in 457,

> the Spartans came to the aid of the Dorians (in Doris), . . . and after compelling the Phocians to restore the town on conditions, they began their retreat. The Athenians were likely to send round a fleet to block their route by sea across the Crisaian Gulf, while the route across Geranea did not seem safe to them since the Athenians held Megara and Pegae. For the pass was a difficult one and was always guarded by the Athenians, and they had then heard that the Athenians intended to stop them using this route too. So they decided to stay in Boeotia and consider how they could get through most safely. (Thucydides 1. 107. 2–4)

Moreover, both of the aims I impute to the Athenians were inherent in the long-term regional geopolitics of Central Greece. A link between Athens and Boeotia was sought again in 424 and nearly came off, and was indeed re-created in an alliance of 395 and again in 378. Each time its threat or creation placed Sparta in acute difficulty, and each time its dissolution allowed Sparta to wield influence in Central Greece. Equally, the possibility that Corinth might leave the League was a real one. In July 432 her envoys begged Sparta to 'assist your allies and Potidaea in particular, as you promised, by a speedy invasion of Attica, and do not sacrifice friends and kinsmen to their bitterest enemies and drive the rest of us in despair to some other alliance' (Thucydides 1. 71. 4). In 421, affronted by Great Power détente, she did break temporarily with Sparta and allied herself with Argos and Boeotia instead. In 395 she did the same again, and in 391 amalgamated completely with Argos. It is probably true that though Sparta was placed in acute difficulty each time, this alternative alignment was a sign of Corinth's growing weakness through the fifth century, while for Boeotia it was a sign of her growing strength. However, what matters here is the continuity of the tactical options of both states vis-à-vis Sparta and Athens over several generations.

It is the medium term, the fifteen years after 446, which provides the best support. By July 432 the Corinthians were exerting strong pressure on Sparta to move against Athens (see p. 65), and this time Thucydides' much more detailed narrative of events in the 430s (1. 25–67) helps us to see why. He describes two main incidents. One was a quarrel between Corinth and her colony Corcyra over their joint colony Epidamnos, which led to Corcyra seeking Athenian help and to a confrontation between Athenian and Corinthian ships off the mainland coast at Sybota in August or September 433. The second concerned Potidaea, a colony of Corinth in Chalcidice but also a tribute-paying ally of Athens, where rough Athenian reactions to a threatened revolt provoked active Corinthian support for Potidaea by June 432 against an Athenian siege. Thucydides also says, with infuriating brevity, that alongside Corinth's complaints

> the Aeginetans, formally unrepresented from fear of Athens, proved not the least urgent of the advocates for war, asserting that they were not autonomous as the treaty specified. After extending the summons to any of their allies and others who might have complaints to make of Athenian aggression, the Spartans held their ordinary assembly and invited them to speak. There were many who came forward and made their several accusations. Among them the Megarians, in a long list of grievances, called special attention to the fact of their exclusion from the ports of the Athenian Empire and the market-place of Athens contrary to the treaty. (Thucydides 1. 67. 2–4)

(One other 'accusation' may have stemmed from an undatable Athenian naval expedition, which Thucydides mentions later *en passant*, to Acarnania at the mouth of the Corinthian Gulf.) In spite of much scholarly argument and of the fact that other authors (Aristophanes, Diodorus, Plutarch) thought, probably wrongly, that they had more information, these latter complaints remain hopelessly obscure. We still have to start and finish with Thucydides' presentation if we are to make sense of what is going on. Matters are not helped by his own equivocation, for he introduces his narrative by saying, 'The real cause I consider to be the one which was formally most kept out of sight. The growth of the power of Athens, and the fear which this caused to the

Spartans, compelled them to go to war. Still, the following were the grounds alleged by each side, which led to the dissolution of the treaty and the breaking out of war' (1. 23. 6). Here he describes as 'kept out of sight' a motif which runs repeatedly through the speeches which he then gives to participants in the debates at Sparta in July and September 432. Nonetheless, some things are clear. In the first place, the terms of the treaty of 446–5 did matter, even if it was arguable whether Athens had broken them. The trouble was that they seem, though we do not have the exact text, to have been so unspecific that they allowed too much freedom of interpretation. Secondly, both sides are presented as thinking themselves the victims of aggression. 'Vote therefore, Spartans, for war, as the honour of Sparta demands, and neither allow the further aggrandizement of Athens, nor betray our allies to ruin, but with the gods let us advance against the aggressors,' said the bellicose Spartan Sthenelaidas (1. 86. 5). 'The Spartans were plainly plotting against us previously, and it is still more clear now,' said Perikles in reply (1. 140. 2). All the same, the initiatives which had led to the crisis of 432 were undeniably Athenian, and do seem to have been not so much forced on her as suggested by circumstances which left room for manoeuvre and for choice from among alternative options. Thirdly, if one again resorts to a map, the initiatives again consisted of Athenian penetration outside 'her own' Aegean region into Central Greece, and the geographical or political epicentre of them all was again Corinth. The continuity of target and strategy is plain enough. Plainly, too, Athens' power had now to be measured not on a regional scale, but on a national, indeed Mediterranean scale. That power now needs more detailed assessment.

VI

Athenian Society in the Fifth Century

WE SAW IN Chapter Four how the documentary source-material throwing light on Athenian public life increased dramatically in bulk soon after 460. The same is true for nearly all other types of evidence about Athens. Of the 35 fully or partly extant tragedies, only three predate 460. Of comedy there is nothing but scattered fragments till 425. Extant prose writing begins in the 440s and 430s with Herodotus, the 'Old Oligarch', and the early speech-writers such as Antiphon from *c.* 420 onwards. The same is true of sacred and secular buildings and even of coinage. The only exceptions are lyric poetry and vase-painting, and even the latter declined in quality rather than in quantity. The problem is how to grasp this source material and to make it yield interpretations of the society that produced it which are neither unhelpfully specialized analyses nor irretrievably unrealistic encomiums. We must select and simplify, and fortunately can do so, for behind the concentration of source-material lies a major historical fact, the concentration of talents and resources at Athens. This concentration lies in the historian's province and needs to be explored and explained. Three aspects are salient: people, money and power.

First, people. It was above all in the fifth century that Athens became what she remained ever after till the emergence of Constantinople, *the* place above all others in the European East Mediterranean which people visited or gravitated towards. Some came by choice. The majority did not, and it is a commentary on our sources that we hear about the various groups of immigrants in inverse proportion to their numbers and importance, for the biggest group was certainly the slaves. Our knowledge about them is mostly a patchwork of incidental references and allusions, and the problem of how many there were at any one time is as virtually insoluble as it is fundamental. Evidence is casual and anecdotal. Thucydides says that after the Spartans had set up a fort at Decelea in spring 413, by midsummer 'great mischief was . . . done to the Athenians. They were deprived of their whole country(side); more than 20,000 slaves had deserted, most of them trained to a craft, and all their sheep and beasts of burden were lost' (Thucydides 7. 27. 3). Xenophon wrote *c.* 354 that:

> I suppose those of us who are interested have heard that long ago Nikias son of Nikeratos had 1000 slaves employed in the silver mines: he hired them out to Sosias the Thracian on condition that Sosias was to pay him the rent of an obol a day nett per man and was to keep the number up at the same level. Hipponikos had 600 slaves hired out on the same terms, who brought him a nett income of 100 drachmai a day, Philemonides got fifty drachmai a day from 300 slaves, and others, I imagine, according to what their resources allowed. (*Revenues* 4. 14–15)

Later, in 337 after Chaeronea, Hypereides was ruled out of order when he proposed to give freedom 'first to more than 150,000 slaves, both those from the silver-mines and those throughout the rest of the country, and then to the public debtors, the exiles, the disfranchised and the resident aliens' (Hypereides F 29). Since this comes from a period of intense renewed exploitation of the silver-mines, there is a case for the accuracy of the transmitted figure, but the far higher figure of 400,000 found in another source is generally disbelieved.

We are on firmer ground in investigating where they came from. A major scandal erupted in 415, and some fifty-three men are known to have been found guilty of profaning the Eleusinian Mysteries and/or of mutilating the phallic statues, or Hermai, which stood in front of each house and were thought to ward off evil. Their property was confiscated and sold off in 414, and the records of the Auctioneers were published. One fragment reads:

Property of Kephisodoros resident alien living in Piraeus:

165 *dr.*	Thracian woman	144 *dr.*	Scythian
135 *dr.*	Thracian woman	121 *dr.*	Illyrian
170 *dr.*	Thracian	153 *dr.*	Colchian
240 *dr.*	Syrian	174 *dr.*	Carian boy
105 *dr.*	Carian	72 *dr.*	Carian child
161 *dr.*	Illyrian	301 *dr.*	Syrian
220 *dr.*	Thracian woman	151 *dr.*	Melitt [–]
			(? = Maltese)
115 *dr.*	Thracian	85 *dr.*	Lydian
			woman
			(M-L 79A,
			lines 33–49)

Such other evidence as there is from the fifth and fourth centuries suggests that this group comprises a very typical cross-section, both for origins, sex-ratio and prices. The only significant, though small, group unrepresented is the 'house-bred', presumably as often as not the master's bastard children, who would take the legal status of their mother.

One can also see, at least roughly, where they were needed. The silver-mines, pumping out the bullion which formed the coins which paid for the corn imports which kept Athenians alive, seem to have swallowed slave-workers insatiably. The prayer of the newly gentled Furies, 'May the produce of the wealth of Earth always do honour to the unlooked-for gift of the gods!' (Aeschylus, *Eumenides* 946–8), needs to be read in the light of Nikias' contract with Sosias. Agricultural slavery is unquantifiable but was certainly the norm for an estate of any size, as our one extant treatise dealing in part with farming, Xenophon's *Oikonomikos*, reveals. Such slavery gave peasants the leisure to exercise their political rights and gave aristocrats the means to cut a dash, to live the good life and to hope to control public affairs. Craftsman slaves, often 'living outside' (the technical phrase) the household of their master but paying rent to him for the precarious privilege of *de facto* liberty, were not only another source of rentier income but must also have made many of the basic artefacts of life, e.g. domestic utensils and weapons. They certainly helped to build the temples and to form the occupational groups of small tradesmen and retailers. The most explicit, and always quoted, fifth-century source, the accounts of the Building Commission for the Erechtheion, records payments in May 407 as follows:

> For Stonework. For channelling the columns at the East end, by the altar: the column next to the altar of Dione, Laossos of Alopeke, Philon of Erchia, Parmeaon slave of Laossos, Karion slave of Laossos, Ikaros – 110 *dr*. The next column, the second one, Phalakros of Paiania, Philostratos of Paiania, Thargelios slave of Phalakros, Gerys slave of Phalakros – 110 *dr*. The next column, Ameiniades living in Koile, Lysanias, Somenes slave of Ameiniades, Aischines, Timokrates – 110 *dr*. The next column, Simias living in Alopeke, Kerdon, Sindron, Sokles, Sannion, Epieites, Sosandros – 60 *dr*. The sixth column from the altar of Dione, Theugenes of Piraeus, Kephisogenes of Piraeus, Teukros living in Kydathenaion, Kephisodoros, Nikostratos, Theugeiton of Piraeus – 110 *dr*. Total for stonework 500 *dr*. (*IG* i³ 476, lines 304–27)

We can see here both the contribution being made by slaves (at least 20 of the 107 employees whose names survive) and their apparent equality in terms of earnings with citizens and resident aliens. However, free men were so scarce in 407 that slaves may be more prominent, and better treated, than was normally the case. Lastly, domestic slaves are portrayed universally in Old and New Comedy and through countless incidental references in orators, essayists and philosophers. Though there is the important source-bias that the households represented are rarely poverty-stricken, the material probably reflects accurately enough both the predominant pattern of slave domestic servants and the paranoid combination of easy familiarity and casual violence to which they were subject.

We cannot see directly from the sources how much the slaves were needed, and many scholars have inclined to minimize the dependence of Athenian society on the labour and the services of the slave population. There are, however, at least three counter-considerations. At prices which made an average slave cost the equivalent of seven months' wages for a skilled man, even the comparatively poor could gain both economically and in terms of status and leisure by buying as many as possible. 'Those who can do so buy slaves so that they can have fellow-workers', says Xenophon's Sokrates, as if stating a self-evident truth (*Memorabilia* 2. 3. 3). The predominant value-system had long since outlawed serfdom, regarded the private employment of free men by free men as an unacceptable subordination, and looked askance at the enslavement of fellow-Greeks. Only one of the slaves sold off in 414 is Greek (a Messenian), and another of Xenophon's reminiscences is of a conversation between Sokrates and a certain Eutheros, who had been reduced to penury in 404, was working as a labourer and was facing a grim old age when his physique broke down. 'Would it not be better to apply yourself to the sort of job which will give you a living even when you are older, by going to a rich man who needs an assistant and help yourself and help him by supervising his affairs, helping to get in the crops and protecting his property?' 'I could hardly endure slavery, Sokrates.' 'But surely those who are in charge of cities and supervise public affairs are thought to be more respectable, not more servile, on that score?' 'I simply do not submit to being responsible to someone else, Sokrates' (*Memorabilia* 2. 8). Again it is true that improvements in what we should call productivity were intermittently made, e.g. a form of building-crane *c.* 515, and the fuller development of the larger-capacity merchant sailing ship by the late sixth century. Nonetheless, existing techniques were and went on being highly labour-intensive, whether in agriculture, craftsmanship, transport or extractive industry. What could be done with a purely citizen labour force was therefore limited in any case, so that the only way of exploiting this or that resource or opportunity, or of increasing the elegancies of one's domestic services, was by recourse to forced imported labour. It was easily available ('The Thracians sell their children for exportation abroad', said Herodotus matter-of-factly (5. 6)) in quantities limited only by the Athenian ability to pay, and that ability, thanks to the silver-mines, was virtually unlimited.

Slaves, then, were brought to Athens, and had no choice. Freemen did. Theirs was certainly a large-scale movement, though (as usual) scarcely quantifiable. Such resident aliens as were in Attica in 508–7 may then have been incorporated into the citizen body, but the inflow of others thereafter must have been considerable. They came to be referred to as *metoikoi*, 'metics', and Aeschylus was using the technical word freely in his *Suppliants* of 465–4. The effect, and perhaps the intention, of Perikles' citizenship law of 451–50, 'that those whose parents were not both citizens should not themselves be citizens' (*Athenian Constitution* 26. 4), was to make rigid the status distinction between citizen and metic. In autumn 431 the Athenian army which invaded Megara included at least 3000 metic hoplites. The only figure we have from any period for the total metic population, though coming from the census of 317 after a period of internal and international disruption, estimates it at no less than 10,000, presumably though not certainly adult males only. On this evidence they must have formed a very substantial element in the population. The Erechtheion accounts (see p. 90) and much else shows that they gravitated towards craftsman occupations and retail trading, *faute de mieux* since they could not own real property in Attica. However, some at least are attested in farming (as tenant-farmers, therefore). It is likely, and it is generally assumed, that most metics had originally come to Athens because attracted by the rather better opportunities for a livelihood than were available elsewhere in the Aegean, and that they moved into the gaps left by the general rise in status and wealth of the citizen population. Most may have remained comparatively poor, but the 3000 metic hoplites will have had some economic standing. A much wealthier element is represented not only by Kephisodoros (see p. 89) but also by the orator Lysias, whose property was sold off for no less than 70 talents during the oligarchy of 404–3 and who till then 'had been the richest of the metics' (Lysias, *P.Oxy.* XIII 1606, lines 30 and 153–5). The contrast between metic and citizen is a status difference, not an economic class difference.

Other motives are attested. We happen to know that Lysias' father Kephalos 'was by birth a Syracusan but moved to Athens because he wished to live in that city and also because Perikles son of Xanthippos persuaded him to do so, as he was a personal friend of Perikles and they were connected by ties of hospitality, and he was a man of great wealth. But some say that he moved because he was banished from Syracuse when Gelon was tyrant' ([Plutarch],

Moralia 835 C). Whether or not Kephalos was a refugee, others undoubtedly were, either attracted by a stabler and more congenial political environment or more nakedly forced into exile. It is the upper-class immigrants whom we hear most of individually, and their historical importance was out of all proportion to their numbers. Remarkably enough, our best single source about them is Plato, whose *mises-en-scène* and passing references throw all the more light for being incidental and casual. Two salient aspects emerge from the very first words of the *Republic*. Sokrates relates that he 'went down yesterday to Piraeus with Glaukon the son of Ariston, so that I could offer my prayers to the goddess and also because I wanted to see how they would celebrate the festival, since this was going to be the first celebration. The procession by the local inhabitants did indeed seem a fine thing, but the one which the Thracians organized was no less splendid. When we had made our prayers and seen the procession, we started back towards Athens. Polemarchos the son of Kephalos caught sight of us from a long way off as we were starting home, and told his slave to run and tell us to wait for him' (*Republic* 327 a–b). The goddess is the Thracian deity Bendis, of whose naturalization in Attica in the later fifth century we know a little from other evidence. She was only one of several foreign deities (Egyptian Isis is another) whose worship was brought to Attica in the fifth century by foreign communities influential enough to secure their recognition by Athens. Polemarchos, like his brother Lysias or their father or many another metic then and later, is moving easily within the Athenian social framework. A handful of men got even further, as Plato reveals casually elsewhere in the course of Sokrates' conversation with Ion. 'My dear Ion', said Sokrates, 'have you not heard about Apollodoros of Cyzicos?' 'No, who is he?' 'A man whom the Athenians have often elected as their general, foreigner though he is; and there are Phanosthenes of Andros and Herakleides of Clazomenae, who though foreigners have shown themselves worthy of remark, and the City has appointed them to generalships and other magistracies' (Plato, *Ion* 541 c–d). Moreover, the *Ion* illustrates something else. In depicting a visiting artist, in this case the Homer-reciter Ion of Ephesus, showing off to an admiring or, as here, sceptical audience, it both shares the same basic format as many other dialogues of Plato and foreshadows a permanent and fundamental reorientation of Greek culture. Attracted by public patronage offered by the Athenian musical festivals, by commissions for temple decoration or works of art, or by the private patronage and social lionizing offered by wealthy Athenian aristocrats, the previously scattered Greek intellectual aristocracy of painters, sculptors, performing artists, writers, teachers, and philosophers began increasingly to use Athens as a *pied-à-terre* and to contribute to that concentration of talent which was formalized in the fourth century in the artists' studios and the schools of rhetoric and philosophy.

Patronage costs money. The money was there. If the documentation about fifth-century Athens leaves any one overall impression, it is that of a concentration of monetary resources, in both public and private hands, previously unheard of in Greece. When war broke out in 431, Perikles told the Assembly that:

they had no reason to despond. Apart from other sources of income, an average revenue of 600 talents of silver was drawn (annually) from the tribute of the allies; and there were still 6000 talents of coined silver in the Akropolis, out of 9700 talents that had once been there (from which the money had been taken for the Propylaia, the other public buildings and for the Potidaea campaign). This did not include the uncoined gold and silver in public and private offerings, the sacred vessels for the processions and games, the spoils from the Persians and similar resources to the amount of 500 talents. To this he added the treasure of the other temples. These were by no means inconsiderable and might fairly be used. Nay, if they were ever absolutely driven to it, they might take even the gold ornaments of Athene herself; for the statue contained forty talents of pure gold and it was all removable (Thucydides 2. 13. 3–5)

Also, we have reason to think that the revenue raised internally from all sources was at least 400 talents a year. Aristophanes, indeed, in early 422 makes Bdelykleon say to his father '. . . first calculate roughly, not with pebbles but on your fingers, the total of the tribute which comes to us from the allied cities, and besides this reckon up the taxes and the many one-per-cents, the court-dues, silver mine revenues, market-taxes, harbour-dues, rents from property, and sales of confiscated property; we get a total for all these of nearly 2000 talents' (Aristophanes, *Wasps* 657–660). That figure may well be pitched a bit on the high side, but since we can see two sharp jumps (in 428–7 and spectacularly in 425–4) in the level of tribute being exacted, it may not be so far out.

From Bdelykleon's list of revenues there are two notable absences: income-tax and property-tax. The former was impracticable. Mining slave owners such as Nikias (see p. 88) might have income in coin and might know how much it was, but even in Attica most people, and certainly most citizens, were farmers for whom transactions involving money were marginal and infrequent. Their 'income' was agricultural produce, which they largely consumed themselves. We do hear of a levy on produce being exacted for the agricultural goddesses of Eleusis, Demeter and Kore, but, at rates of 1/1200 for wheat and 1/600 for barley, such levies had cultic rather than fiscal importance. Property-taxes in contrast were practicable, for the concept *telos* (see below) had long since been used to divide the citizen body into four property-classes. However, such taxes were levied in fifth- and fourth-century Athens (as elsewhere) only for military emergencies, and only on the wealthier classes. They remained rare enough for paying them to be a sign of civic virtue (see p. 97) and even in the fourth century, when they were needed more, they apparently yielded about the same as a one per cent annual property-tax.

The other side of the balance can only be drawn very sketchily. Bdelykleon goes on to reckon pay for the 6000 jurors at 150 talents a year (probably a high maximum), while salaries and maintenance for the Councillors, magistrates, administrative boards, and public slaves might have absorbed another fifty talents (again a maximum), but the main recurrent, though fluctuating, expenditure must have been for the armed forces. It is worthwhile to dwell for a moment on this phenomenon. When an archon-elect was asked whether he 'pays his taxes and has gone on campaign when required' (*Athenian Constitution* 4. 3), the word translated as 'tax', *telos*, in fact conveys rather more, denoting the whole complex of obligations and privileges which derived from his membership of the citizen descent-group, from his ownership of an estate, and from his membership of one of the four property-classes. Since military service was a cardinal element of that complex, while the form his obligations took varied according to the size of his estate, maintenance or pay during its performance should have been inappropriate. Yet the surviving accounts for the expenses of the war against Samos and Byzantium in 440–39 shows that the principle of maintenance while on active service had been established by then. Its introduction was presumably linked on the one hand with mercenary service in the true sense, where it had long been familiar, and on the other with the equally revolutionary establishment after 460 of the principle of maintenance during the performance of civilian public duties. Whatever the date, the consequence was a scale of expenditure hitherto unheard of. To keep a trireme at sea for a month cost at least 3000 drachmai, even if the sailors got only three obols a day each; at least by 415 they could hope for a drachma a day. Hoplites were paid too, and at a higher rate than the sailors. Known figures for the major campaigns of the 430s (over 1400 talents for Samos and Byzantium; over 2000 talents for Potidaea; and 76 talents even for the comparatively brief and minor expedition to Corcyra in 433) make it easy to understand how the reserves dwindled with alarming rapidity in the 420s, in spite of drastic action concerning the tribute. Even in 431 Perikles had perhaps not fully appreciated how ruinously expensive a new-style war could be.

There remains the non-recurrent expenditure, *imprimis* on the temples and public works which transformed Athens. A few sets of accounts survive, but in badly broken form, and most of the figures are missing. The firmest is that for the gold and ivory statue of Athene in the Parthenon, between 700 and 1000 talents. Given informed guesses that the Parthenon might have cost about 500 talents, a very late and indirect tradition can be doctored to imply that the statue, the Parthenon and the Propylaia cost together over 2000 talents. This tradition may preserve some truth, as may another, known only to Isokrates (7. 66), that the ship-sheds in Piraeus cost 1000 talents. No figures survive for other monuments, which include the statues of Athene Promachos; the Long Walls; the Odeion; the temples of Hephaistos and Ares in the Agora; those of Poseidon at Sunium, of Nemesis at Rhamnous and Artemis at Brauron; and the initiation-building (telesterion) at Eleusis. We simply do not know how much they all cost, nor where the money came from, even if they comprise the 'other public buildings' which Perikles mentioned. We have already reached the point where the documentation fails us, and the tangible facts of the surviving remains are all we have to go on.

Such buildings were paid for through the public exchequer, whether from tribute, or booty, or general revenue, for their expense made impossible private patronage of the kind practised by Kimon in the 460s (see p. 49). By good fortune an extant document illustrates the transition. To a decree of the 430s concerning the construction of a well-house, someone moved the amendment 'In other respects in accordance with the motion of Nikoma[chos; praise Perikles and Par]alos and Xanthippos and the b[oys, but meet the expenses from the moneys] which are paid into the tribute of the Athenians, [after the goddess has] taken her customary share [from them]' (*IG* i³ 49, lines 13–16). We have moved explicitly from private patronage to public-imperial funding. However, at a lower level more could and did combine duty with display. One way was an energetic and appropriately open-handed discharge of the obligation to commission and command a trireme for a year (trierarchy). Another was to act as impresario for the staging of a tragic trilogy, a lyric chorus, or a comedy at a dramatic festival (choregia). These liturgies, which were performed by the few hundred richest men in Athens and could cost up to a talent a time, came to be a fundamental part of Athenian public life. The financial outlay acted both as effective artistic patronage and as a redistribution of wealth to the poorer people who formed the choruses or crewed the ships. The beauty and display thus created both honoured the gods, satisfied the human need for spectacle and provided an appropriately magnificent setting for the art forms of tragedy and comedy which Athenian writers had made their own. The goodwill created among the citizenry by the efficient and willing discharge of each liturgy was an asset aimed at, and used for advancement in public life, by the wealthy men involved. 'As for me, you will perceive from my previous actions that I am no plotter, nor do I have my eyes on what does not belong to me. On the contrary, unlike my opponents I have paid many heavy property-taxes (see p. 95), been trierarch many times, performed the choregia munificently, made interest-free loans to many men, and redeemed large pledges on behalf of many men. The wealth which I possess is the product of my own energies, not of law-court proceedings; I am fond of sacrifices and law-abiding. You must not convict a person such as myself of anything impious or disgraceful' (Antiphon, *Tetralogy* 1. B 12). This speech, perhaps written in the 420s, is merely the first preserved example of many which use such arguments. They were arguments which a massed Athenian jury could expect to hear and which a speaker could expect to be persuasive.

Private wealth was not always diverted to civic use, nor were the very rich the only spenders. In observing that 'the Athenians have mingled with peoples in different areas and discovered various gastronomic luxuries; the specialities of Sicily, Italy, Cyprus, Egypt, Lydia, the Peloponnese or any other area have all been brought to Athens because of their control of the sea,' the 'Old Oligarch' (2. 7) touched briefly on a theme which became an obsession in comedy. Here, for example, is a catalogue, interlarded with political overtones, from an almost contemporary play:

Tell me now, ye Muses that dwell in Olympian mansions, all the blessings (since the time when Dionysus voyaged over the wine-coloured sea) which he hath brought hither to men in his black ship. From Cyrene silphium-stalks and ox-hides, from the Hellespont mackerel and all kinds of salt-dried fish, from Thessaly salt and sides of beef, from Sitalkes an itch to plague the Spartans, from Perdikkas lies by the ship-load. Syracuse provides hogs and cheese – while as for the Corcyreans, may Poseidon destroy them in their hollow ships, because they are of divided loyalty. These things then come from those places; but from Egypt we get rigged sails and papyrus, from Syria frankincense, while fair Crete sends cypress for the Gods, and Libya provides plenty of ivory to buy. Rhodes provides raisins and dried figs, while pears and fat apples come from Euboea, slaves from Phrygia, mercenaries from Arcadia. Pagasae (in Thessaly) furnishes slaves, and branded rascals at that.

The acorns of Zeus and glossy almonds come from the Paphlagonians, and are the ornaments of a feast. Phoenicia provides the fruit of the palm and the finest wheat flour, Carthage supplies carpets and cushions of many colours. (Hermippos, *Stevedores*, F 63)

Here, largely at the level of private consumption, one can see the concentration of goods and services made available by the drawing-power of the wealth which diffused through the whole population, attracted trade from far and wide, and made some Athenians the richest individuals in Greece.

This concentration had other consequences too. Even such frustratingly limited excavation of the inhabited areas of Athens and Piraeus as has so far been done has revealed large-scale new building of the fifth century on what had been farmland inside the Themistoklean walls of Athens, and the explosive growth of Piraeus from a medium-sized village to a huge planned city, the biggest port of Greece. Presumably it was the immigrant influx which precipitated such dramatic urban growth, just as it deepened Athens' dependence on imported food, and on the mines for her ability to pay for it.

Even more far-reaching were the consequences of the influx of money. The existence of the reserve as Perikles described it (see p. 94) had the overwhelming advantage that it allowed immediate action by land or sea. Money did not have to be raised from other sources overnight, so that Athenian policy was independent, as it later was not, of any veto from the subject allies or from the only other possible source, the Athenian upper class itself. However, the size of the sums being handled imposed new responsibilities and exposed new temptations. A traditional society could be governed by people whose claim on public recognition lay in their wealth, or athletic prowess, or descent from a god or hero. A complicated, Assembly-based, political society such as Athens had rapidly become needed men to run it who could compile a set of accounts and check that they were right, who had enough sense of logic to put a case persuasively, and who could cope on their feet with malicious opponents and a bloody-minded Assembly. It is no accident that two of Plato's dialogues which deal most with education, the *Laches* and the

Meno, single out the lack of political success attained by the sons of Themistokles, Aristeides, Perikles and Thoukydides (not the historian, but a politician who was an older relative). Brought up in the traditional way to be good horsemen, wrestlers, musicians and gymnasts, two of them, Thoukydides' son Melesias and Aristeides' son Lysimachos, had learnt inappropriate skills. They told Laches how

> both of us often talk to our sons about the many noble deeds which our own fathers did in war and peace, in the management of the allies and in the administration of the city. Neither of us has any deeds of his own which he can show. The truth is that we are ashamed of this contrast being seen by them, and we blame our fathers for letting us be spoiled in the days of our youth, while they were occupied with the concerns of others; and we urge all this upon the lads . . . They, on their part, promise to comply with our wishes; and our care is to discover what studies or pursuits are likely to be most improving to them. (*Laches* 179 c–d)

The training which the sophists were later to offer went some way to remedy the situation, and there is no more salient aspect of fourth-century philosophy than its logical and mathematical modes of thinking. Yet the leisure-class presuppositions of the intellectual tradition were so strong that the greater emphasis on numeracy went on to lean far more towards abstraction and geometry, as spectacularly in Plato's *Republic*, than towards accountancy. So the gap at the level of political expertise remained. It was perforce filled by men who had more of the requisite political and administrative skills.

These were the so-called demagogues. Kleon is the most famous; others were Hyperbolos, Androkles and Kleophon. Our main sources, Thucydides and Aristophanes, paint a lurid portrait of them. Thucydides writes of Kleon with more personal animus than he allows himself anywhere else, and comments bitterly that Perikles' successors, who included all three named above, lost the war for Athens by turning Perikles' strategic thinking upside down (see p. 120). Aristophanes portrays Kleon twice, as the Paphlagonian slave in the *Knights* of 424 and as the dog (*Kyon*) of Kydathenaion, Kleon's deme, in the *Wasps* of 422. Both in these plays and in casual allusions elsewhere the tone is so sharp and contemptuous as to suggest that Aristophanes shared Thucydides' view of him. It is tempting to follow them, but for various reasons we should not. Both men had probably run foul of him in the lawcourts, and both stood by origin and inclination on the 'noble and good' wing of Athenian society, as the demagogues did not. Social prejudices were strong, and were expressed in repeated, but so far as we know quite false, allegations that the demagogues were of foreign or bastard birth. What is more, the contrast between them and Perikles needs to be put more subtly. Certainly, Perikles achieved an unchallenged leadership as no other Athenian did. Thucydides concentrated on, and admired, this aspect:

> Being powerful because of his rank, ability, and visible integrity, he held down the multitude as befits a free man, and was not so much led by it as himself led it: for as he did not gain possession of power from improper sources he did not have to flatter it . . . In short, what was nominally a democracy became rule by the first man. His successors were more equal with each other and were each striving to become the first. (2. 65. 8–11)

However, Thucydides is less helpful in telling us how this position was achieved. Honesty evidently mattered, as it had done for Ephialtes (see p. 51), but to see more of Perikles' own 'demogogic' techniques we must turn to Plutarch's life of him. There, in one of Plutarch's most brilliant re-creations, we can see Perikles' single-minded devotion to full-time politics; his 'Olympian' style of speaking; his diversion of the tribute surplus to the Parthenon and the rest of the building programme; his caution as a general and in foreign policy; his colonization programme; his judicious use of bribery on one occasion; and his populist instinct for the melodramatic gesture:

> One of the workmen on the Propylaia, the most active and energetic among them, slipped and fell from a great height. He lay for some time severely injured, and the doctors could hold out no hope that he would recover. Perikles was greatly

distressed at this, but the goddess Athene appeared to him in a dream and ordered a course of treatment, which he applied, with the result that the man was easily and quickly healed. (*Perikles* 13. 13)

True, we are also told of his association with intellectuals such as Damonides (see p. 52), Zeno and Anaxagoras. From this link Plutarch derives Perikles' sense of dignity:

> From it he derived not only a dignity of spirit and a nobility of utterance which was entirely free from the vulgar and unscrupulous buffooneries of mob oratory, but also a composure of countenance that never dissolved into laughter, a serenity in his movements and in the graceful arrangement of his dress which nothing could disturb when he was speaking, a firm and evenly modulated voice, and other characteristics of the same kind which deeply impressed his audience. (*Perikles* 5. 1)

Here, expressed in behaviour, we have the cultural ideal of the gentleman. Plutarch rightly saw a tension between it and Perikles' populist policies. Even for Perikles the tension caused trouble towards the end of his life. His successors avoided it only by not being gentlemen and by following to its limits the logic of articulating the ambitions, fears, and prejudices of the Assembly and the lawcourt. They could have been gentlemen. Most of the demagogues were rich from owning craftsmen slaves; some such as Kleon and Kleophon were far more aristocratic than any source would have us think, and other men with the same background but different temperament, such as Nikias, were willingly accepted on the conservative wing of politics. In contrast, for a populist it helped to be abrasive and anti-intellectual, and even to bully the audience. Thucydides makes Kleon begin a speech with startlingly undemocratic sentiments:

> I have often before now been convinced that a democracy is incapable of running an Empire, and never more so than by your present change of mind in the matter of Mytilene . . . The most alarming feature in the case is the constant change of

measures with which we appear to be threatened, and our seeming ignorance of the fact that bad laws which are never changed are better for a city than good ones which have no authority. (3. 37. 1 and 3)

The hint should be taken seriously. Demagogues were radical, in the sense of attacking aristocratic pretensions and of being merciless towards aristocratic incompetence. They were a new breed of politician, in the sense of having the administrative and oratorical skills which Melesias and Lysimachos lacked. But fundamentally they articulated the old-fashioned values and attitudes of the peasant core of Athenian society. It is no accident that one of the best of Aristophanes' heroes, an elderly resourceful buffoon, passionately addicted to jury-service, with a strong preference for the older poets and little taste or aptitude for the new learning of the intellectuals, should be called Love-Kleon: Philokleon in the *Wasps*.

Competence does not entail honesty. Financial corruption is a recurrent theme in the sources for fifth- and fourth-century Athens. We have already seen how Thespieus' amendment (see p. 55) probably reflects some kind of dishonesty, but there were more spectacular cases of it, or of the suspicion of it. About 420 Antiphon reminded a jury of an old scandal:

The Hellenotamiai were once put to death, all but one, on a false charge concerning the funds, out of anger rather than considered judgement. The matter later came to light. The sole survivor, whose name we are told was Sosias, had been condemned to death, but had not actually been executed. When it was found out how the money had disappeared, he had actually been handed over to the Eleven (executioners) by the people. He was released, but the others had been put to death, for all that they were innocent. (Antiphon 5. 69–70)

The incident probably happened in 440–39, since there is a very peculiar erasure in the heading of the Tribute List for that year. Most politicans were alleged, often justly, to have accepted bribes, favours and kickbacks. For a politician to die poor, as Kleophon did, was an event. The honesty of those politicians who were honest (Aristeides, Ephialtes, Perikles) was an important part of their claim to public recognition. 'Some say that if you approach the Council or the People with money, then things get considered. Now I would agree that money plays a considerable part in getting things done at Athens, and it would be even more influential if more people employed it' (*Old Oligarch* 3. 3).

If corruption is a recurrent theme, power – its concentration, justification, exercise, effects, and control – is nothing short of an obsession, palpable in contemporary thinking at all levels. We have already seen (see p. 94) how Thucydides makes Perikles dwell in detail on its financial basis, just as he went on to catalogue in comparable detail the fighting resources available in ships and men. Similarly, the 'Old Oligarch' singled out the political consequences in remarking that 'it is right that the poor and the ordinary people in Athens should have more power than the noble and the rich, because it is the ordinary people who man the fleet and bring the city her power; they provide the helmsmen, the boatswains, the junior officers, the look-outs and the shipwrights; it is these people who make the city powerful much more than the hoplites and the noble and respectable citizens' (1. 2). This awareness yielded a spectrum of reactions. In the last speech which Thucydides gives Perikles just before the latter's death in 429, he made him say:

Again, your country has a right to your services in sustaining the glories of your position. These are a common source of pride to you all, and you cannot decline the burdens of Empire and still expect to share its honours. You should remember also that what you are fighting against is not merely slavery as an exchange for independence, but also loss of Empire and danger from the animosities incurred in its exercise. Besides, to recede is no longer possible, if indeed any of you in the alarm of the moment has become enamoured of the honesty of such an unambitious part. For what you hold is, to speak somewhat plainly, a tyranny; to take it perhaps was wrong, but to let it go is unsafe. (Thucydides 2. 63. 1–2)

The speech ranks among Thucydides' most complex creations, but one motif which stands out clearly here is the uncritical acceptance of the benefits of Empire: status, pride and honour. The motif is echoed so often elsewhere that it must have reflected a reality. Aristophanes in early 422 gives Bdelykleon a crude version of it:

> Just consider how, while you and everyone could be wealthy, you have been hemmed in somehow or other by the politicians. You who rule over countless cities, from the Black Sea to Sardinia, get no advantage from them at all, except your pay: and this they keep dripping into you with wool, like oil, a little at a time, just to keep you alive. They want you to be poor, and I'll tell you why: to make you realize who's boss, so that when they whistle at you to set you growling at an enemy, you leap on them fiercely. If they really wanted to give the people a decent living, it would be easy enough. There are 1000 cities which bring you tribute at the moment. If someone told each of them to maintain twenty men, then 20,000 of the common people could have been living on jugged hare with garlands of every kind and cream and cream-cheese, enjoying things worthy of our country and of the trophy at Marathon. (Aristophanes, *Wasps* 698–711)

Here, appropriately in so egregiously repulsive a piece of demagogic rhetoric as this is meant to be, there lurks the theory that Athens' victories in the Persian Wars entitled her, and her citizens, to a privileged status and position. Again:

> In strict truth we have done nothing unfair in reducing to subjection the Ionians and islanders, the kinsfolk whom the Syracusans say we have enslaved. They, our kinsfolk, came against their mother country, that is to say against us, together with the Persians, and instead of having the courage to revolt and sacrifice their property as we did when we abandoned our city, chose to be slaves themselves, and to try to make us so. We therefore deserve to rule our empire, because we placed the largest fleet and an unflinching patriotism at the service of the Greeks, and because these, our subjects, did us mischief by their ready subservience to the Persians. (Thucydides 6. 82. 3–83. 1)

This, by an Athenian diplomat in Sicily in 415, is the clearest expression of a 'charter myth' which Thucydides was clearly not the first to formulate. It was resuscitated by Isokrates and others in the fourth century, and had an extraordinarily long life, cropping up in rhetorical encomiums of Athens well on into the Roman Empire.

There were other justifications too. At least three are to be found in Thucydides (whether formulated by him, or merely echoed by him, is an endlessly debated problem). The classic form of one of them is the claim, put into Perikles' mouth in the famous Funeral Speech of winter 431–30, that Athenians were culturally superior, combining civility with versatility and daring with deliberation in a way that no other Greek state could emulate. A second justification was the claim which he has the Athenian envoys make at Sparta in summer 432, that the Athenians exercised over their subjects a control far less brutal and explicit than their superiority would have allowed. Both claims clearly echoed and reinforced that complacent and self-satisfied strand in Athenian attitudes which, as sardonic critics observed, made it so easy to flatter and beguile Athenian audiences with a judicious quotation from Pindar. 'In the old days envoys from the subject cities used to deceive you by calling you "violet-crowned"; and whenever somebody said that, you at once sat up straight on the points of your buttocks because of the "crowns". And if anybody really laid it on thick and called Athens "glistening", he got everything he wanted because of this "glistening", when it's a label fit only for sardines' (Aristophanes, *Acharnians* 636–40).

The third justification was formulated in very different terms. The concentration of Athenian power, and especially the form it took as seapower, became during the fifth century an intellectual paradigm of the way human beings behaved in practice. As such it posed (for some, at any rate) a searing moral problem.

For ourselves, we shall not trouble you with specious pretences – either of how we have a right to our Empire because we overthrew the Persians or are now attacking you because of wrong that you have done us – and make a long speech which would not be believed . . . You know as well as we do that right, as the world goes, is only in question between equals in power, while the strong do what they can and the weak suffer what they must . . . Of the gods we believe, and of men we know, that by a necessary law of their nature they rule wherever they can. And it is not as if we were the first to make this law, or to act upon it when made. We found it existing before us, and shall leave it to exist for every after use. All we do is to make use of it, knowing that you and everybody else, having the same power as we have, would do the same as we do. (Thucydides 5. 89 and 5. 105. 2)

This is the third justification: thus Thucydides would have us believe the Athenians negotiated (vainly) with the hitherto independent community of Melos in 416 before proceeding to besiege the city and capture, kill or enslave the entire population. Few scholars suppose that the words can be a verbatim transcript, though they are presented as such. All the same, the motifs which are emphasized – the relationship between power and justice, and the role of 'necessity' – had become, and were to go on being, central preoccupations of Athenian intellectuals, while the motif of necessity comes, *inter alia*, from Perikles' own last speech (see p. 104).

Two other factors made the moral problem worse. One was that Athenians were exercising power over *Greeks*. There would not have been the least compunction about lording it over non-Greeks. To put it somewhat cynically, barbarians were either dangerous, and therefore deserved to be the object of hostile portrayal and offensive action, or they were militarily inferior, in which case they were slaves by nature and, if need or opportunity arose, slaves by law. Yet the Athenians had begun as liberators, and the imperial myth which had come to prevail emphasized, indeed overemphasized, the ethnic homogeneity subsisting between the Athenians and their subject allies. The contradiction was fundamental: Athens could not subject the Aegean states to what was widely called 'slavery' while simultaneously claiming them as fellow-members of a community. The second factor was the realization, most clearly presented for us in the ethnographic books of Herodotus, that moral systems differed throughout the world; that one needed more, in order to validate one particular system, than the *imprimatur* of a god or a lawgiver or the fact of its antiquity; and that the natural order and the moral order were not only logically separable but could even be formal contraries. Here is one classic formulation of the consequences which could be thought to ensue in the sphere of private behaviour:

> Justice consists in not transgressing any of the ordinances of the state of which one is a citizen. A man would therefore exercise justice with most advantage to himself if in the presence of witnesses he held in esteem the laws, but in the absence of witnesses, the precepts of nature. For the precepts of the laws are adventitious, whereas those of nature are necessary, and the precepts of the laws are the product of agreement, not of growth, while those of nature are the product of growth, not of agreement. Thus in transgressing legal ordinances, whenever he is unobserved by the parties to the agreement, he is free both from shame and punishment, but not if he is observed. On the other hand, if he strain any of the innate principles of nature more than it can bear, the evil is no less, if he is unobserved by everyone, nor any greater, if everyone sees. For the injury does not depend on opinion but on fact. All this is the object of our enquiry: because most of what is just according to law stands in opposition to nature. (Antiphon the Sophist, *On truth*, DK 87A 44A, cols i–ii)

Another formulation, given by Plato to Kallikles in his *Gorgias*, brings us back even more starkly to public behaviour and to the distribution and control of power:

> How can a man be happy who is the servant of anything? On the contrary, I plainly assert, that he who would truly live ought to allow his desires to wax to the uttermost and not to chastize them; but when they have grown to their greatest he should have courage and intelligence to minister to them and to satisfy all his longings. And this I affirm to be natural justice and nobility. To this however the many cannot attain; and they blame the strong man because they are ashamed of their own weakness, which they desire to conceal, and hence they say that intemperance is base.

Or again, a little earlier:

> The makers of laws are the majority who are weak: and they make laws and distribute praises and censures with a view to themselves and to their own interests; and they terrify the stronger sort of men, and those who are able to get the better of them, in order that they may not get the better of them; and they say, that dishonesty is shameful and unjust, meaning, by the word injustice, the desire of a man to have more than his neighbours, for knowing their own inferiority, I suspect that they are only too glad of equality. And therefore the endeavour to have more than the many is conventionally said to be shameful and unjust, and is called injustice, whereas nature herself intimates that it is just for the better to have more than the worse, the more powerful than the weaker; and in many ways she shows, among men as well as among animals, and indeed among whole cities and races, that justice consists in the superior ruling over and having more than the inferior:
> (*Gorgias* 491e–492a and 483b–d)

We do not know who Kallikles was, save that he and Antiphon must have been near-contemporaries, nor do we know whether he really held these and other views imputed to him. However, that they made a powerful impression, and reflected a major and influential current of thinking, emerges not only from the ferocious intellectual efforts which Plato repeatedly made to prove him wrong, or from their echo in the oligarchic coups d'état of 411 and 404, but also from the prominence which mechanisms for the exercise and control of power came to have in contemporary Athenian political life. Of course, the problem of evolving or retaining effective mechanisms is always present in any society, but it was especially urgent in an Athens whose decisions had come to matter on a European and Mediterranean scale.

To identify and classify such mechanisms, especially those of control, is also to identify the main tensions and oppositions which they serve to mediate. We can here move straight from the motifs visible in the sources to the analysis of the society they reflect. One, inevitably, was the tension between rich and poor. That the tension existed and was felt is clear from the language of

Kallikles and the 'Old Oligarch', and became visible in action in the ruthless bitterness generated in 411. The problem indeed is rather what had hitherto kept it in check. It may well be that the tension was overlaid by the common interest which all citizens shared in keeping power in their own hands and away from immigrants and foreigners. Another opposition, between the politicians and 'us', comes out very clearly in Bdelykleon's speech (see p. 105). Again inevitably, even in a state where so much was decided in the citizens' assembly, the opposition goes back to Solon and becomes a commonplace in fourth-century oratory. It generated two sets of inherently conflicting techniques and institutions, those by which the people at large hoped to control the politicians, and those by which the politicans hoped to control the people at large. The threat of exile for ten years by 'ostracism' was one example of the former. Another applied especially to the generals: 'There is a vote in every prytany on their conduct of their office, and if the people vote against a man, he is tried in the lawcourt, and if condemned, the jury assesses the appropriate penalty or fine, while if he is acquitted he resumes his position' (*Athenian Constitution* 61. 2). There were other legal procedures too, available against magistrates. More generally, though some forms of legal action ('suits') could only be initiated by the injured party or, in the case of homicide, by a relative, others ('writs') were available by which any citizen of good standing could prosecute another. Such prosecutions could be on specifically political charges, e.g. the 'writ of proposal contrary to existing law' or the 'writ of proposing an unsuitable law', or they could be on charges such as impiety, false witness, or insult, where the political element was simply the motive of the prosecutor or the status of the defendant. As a last resort prosecution by 'impeachment' could be initiated by anybody, citizen or not, free or not, on any charge whatever which could be held to affect the stability of the state and the constitution. By these means public figures were permanently vulnerable to sanctions via the lawcourts, which gave a formidable veto-power to the citizenry on the juries. In that sense Aristotle was quite right to observe that 'when the people have the right to vote in the courts they control the constitution' (*Athenian Constitution* 9. 1). It is no accident that the literature about Athenian public life (Aristophanes: the orators: *Athenian Constitution*), and the analyses of the system by the 'Old Oligarch' and by Aristotle in his *Politics*, gave the courts so central a position. To suspend the popular courts was among the first acts of any authoritarian régime. The *ne plus ultra* was reached by a well-known politician whose active career stretched from 404–3 to the 330s: 'The famous Aristophon of Azenia once had the nerve to boast in your presence that he had been acquitted on 75 writs of proposal contrary to existing law' (Aeschines 3. 194). No politician was safe.

The challenge to the politician was therefore to build as strong a power-base as possible, a task made even harder by the fact that, in the generation we are looking at, the relative value of its various possible components was changing so fast. We have already seen how financial and administrative expertise and probity were outmoding other cultural accomplishments (see p. 99ff). Equally inappropriate were becoming claims such as those of the Praxiergidai in the 450s (see p. 57) to a recognized position in public life by virtue of descent from a god or hero. Plato makes Ktesippos describe with amused and condescending scorn how Hippothales, madly in love with young Lysis,

> can only speak of the wealth of Demokrates, which the whole city celebrates, and grandfather Lysis, and other ancestors of the youth, and their stud of horses, and their victory at the Pythian games, and at the Isthmus, and at Nemea with four horses and single horses – these are the tales which he composes and repeats. And there is greater twaddle still. Only the day before yesterday, he made a poem in which he described the entertainment of Herakles, who was a connexion of the family, setting forth how in virtue of this relationship he was hospitably received by an ancestor of Lysis; this ancestor was himself begotten of Zeus by the daughter of the founder of the deme. And these are the sorts of old wives' tales which he sings and recites to us, and we are obliged to listen to him. (Plato, *Lysis* 205 c–d)

Plato cannot have been writing in a climate which took such aristocratic pretensions seriously. In contrast, and naturally enough, military skills were taken seriously. The line between politican and general was nothing like as clearly drawn as it was later to become, and most, though not all, politicians either were also commanders or moved into the generalship when opportunity offered. Yet even generals had to speak effectively in public, not just to encourage their troops before battle (the occasion of many a speech in Thucydides and every later historian) but also to persuade Council and Assembly to adopt this or that plan of naval or military action. Still more was it true for all civilian politicians.

Oratory became the vehicle of power. Such a role was not wholly new, for no one can read the Homeric poems without sensing the power recognized even then to come from the persuasive spoken word. However, after the 450s, in Athens and elsewhere, the formal sovereignty of Council and Assembly and lawcourts, and the size of the audience involved in each institution, diverted a massive and continuing intellectual investment, essential for any public figure, into the techniques of effective persuasion. We can see the results of this effort in the speeches, both those transmitted directly and those reported, or re-created, or freely invented, in historians' narratives. They show how the power of public speaking was wielded. In so doing they lay open Athenian society far more nakedly than historians or inscriptions can, for to be persuasive an orator had to move within the attitudes, values and prejudices of his audience. Of course, that is precisely why in one sense such speeches are very treacherous ground for the historian. We usually have only one side of the argument, and the orators are spectacularly bad witnesses of truth, for their object was to persuade, not to record. Inconvenient facts are glossed over; systematic presentation is sacrificed for a shock start or a knockout punch line; appeals to the prejudice or self-interest of the audience abound (as in Bdelykleon's speech, see p. 105), arguments balance precariously on implausible claims of probabilities (as in Antiphon's argument, see pp. 97–8); extraneous matter is brought in to create a favourable picture or to excite ridicule; and historical perspectives are foreshortened or floodlit in the warm glow of patriotic and sentimental myth-mongering. Yet, paradoxically, this very treacherousness is historical evidence of the first rank. Whatever the relationship between recorded utterance and fact on any one occasion, we can be reasonably confident that we are seeing how the best practitioners of the art of persuasion went about their business. If Antiphon's arguments turn more on likelihood than on evidence, they reflect thereby both the ease with which complaisant witnesses could be bought and the new liberating possibilities of making human problems manageable by appeal to logic and system. Or, again, Andocides could argue in favour of peace with Sparta in the winter of 392–1 by saying that:

Having made war again because of the Megarians and abandoned our land to be ravaged, after being deprived of many good things we again made the peace which Nikias son of Nikeratos negotiated for us. I think all of you know that because of this peace we transferred 7000 talents of currency to the Akropolis, possessed more than 300 ships, had more than 1200 talents of tribute coming in every year, and we possessed Chersonese and Naxos and more than two-thirds of Euboea: it would be a long story to list the other colonies individually. With all these good things in our hands, we were again drawn into war with the Spartans, then too under Argive persuasion. (Andocides 3. 8–9)

As history this is frightful, for there are five or six major errors or over-simplifications in this passage. Yet as another sort of history it is invaluable, for it shows us that most people's memory of the past was vague enough for arguments like these to be persuasive.

Or again, Gorgias' funeral speech could say of the dead that:

They doubly excerised, above all, as was right, mind and body, the one in counsel, the other in action; helpers of those in undeserved adversity, chastizers of those in undeserved prosperity; bold for the common good, quick to feel for the right cause, checking with the prudence of the mind the imprudence of the body; violent towards the violent, restrained towards the restrained, fearless towards the fearless, terrifying among the terrifying. As evidence of these things, they have set up trophies over the enemy, an honour to Zeus, a dedication of themselves: men not unacquainted with the unborn spirit of the warrior, with love such as the law allows, with rivalry under arms, with peace, friend of the arts; men showing reverence towards the gods by their justice, piety towards their parents by their care, justice towards their friends by keeping faith with them. Therefore, although they are dead, the longing for them has not died with them, but immortal though in mortal bodies, it lives on for those who live no more. (Gorgias, DK 82 B 6)

This is indeed the incantation of someone drunk on words and antitheses (later Greek critics called it 'childish'), but its vision of the ideal citizen would find immediate acceptance in any Greek state. Incidentally it also shows how a speech can be a performance just as much as a symphony or a sonata, and can be composed, performed and judged in much the same way. In other words, surviving speeches gives us direct access to the modes by which power was wielded, increased and indeed created. No public man, however honest, could avoid using the available techniques and consciously creating a *persona* for himself, reflected above all in the style and presentation of his public utterances: and no member of the Assembly or jury, however stupid, could avoid having to make repeated choices among competing *personae*.

It is this motif of competition between individuals which provides the last and most important tension, but it also presents a major conceptual difficulty. Competition for power was very generally seen as, or transformed into, competition for *honour*. Granted, this is not always the case. In talking of Perikles and his successors, Thucydides used straight power-language (see p. 101). Much of the analysis of the 'tyrant' concentrates, to the point of grotesque caricature, on his unbridled power to do what he wishes, while we have already seen the starkness of the language of Kallikles (see p. 108ff.). But by and large Aristotle was reflecting current vocabulary in saying: 'People of superior refinement and of active disposition identify happiness with honour: for this is, roughly speaking, the goal of the political life' (*Nicomachean Ethics* 1095^b 22–3). That most people would have seen it this way emerges from innumerable casual remarks in the sources, or from the way in which offices carrying power and responsibility were commonly called 'honours', or even in the way in which tyranny could be seen as a concentration of honour. As Xenophon makes the poet Simonides say to Hieron of Syracuse,

> A man seems to me, Hieron, to differ from the other animals in this respect, by his striving for honour. All living things seem to take equal pleasure in food and drink and sleep and sex, but love of honour is not rooted in irrational living things or even in all humans. The people who are endowed with the love of honour and praise are precisely those who differ most from the beasts and can be regarded as real men, not just human beings. So I think you tyrants are quite right to endure all the disadvantages which you endure in your tyranny, since you are given exceptional honour by other men. For there is no human pleasure that approaches more nearly to the divine than glad festal thoughts concerning honours. (Xenophon, *Hieron* 7. 3–4)

True, Hieron disagrees, distinguishing between flattery of a tyrant through fear and honours freely and willingly accorded, but the point remains, expressed in (for Xenophon) very strong and poetic language. The term he uses, 'love of honour' (*philotimia*), came to be used universally to denote ambitiously energetic public activity, sometimes pejoratively but increasingly as commendation. Pindar indeed could speak blackly of how 'men too apt to woo love of honour in cities set up a visible pain' (F 210), and Thucydides uses the word bitterly of Perikles' successors. Yet he also makes Perikles say, in his own Funeral Speech, that 'it is only the love of honour that never grows old; and honour it is, not gain, as some would have it, that rejoices the heart of age and helplessness' (2. 44. 4). It is most striking, too, how the word *philotimia* suddenly appears in Athenian decrees from the 340s onwards, as soon as the city began to pass decrees in honour of her own citizens.

The pattern of thought should not surprise us, for its roots lay deep in Greek thinking. The heroic code, 'Always to strive to be best and to be superior to others' (*Iliad* 6. 208 and 11. 783), had been a cliché of thought since Homer. Transferred from war to the sphere of ritualized violence, it figured among the ideals of action and personal qualities institutionalized in the Panhellenic

Games. It was transferred, too, to the festivals of the state, for the dramatic productions were contests among poets and among choregoi, and the other contests, whether musical (as here) or athletic/ military (at other festivals), were linked still more closely to the main institutions of the state by being contests among teams from the ten tribes.

Yet, though clear in its para-political aspect, the contest for honour and prestige does make the battle for power between politicians elusive. We can make a functional analysis well enough, by seeing the effect of the conviction of an opponent in court, for example, or by seeing how the triangle 'politician: opponent: people (Assembly or jury)' could be exploited by representing oneself as the 'friend of the people' against one's opponent who (by implication or explicit allegation) is not, or by seeing how politicans got and kept the initiative, as Perikles did by making well-thought-out and well-spaced-out proposals, or as the politicans of the 420s tried to do, each overtrumping the other with successively more ambitious schemes. The difficulty rather is in integrating the use of these and of the other techniques of power with the pursuit of honour as an attitude and an ideal. That the men involved may have felt the same difficulty, its unresolvability contributing to the electric tensions of Athenian political life, is perhaps some consolation to the historian.

VII

The Peloponnesian War

THE PELOPONNESIAN WAR presents the historian with three major problems. One, oddly enough, is that of identifying the war as an entity. Conventionally, indeed, it began in 431 and ended in 404. Yet it fell into several distinct phases. First came the Archidamian war, so named after King Archidamos of Sparta, which ended with the Peace of Nikias in spring 421. Then came a period of desultory political and military activity till the end of the Athenian expedition to Sicily in 413. There then followed the naval war in Ionia and the Aegean, which ended with the Athenian capitulation. The first two phases belong together, but there is a very real break in the years 413–11, when Athenian superiority had been broken, Persia entered the war, and Sparta became a sea-power. Thereafter the new configuration of international politics remained stable for a generation till the 370s, and the actual ends of wars in 404 and 386 were comparatively unimportant. Hence, though unorthodox, to end this chapter in 413 and to let Chapter Eight straddle the years 412–380 does correspond to the military and political facts.

It also roughly corresponds to the evidence, for the second problem is that of the sources. For the years of the war we have Aristophanes' comedies, early speeches and pamphlets, Plutarch's lives of Nikias, Alkibiades, and Lysandros, and a continuous flow of documents from Athens. Yet the importance and authority of one source – Thucydides' *Histories* – till it breaks off, never completed, in 411 is so paramount that there seems little to do but to take it as a true and complete record of events till that point. Yet the more we so take it, the harder it is to keep our distance and to emancipate ourselves from Thucydides' attitudes and biasses. To do that, we can bring into play events, themes, and documents which he fails to mention; we can study his text closely so as to re-create a detailed profile of his mind, to see his concentrations, omissions, and obsessions, and then to apply correction factors; and we can use the information he provides in order to develop an entirely different framework of analysis.

The third of these techniques perhaps matters most, for it merges with our remaining problem, that of determining what counts as understanding the war. Thucydides concentrates either on dense, full narrative of military action, so chronologically and otherwise exact that it sometimes becomes disjointed, or on stylistically elaborated set pieces. These last are often laid out as speeches or as assembly debates, and occasionally as editorial comment. They repeatedly set out to explore the impact of events on community, as for example in his descriptions of the plague at Athens in 430 (2. 47 ff.), of civil war at Corcyra in 427 (3. 70–83), or of the witchhunt in Athens in 415 (6. 53–61). Sometimes, instead, they give his reading of the psychological springs of action. To explain satisfactorily why actions took place in this theatre of war rather than that, or to account for repeated patterns, are not his real strengths, any more than he spells out what he, like all Greek writers, took for granted, the relationship between the logistics of warfare and its technology. In consequence, the interpretative responsibility is far more wholly ours than appears at first sight.

The basic feature of action was obvious enough. Sparta and her allies were unchallengeable by land but weak by sea, the Athenians the precise contrary. Strategies could either be formulated in terms of this fact, or they could seek to alter it. Not surprisingly the early years of the war largely saw action in terms of it. The first and principal Spartan ploy was to invade Attica and ravage the countryside. This they did in 431, 430, 428 (twice), 427, and 425. Thereafter the Athenians used as hostages the 292 Spartan soldiers captured on Pylos and 'determined . . . if the Peloponnesians invaded their country before peace was made, to bring them out and kill them' (Thucydides 4. 41. 1). It was a rational enough tactic. In 446 the mere threat of invasion had brought Athens to make peace on disadvantageous terms; in 431, the shock of the first invasion nearly lost Perikles his position

of leadership when he refused to authorize a sortie. Correspondingly, 'at the start of the war some thought the Athenians might
hold out for a year, some for two, none for longer than three years
if the Peloponnesians invaded their territory' (Thucydides
7. 28. 3). Yet by 421 'the Spartans had found the course of the
war falsify her notion that a few years would suffice for the
overthrow of Athenian power by the devastation of their land'
(Thucydides 5. 14. 3). King Archidamos had been made to say in
432 that 'confidence might possibly be felt in our superiority in
heavy infantry and population, which will enable us to invade and
devastate their lands. But the Athenians have plenty of other land
in their Empire, and can import what they want by sea . . . Let us
never be elated by the fatal hope of the war being quickly ended
by the devastation of their lands. I fear rather that we may leave it
as a legacy for our children' (Thucydides 1. 81. 1–2 and 6).

Yet Perikles' own ideas were equally unproductive. The
Athenians, he said on various occasions, were:

'not to combine schemes of fresh conquest with the conduct of
the war, and abstain from wilfully involving yourselves in other
dangers.' 'They were not to go out to battle, but to come into
the city and guard it, and get ready the fleet, in which their real
strength lay. They were also to keep a tight rein on their allies,
the strength of Athens being derived from the money brought
in by their payments.' 'They were to wait quietly, pay attention
to the navy, to attempt no new conquests, and to expose the
city to no hazards during the war.' (Thucydides 1. 144. 1, 2.
13. 2, and 2. 65. 7)

Such advice evidently permitted both the seaborne expeditions,
which ravaged various coastal areas of the Peloponnese in the
early years of the war, and the invasions of Megara which were
made annually after the main Peloponnesian army had gone
home. Yet the cost was high and the gain small. Not a single
Peloponnesian town was captured or held, and at length an
oligarchic revolution in Megara in 424 anchored her more firmly
to the Spartan alliance.

Initial strategies, then, produced deadlock. We can see,
implicit in Thucydides' narrative, how the more intelligent

military men on each side tried to break the deadlock, by encroaching on and mastering the other side's element and territory, even at the cost of some rashness and ambitious adventurism. Thucydides indeed is scathing:

> What the Athenians did was the very contrary [of Perikles' advice], allowing private ambitions and private interests, in matters apparently quite foreign to the war, to lead them into projects unjust both to themselves and to their allies – projects whose success would only conduce to the honour and advantage of private persons, and whose failure entailed certain disaster on the country in the war . . . Perikles' successors, more on a level with each other, and each grasping at supremacy, ended by committing even the conduct of state affairs to the whims of the multitude. This . . . produced a host of blunders, and among them the Sicilian expedition; though this failed not so much through a miscalculation of the power of those against whom it was sent, as through a fault in the senders in not taking the best measures afterwards to assist those who had gone out, but choosing rather to occupy themselves with private cabals for the leadership of the commons, by which they not only paralysed operations in the field, but also first introduced civil discord at home. (Thucydides 2. 65. 7 and 10–11)

Many would agree with this (for him) highly personal statement, but we can also see that doubts whether the war could be won by Periklean or Archidamian strategy were widely shared.

However, effective Spartan innovation till 413 was limited, for ideas outran capacity. Attention was paid to the navy, in spite of Hetoimaridas' qualms forty years previously (see p. 43), and a major ship-building programme was begun in 431. Yet it seems to have achieved little. Though Corinth and her allies had commissioned 150 ships in 433, the largest fleet deployed thereafter till 412 was one of 100 ships in summer 429; and Peloponnesian fleets either came off badly against smaller forces or flatly declined battle. We can readily see why. Their tactics lagged far behind current Athenian practice, as Thucydides notes on several occasions. There were few skilled rowers available.

Most of all, there was no money and no reserve. The idea of 'borrowing' the treasures of Olympia and Delphi was mooted but no more. An inscription from Sparta, perhaps dating from 427, seems to record contributions made by communities and individuals outside Sparta, including, interestingly, the Melians and 'the friends (of Sparta) among the Chians' (ML 67), but the sums amount to little, and the obvious source both of ships and of money, Persia, proved unhelpful. In the winter of 425–4 the Athenians

> arrested at Eion on the Strymon Artaphernes, a Persian, on his way from the Persian King to Sparta. He was conducted to Athens, where the Athenians got his despatches translated from the Assyrian script and read them. With numerous references to other subjects, they in substance told the Spartans that the King did not know what they wanted, as of the many ambassadors they had sent him no two ever told the same story: if however they were prepared to speak plainly they might send him some envoys with this Persian. (Thucydides 4. 50. 1–2)

'To speak plainly' probably meant to spell out the diplomatic price which the Spartans were prepared to pay, but Spartan public opinion seemed unable to face the compromise involved till 412.

The other main Spartan activity, to try to detach or neutralize Athenian allies, had rather more success. In most cases indeed the initiative lay not with Sparta but with locals, usually oligarchs. Such cases exemplified the pattern which Thucydides derived from the civil war in Corcyra:

> Struggles were made everywhere by the popular leaders to bring in the Athenians, the oligarchs the Spartans. In peace there would have been neither the pretext nor the wish for such an invitation; but in war, with an alliance always at the command of either faction for the hurt of their adversaries and their own corresponding advantage, opportunities for bringing in the foreigner were never lacking to those who wished to begin a revolution. (Thucydides 3. 82. 1)

Yet attempts which needed access by sea broke down. Descents on Cephallenia and Zacynthos in 431, 430, and 429 failed, and though Sparta encouraged the revolt of Mytilene in 428–7 her admiral Alkidas showed such timidity and insensitivity when he ventured into the Aegean that he did more harm than good. As some sympathizers said after he had massacred some prisoners, 'he was not going the right way to free Greece in massacring men who had never raised a hand against him, and who were not enemies of his, but allies of Athens against their will, and that if he did not stop he would turn many more friends into enemies than enemies into friends' (Thucydides 3. 32. 2). Similarly, the Spartan backing for the oligarchs in Corcyra during the civil war between 427 and 424 was ineffective, since Athenian fleets impeded access at the critical moments.

Actions by land went better. Spartan and Corinthian help was continually being asked in the zone north of the Corinthian Gulf. Here their help in 430, 429, and 426 to Ambracia and Aetolia against Acarnania, Argos, and the Athenian colony of Naupactus at least prevented Athenian influence from spreading out from Naupactus. North of the Isthmus, the siege and capture of Plataea between 429 and 427, was intended, as Thucydides tells us (3. 68. 4), to keep happy Sparta's most important and vulnerable allies, the Boeotians. Whose idea it was we cannot tell, but we are told more about the one real Spartan achievement before 413, Brasidas' success in 423 and 422 in detaching many cities in Chalcidice and the North Aegean from Athens after his long march through Thessaly with 700 enfranchised helots in the winter of 424–3. So far, though his career since 431 had been by far the most distinguished of any non-royal Spartan, his actions had been mainly rescue operations. Now, however,

he was sent out by the Spartans mainly at his own desire, although the Chalcidians also were eager to have a man so thorough as he had shown himself whenever there was anything to be done at Sparta, and whose after-service abroad proved of the utmost use to his country. At the present moment his just and moderate conduct towards the towns generally succeeded in procuring their revolt, besides the places which he managed to take by treachery; and thus when the Spartans desired to treat, as they ultimately did, they had places to offer in exchange, and the burden of war meanwhile shifted from Peloponnese. Later on in the war, after the events in Sicily, the present valour and conduct of Brasidas, known by experience to some, by hearsay to others, was what mainly created in the allies of Athens a feeling for the Spartans. He was the first who went out and showed himself so good a man at all points as to leave behind him the conviction that the rest were like him. (Thucydides 4. 81)

Yet Thucydides' warmth does not stop him from remarking later that 'the success and honour which war gave him' had made him, with the Athenian Kleon who died simultaneously with Brasidas in battle outside Amphipolis, 'the two principal opponents of peace on either side' (5. 16. 1). Indeed, Brasidas may not have been fully trusted in Sparta. His forces were expendable, like all helots, and were not reinforced. There is much in him, as in his younger Athenian contemporary Alkibiades, which foreshadows the independent and ambitious fourth-century 'generals with full powers' (see p. 188). Not for the first or the last time in Spartan history, successful military action involved a new and perhaps tense relationship between commander and State.

Athenian attempts to break the deadlock are best dealt with regionally, to bring out the continuity of interests and pressures which stem from well back in the past. Four regions need noting. In the Aegean, at least, Perikles' advice was followed to the letter. The strenuous efforts made to regain defected allies such as Potidaea between 433 and winter 430–29, Mytilene in 428–7, and the cities of Chalcidice and Thrace between 423 and 421, are fully described by Thucydides. So too are moves to head off disaffection at Chios in winter 425–4 or Colophon in 427. The cost of these operations also emerges in part. He notes that the siege of Mytilene needed a special tax levy, but the facts that the tribute was raised in 428–7 and again very sharply in 425, or that the rate of interest levied on borrowings made from Athene's treasury to the state was cut in 426–5 from about 7 per cent per annum to just over 1⅕ per cent per annum, come not from Thucydides but from complicated detective work by modern scholars on the Tribute Lists and Treasurers' accounts. Most illuminating of all is the reassessment decree of 425, a pugnacious document probably based on the correct calculation that after Athenian success at Pylos they could get away with it. It lays down:

> [The present assessments of the tribute, since] it has become too little, [are to be] assessed jointly by the jurymen and the Council, [and, as in the la]st administrative period, assessments [on all the cities in due] proportion (are to be completed) within the month Poseideion (Jan–Feb). The bu[siness is to be conducted daily] from the beginning of the month in the [same way, so that the assessment of] the tribute may be completed in the [month] Po[seideion: the Council in full session is to] conduct the business [of assessments without interruption until] they are completed, unless [the demos passes any decree to the contrary.] No c[ity is to be assessed for] the tribute [at a rate less] than that [which they have previously paid], unless a [shortage] be [proved such that it is] impo[ssible for more to be paid from] the country's [total resources]. (ML 69, lines 17–22)

Moreover, the attached roster goes on to assess cities hitherto outside the Empire. Yet the tribute was cut to lower levels after the Peace of 421, and in the event remarkably little was done throughout the war to bring new states into the Empire. The only exceptions were brief forays on Crete in 429 and against Melos in 426, followed by the siege and reduction of Melos in 416. Thucydides makes the latter into his most elaborate and famous set piece (5. 84–116), pointedly setting success in the rationalized and amoral use of power at Melos against its spectacular failure in his narrative of Sicily (Books 6–7).

However, intense activity by Athenian generals and politicians in three other areas did go well beyond Periklean bounds, no doubt intentionally. The first area chronologically was the north shore of the Corinthian Gulf, where Naupactus had been colonized *c.* 460 by Messenian refugees in Athenian interests. Pre-war operations from there had brought Acarnania into alliance and promised to break the area's traditional links with Corinth. Ambraciot and Aetolian opposition had achieved little by 426, when a general newly arrived at Naupactus,

Demosthenes, was persuaded to attack Aetolia. For once Thucydides reveals the strategic thinking:

> Demosthenes consented, not only to please the Messenians, but also in the belief that by adding the Aetolians to his other mainland allies he could be able, without aid from home, to march against the Boeotians by way of Ozolian Locris to Kytinion in Doris, keeping Parnassus on his right until he descended to the Phocians, whom he could force to join him if their ancient friendship for Athens did not, as he anticipated, at once decide them to do so. Arrived in Phocis he was already upon the frontier of Boeotia. (3. 95. 1)

The attack miscarried, his hoplites significantly being no match for lightly armed Aetolians in wooded and mountainous country, but the idea both goes back to the 450s, when Athenian-held territory had extended right through Central Greece, and was revived in November 424. Then Demosthenes, again starting from Naupactus, the main Athenian army, starting from Attica, and Boeotian exiles, starting from Phocis, were to invade Boeotia simultaneously. The timing went wrong, the Athenian forces were decisively defeated at Delium, and the net result was to strengthen Theban self-confidence and control of Boeotia. All the same, the basic idea, that of backing local dissidents so as to deny Boeotian hoplite forces to Sparta and thereby create a more tolerable balance of land-power, had proved viable 30 years previously and might well have decided the war.

The second area was Peloponnese itself. Seaborne raids had achieved little, but the capture and garrisoning of Pylos on the south-western coast in 425 by Kleon and Demosthenes, and of the island of Cythera in 424 by Nikias, demoralized Sparta very effectively, to judge from Thucydides' description (4. 55–56). Other ideas seem to have been current too. In January 424 Aristophanes made the sausage-seller say of Kleon:

> The sorts of thing he is doing in Argos do not escape me. Nominally he is making the Argives friends of ours. But privately he's consorting there with the Spartans. (*Knights* 463–5)

Kleon was certainly being premature, for Argos had had a treaty with Sparta since 451 by which she agreed not to make alliance with Athens, but he was not being stupid. The fact that the treaty expired in 421 both gave Sparta a major reason to make peace in that year, as Thucydides explicitly says, and triggered off major political realignments in Peloponnese. They followed a complex evolution which Thucydides recounts in great detail in 5. 25–83, and since in the short run they proved abortive, things having returned by 417 to the status quo of the 420s, their effect was small. However, they came to matter in Athenian politics, and motifs recognizable in them were to recur importantly in Peloponnesian politics over several generations.

Two of these motifs, Corinthian willingness to abandon the Spartan alliance, and general resentment at Great-Power détente, emerged at once, for peace between Athens and Sparta in spring 421 was quickly followed by alliance between them.

> The Corinthians . . . opened negotiations with some of the men in office at Argos, pointing out that Sparta could have no good end in view, but only the subjugation of Peloponnese, or she would never have entered into treaty and alliance with the once detested Athenians, and that the duty of consulting for the safety of Peloponnese had now fallen upon Argos, who should immediately pass a decree inviting any Greek state that chose, such state being independent and accustomed to meet fellow powers upon the fair and equal ground of law and justice, to make a defensive alliance with the Argives. (Thucydides 5. 27. 2)

A third motif, which came to destroy the détente of 421, was Athenian adventurism in Peloponnese. Themistokles and Kleon had both rightly seen that Argos could give Athens the political entrée to Peloponnese. By summer 420 Athens had allied with Argos, Elis and Mantinea, and had begun to commit her land forces to support her allies' interests. The prime mover in Athens was Alkibiades:

> He thought that it really was better to go over to the Argives, not that personal pique had not also a great deal to do with his

opposition. He was offended with the Spartans for having
negotiated the treaty [of 421] through Nikias and Laches, for
having overlooked him on account of his youth, and also for not
having shown him the respect due to the ancient connexion of
his family with them as their proxenoi. (Thucydides 5. 43. 2)

We know much about Alkibiades from Thucydides, Xenophon,
Plato, and Plutarch's *Life* of him, enough to see in him an
acutely unstable combination of ego-defined with society-defined
ambitions. All was well if public and private drives coincided with
the honour accorded him, but he could also say, as an exile to the
Spartans in 414, 'I am an outlaw from the iniquity of those who
drove me forth, not, if you will be guided by me, from your
service; my worst enemies are not you who only harmed your
foes, but they who forced their friends to become enemies; and
love of country is what I do not feel when I am wronged, but
what I felt when secure in my rights as a citizen' (Thucydides
6.92. 3–4). He could turn his talents as coolly to helping Sparta
against Athens (in 414–12), or to advising a Persian Viceroy to
play one off against the other (in 411), as to rebuilding Athenian
naval power in the Aegean (after 410). Yet he was also a product
of the spoiling competitiveness of current Athenian politics (see
pp. 114–16f.). If Nikias captured Minoa, Demosthenes countered
by attacking Aetolia; if Demosthenes captured Pylos, Kleon helped
to take 292 Spartans prisoner and 'unscrupulously snatched up
the Spartan cake I baked at Pylos, and served it up on his own', as
Aristophanes made Demosthenes say in January 424 (*Knights*
55–7); if Kleon raised the tribute, Hyperbolos suggested sending
100 ships to attack Carthage (*Knights* 1300ff.). Such restless
overbidding was certainly fuelled by war, by ambition and
jealousy, and to some extent also by social tensions in Athens.
Still it was also a desperate search for a way of winning the war,
and the concentration of successive bids in Central Greece and
northern Peloponnese was no accident. To create and head a bloc
of powers in this region was for Athens the long-term alternative,
or complement, to controlling the Aegean. The idea surfaced
again in the 390s, the 370s and the 360s, for it was the only way of
denying Sparta the Isthmus and becoming powerful by land. Yet
it failed each time, and for the same reason, the inherent strength

of Sparta's position in Peloponnese. Here we have the fourth motif of these confused years. Once the Spartans had 'concluded that it was high time for them to interfere if they wished to stop the progress of the evil, and accordingly with their full force, Helots included, took the field against Argos' (Thucydides 5.57.1), they totally demolished the allies' opposition at the battle of Mantinea in mid-summer 418. Thucydides commented that 'the imputations cast upon them by the Greeks at the time, whether of cowardice on account of the disaster in the island (of Sphacteria in 425), or of mismanagement and slowness generally, were all wiped out by this single action; fortune, it was thought, might have humbled them, but the men themselves were the same as ever' (5. 75. 3). Effective resistance to the Spartans in Peloponnese vanished for twenty years.

Alkibiades' 'Argive policy' (see pp. 126–7) picked up and developed an idea formulated long previously. The same is true for his 'Sicilian policy', for Athenian interest in Sicily and the west went back to the 450s if not before. This is the third area (see Map 4) wherein we can see she tried to break the deadlock of the Peloponnesian War. The evidence of her earlier interest is patchy. Herodotus (8. 62) reports a threat by Themistokles in 480 to take the Athenians off to Siris in Apulia, 'which is ours of old', if his views were not accepted by the allies. Athenian inscriptions reveal alliances made with Segesta and Halikyai in Western Sicily, probably in the 450s and 440s, and with Rhegium and Leontini on the Straits of Messina, possibly in the 440s but renewed in 433–2. Diodorus and others give us considerable information about the refoundation of Sybaris as the Athenian colony of Thurii between 446–5 and 443. Thucydides in Books 3–4 recounts in detail how an Athenian expedition, sent to the west in 427 and later reinforced, participated in warfare between their allies and Syracuse until a congress of the Sicilian states at Gela in summer 424 made a peace common to the whole island and prevailed upon the Athenians to withdraw. Thus, we have some basic facts. We need to pattern them by understanding what the Athenians intended and why the region was susceptible to their penetration. For the first, Thucydides says that in 433 they allied with Corcyra not just because of her navy but also because 'the island seemed to lie conveniently on the coasting passage to Italy and Sicily' (1. 44. 3). He also says that the expedition of 427 was sent 'nominally because of Athenian kinship (as fellow-Ionians with Leontini), but in reality to prevent the export of Sicilian corn to Peloponnese and to test the possibility of bringing Sicily into subjection' (3. 86. 4). At the motives of earlier activity we must guess. Athens' own need for corn and wood may be relevant, for the increasing imports of Athenian pottery throughout the region must have been paid for somehow, and coin or slaves are less likely. Athens perhaps also wished to constrict Corinthian intersts in the west in the same way as they were being constricted after 460 and in the 430s in Central Greece.

However, it is the general situation which needs analysing, and here the problem of information is crippling. For Sicily a basic minimum comes from Diodorus' Books 11–12, whose narrative concerning his own island is reasonably coherent and probably goes back via Timaios to fifth-century authors, but information about South Italy is desperately scanty. Diodorus has a little, mostly about the foundation of Thurii, but otherwise we must use the evidence of temples, other archaeological sites, and coins, together with a few casual references such as Herodotus' account of the disastrous defeat, by the tribes of the heel of Italy, of the combined forces of Tarentum and Rhegium in 473. The only other help, if that is the word, comes from the fearful complications of the tradition about Pythagoras and his followers at Croton and elsewhere. This tradition is fully extant only in the three *Lives* of him written by Diogenes Laertios (late third century AD), by the Neoplatonist philosopher Porphyry († *c.* AD 303–5), and by the latter's pupil Iamblichus. Their information goes back layer after layer through sources of the early Roman Empire, Hellenistic historians, and Alexandrian scholars, to pupils of Aristotle, Plato, and the earlier historians of the west. Since succeeding generations each saw what they sought, the authority of Pythagoras' teaching for their own views, the chances of distortion are great but uncheckable. All we can do, therefore, is to pick out such seemingly accurate detail as we can and to allow patterns to emerge, however shaky the documentary foundation.

One recurrent theme is that of the creation and disintegration of 'united states' in various forms. Two call for special notice, because their bases and legitimations were so dissimilar and because the evidence for them is so disparate. The first emerges in part from various series of coins between 480 and 450 which carry the legends KRO(ton) on one side, and SY(baris), PANDO(sia), or TE(mesa) on the other, and in part from the tradition about the Pythagoreans that 'they both preserved the laws and governed certain Italian cities, deciding and counselling what seemed best to them, and abstaining from the public revenues. But though there were many slanders against them, still the gentlemanly merit (*Kalokagathia*) of the Pythagoreans and the will of the cities themselves prevailed for a time, so that the cities wished their governmental affairs to be administered by the Pythagoreans' (Iamblichus, *Life of Pythagoras* 129). Shadowy though the tradition and its chronology are, they suggest both that aristocratic control of politics was exercised through Pythagorean sects and that Croton may have been its centre. Certainly that control ended when the democrats 'carried their plotting against the Pythagoreans so far that when the latter were gathered one day in the house of Milon at Croton deliberating on political matters, they set fire to the building and burned the men to death' (Iamblichus, *Life of Pythagoras* 249). Evidence from the coinages and from Diodorus attesting the full independence of Sybaris, Pandosia and Temesa by about 450 gives us some sort of date for the end of the Pythagoreans' control.

Croton's influence may not have constituted a formal 'Empire', but that of Syracuse in the 470s certainly did. Herodotus and Diodorus tell us how Gelon made himself tyrant first of Gela and then of Syracuse, transferred wholesale to Syracuse the populations of neighbouring cities, beat off the Carthaginians at Himera in 480, made complex marriage alliances with the tyrant house of Acragas, and thereby created a solid Dorian super-state in south-eastern Sicily. We can see too from Diodorus how the pattern was continued by Gelon's brothers after his death in 478, and how political insensitivity and quarrels with Acragas brought the dynasty to an end in 466–5. Then, after much turmoil,

> the peoples who had been expelled from their own cities while Hieron (Gelon's brother) was king, now that they had assistance in the struggle, returned to their fatherlands and expelled from their cities the men who had wrongfully seized for themselves the habitations of others. Among them were

inhabitants of Gela, Acragas, and Himera. In like manner Rhegians along with Zanklians expelled the sons of Anaxilas, who were ruling over them, and liberated their fatherlands. Later on Geloans, who had been the original settlers of Camarina, portioned that land out in allotments. And practically all the cities, being eager to make an end of the wars, came to a common decision, whereby they made terms with the mercenaries in their midst. They then received back the exiles and restored the cities to the original governments. To the mercenaries who because of the former tyrannical governments were in possession of the cities belonging to others, they gave permission to take with them their own goods and to settle one and all in Messene. In this manner, then, an end was put to the civil wars and disorders which had prevailed throughout the cities of Sicily. The cities, after driving out the forms of government which aliens had introduced, with almost no exception portioned out their lands in allotments among all their citizens. (Diodorus (11. 76. 4–6) places this account in 461–0, but he must be describing events spread over several years.)

Thereafter Syracuse remained indeed the leading city in the west, and Diodorus notes that in 439–8 'the Syracusans . . . built 100 triremes and doubled the number of their cavalry; they also developed their infantry forces and made financial preparations by laying heavier tributes upon the Sicels who were now subject to them. This they were doing with the intention of subduing all Sicily little by little' (12. 30. 1). Nevertheless, Syracuse remained only one city among many till the end of the century.

The decline of Syracuse left a vacuum, briefly filled by the non-Greek Sicels of the scarcely colonized hinterland west of Mt Etna. At first in alliance with Syracuse, one of their leaders, Douketios, 'harbouring a grudge against the inhabitants of Catane because they had robbed the Sicels of their land, led an army against them' in 461–60 (Diodorus 11. 76. 3). He went on in the 450s to unite the Sicels into a League; to create towns and a capital; to take on with success the combined forces of Syracuse and Acragas; to be captured and exiled to Corinth; to escape in 466–5 and found Kale Akte on the north-eastern coast of Sicily; and to lay renewed claim to the leadership of the Sicels. His stature emerges from the fact that it was only after his death in 440–39 that the Syracusans felt able to move against the non-Greek cities.

Other themes which emerge can be noted more briefly. One is the ownership of land. It underlay Sicel resentment against Catane, and was the leitmotif of the resettlements of 461–60 (see p. 131). Similarly in 454 'a war arose between the peoples of Segesta and Lilybaeum over the land on the Mazaros river, and in a sharp battle which ensued both sides lost heavily but did not slacken their rivalry' (Diodorus 11. 86. 2). The recolonization of Sybaris and elsewhere in South Italy in the 440s and 430s makes sense in the same terms, and if only Iamblichus' chronology were clearer we could treat very seriously his statement that:

> as long as the people of Croton owned their existing land and Pythagoras lived there, the constitution which went back to the foundation of the city remained, though it was unpopular and (though the people) sought to find an opportunity for change. But when they defeated Sybaris, and he went away, and the government arranged for the land won in battle not to be distributed in allotments in the way the Many desired, the silent hatred broke out, and the masses became opposed to the Pythagoreans (*Life of Pythagoras* 255).

Again, certain other features can be seen, though not easily explained: the comparative rootlessness of populations; the way in which the ability to build temples or maintain mercenaries revealed how régimes could tap and tax the area's agricultural wealth; the oscillation between action taken under common agreements (as in 460 or 424), local hatreds, and antagonisms between Dorians and Ionians; or the ease with which a prominent individual could overshadow or disrupt the constitution of the state.

All this makes Athenian actions intelligible. It is probably no accident that her alliances after 460 were all with cities of Ionian origin or with non-Greek communities such as Segesta or Halikyai. Douketios' escape in 446, and his shift of attention from the Etna region to the north coast, may even have been encouraged by Athens in order to contain Syracuse. The resources of the region gave them a clear motive, and its political fragmentation gave them the opportunity. Thucydides does

Ploughing and sowing scenes.

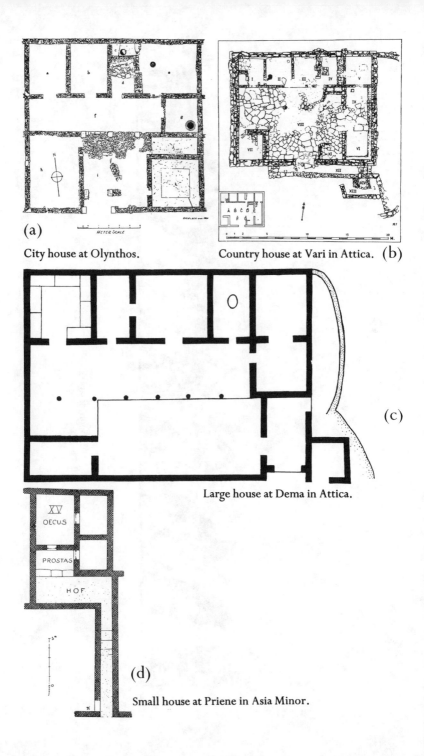

(a)

City house at Olynthos.

Country house at Vari in Attica. (b)

(c)

Large house at Dema in Attica.

(d)

Small house at Priene in Asia Minor.

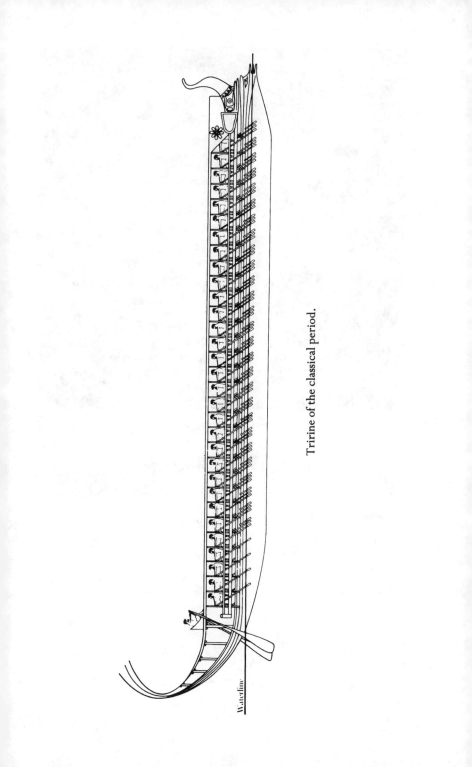

Waterline

Tririne of the classical period.

(a) Chain mail corselet.

Slashing sword.

(b)

(a)   Temple of 'Concordia' at Akragas.

(b)   Part of the Gortyn law code.

(b) Grave monument of ca. 340 from Athens.

(a) Gravestone of Hegeso, from Athens.

(a)   Portrait of an old woman.

(b)   Portrait of Maussollos of Caria.

(a)   The rebuilt city wall at Gela.

(b)

Gold coin of Philip II of Macedon.

indeed make clear that the chief instigator of the great expedition of 415–13 had personal motives: 'By far the warmest advocate of the expedition was, however, Alkibiades son of Kleinias, who wished to thwart Nikias both as his political opponent and because of the attack he had made upon him in his speech. He was, besides, exceedingly ambitious of a command by which he hoped to reduce Sicily and Carthage, and personally to gain in wealth and reputation by means of his successes' (6. 15. 2). Yet Thucydides also shows that the original Athenian design, 'being ambitious in the truest terms to conquer the whole island, although they had also the specious design of succouring their kinsmen and their existing allies' (6. 6. 1), emerged from appeals for help from Segesta, and had its roots and parallels in previous action. From his very detailed narrative in Books 6–7 we can see how the original design was transmuted into an assault on Syracuse and its prolonged siege, how the city almost surrendered in late summer 414, and how the Spartan Gylippos arrived just in time to command the defence. That saved the city and allowed it to defeat the reinforced Athenian army on land, to destroy the Athenian fleet in a battle in the Great Harbour, and to cut off the survivors' retreat in autumn 413. As Thucydides said with appalling simplicity,

> this was the greatest achievement of any in this war, or in my opinion of those we know of in Greek history; at once most glorious to the victors and most calamitous to the conquered. They were beaten at all points and altogether; all that they suffered was great; they were destroyed, as the saying is, with a total destruction, their fleet, their army, everything was destroyed, and few out of many returned home. (7. 87. 5–6)

Those who died may have numbered 40,000 or more, and their deaths signalled the failure of the fourth and greatest attempt by Athens to break the deadlock. Its failure decided the war, and thereby determined that Greek history would not go the way of Italian history. There a dominant power, Rome, imposed its authority, commanded preponderant resources, and ultimately merged its sovereignty in a larger-scale entity. Greece was to continue to be polycentric, competitive, spoiling, and subject to influence and pressure from outside.

VIII

Spartan Supremacy

GREEK POLITICS after 413 kept the same configuration for a generation. The Athenian defeat in Sicily stimulated Sparta and allowed her to reach an understanding with Persia and win the war, to beat off renewed hostilities between 395 and 386 and to dominate Greek politics. Her power lasted until a coup d'état in Thebes in winter 380–79 began to extrude her influence first from Greece in general and then, after 371, even from Peloponnese. Unity of events, then; but not a unity of source, for Thucydides' detailed but unfinished Book 8 begins in autumn 413 and ends in mid-sentence in September 411. We know of three authors who continued him: Xenophon, whose extant *Hellenika* begin by completing the sentence and end in 362; Theopompos, whose lost *Hellenika*, written in the 350s and 340s, probably ended in 394; and *Hellenika Oxyrhynchia* of unknown authorship, whose narrative, partly extant since 1908 (see p. 6), may have begun in 413, probably ended in 386, and may have been written before the 350s. We can now see that Diodorus' narrative ultimately depends on the latter till 386. There are slight hints that Theopompos used him too, and his quality is such that even Diodorus' summary must be taken very seriously. Hence we must now continually calibrate two sources against each other. To them, furthermore, we must add Xenophon's biography of King Agesilaos of Sparta, no less primary for being hagiographic; private and political speeches by Andokides, Lysias and Isaeus; Plutarch's *Lives* of Alkibiades, Agesilaos and Lysandros, themselves a complex *mélange* from Theopompos and other sources; the usual scatter of documents from Athens; and a treatment in Aristotle's *Athenian Constitution* of oligarchic coups d'état at Athens in 411 and 404–3 which incorporates documents and details not the less important for being unknown elsewhere and of dubious reliability. We must as usual simplify, and can best do so by seeing in the material how the Athenian defeat in Sicily affected powers and regions differently.

Reactions in Athens diverged. A decade before, the 'Old Oligarch' had reckoned: 'Given all this, I say that it is impossible for affairs at Athens to be conducted otherwise than they are now, except that it is possible to add something or subtract something. Major change is impossible, so that the democracy cannot be dismantled' (3. 8). Now, however, a minority at least thought otherwise. Much of Thucydides' Book 8 concerns the coup mounted in 411, at first under the slogans of abolishing pay for office, in the interests of the war and of economy, and of creating 'a different sort of democracy', as the coup leaders called it, as the price of gaining Persian help and the return of Alkibiades from exile. Thucydides also reveals the thuggery involved; the determination of the leaders, whose intellectual and political abilities he evidently admired, to create the new régime irrespective of the consequences abroad; the wish of at least some of them to make peace with Sparta at once; the lack of popular support for the régimes; and the adroitness with which the cleverest of the oligarchs, Theramenes, changed sides in September 411, and godfathered the creation of a semi-democratic constitution where at least 5000 men held full citizenship rights. The events of 411, indeed, clearly revealed the underlying drives in Athenian society at large, for the majority showed a formidable will to resist, re-equip, and accept no compromise. In autumn 413 'it was determined to resist to the last, and to provide timber and money, and to equip a fleet as best they could, to take steps to secure their allies and above all Euboea, to reform things in the city upon a more economical footing, and to elect a board of elders to advise upon the state of affairs as occasion should arise. In short, as is the way of a democracy, in the panic of the moment they were ready to be as prudent as possible' (Thucydides 8. 1. 3–4). Ships were commissioned and sent out in dribs and drabs in 412–11, so as to re-create a naval presence in the Aegean. In 410 a fleet commanded by a half-rehabilitated Alkibiades destroyed a Spartan fleet at Cyzicus, and the Spartans sought peace. In response,

The sentiments of the most reasonable men among the

Athenians inclined towards the peace, but those who made it their practice to foment war and to turn public disturbances to private gain chose the war. The leading demagogue of the time, Kleophon, also shared this view. He . . . buoyed up the people, citing the magnitude of their military successes, as if it were not the practice of Fortune to balance military successes against each other. The Athenians, then, took unwise counsel, repented when it was useless, were deceived by words spoken in flattery, and blundered so totally that they were never able to recover properly . . . Elated by their successes, and entertaining many great hopes because they had Alkibiades to lead their forces, they thought that they would quickly win back their supremacy. (Diodorus 13. 53)

Thus Diodorus: the will to resist emerges clearly, even through the political hostility which he transmits from his ultimate source. It emerges too in a badly broken document of 407, which seems to show the unqiue expedient, sponsored by Alkibiades on his return to Athens, of having ships built in Macedon itself. Again, in an emergency of 406, we hear of a staggering feat of mobilization:

When the Athenians heard . . . how (their general) Konon was under blockade (in Mytilene), they voted to send 110 ships to relieve him, and to embark those of military age, everyone both slaves and freemen: they manned the 110 ships in thirty days and set sail. Many of the knights embarked too. After that they reached Samos and took 10 Samian ships from there: they also collected more than 30 other ships from the other allies, forcing everyone to embark. (Xenophon, *Hellenika* 1. 6. 24–5)

Even in 405, as two orators tell us in spectacularly divergent terms:

when your ships had been destroyed (at Aegospotami in 405), . . . those who desired to have a revolution in the State were busy with their plots: they thought their only obstacles were the popular leaders and the generals and the taxiarchs . . . So they began with an attack on Kleophon . . . When the Spartan envoys stated the terms on which they were ready to make peace – on condition that each of the long walls was destroyed for 10 *stades* – you then refused, men of Athens, to stomach what you heard . . ., and Kleophon arose and protested on behalf of you all that by no means could this be done. After that Theramenes, who was plotting against your democracy, said that if you would appoint him as envoy to treat for peace with a free hand, he would arrange that there should be neither a breach made in the walls nor any other abasement of the city. You were persuaded . . . The others . . . brought Kleophon to trial, on the pretext that he did not go to the camp for his night's rest, but really because he had spoken on your behalf against the destruction of the walls. So they picked a jury for his trial, and these promoters of oligarchy appeared before the court and had him put to death on that pretext.

This is Lysias' account (12. 5–12), in a court speech about six years after the event. We can compare it with Aeschines' appeal to his jury in 343 to avoid

the ultimate stupidity (our ancestors committed), when they had been beaten in the war, and the Spartans were calling on them to make a peace which would leave them Lemnos, Imbros, and Scyros as well as Attica and would let them have a democratic constitution. They refused to do this, preferring to make war though they could not. Kleophon the lyre-maker, whom many remembered [as a slave] with foot-irons, who had scandalously had himself made a citizen and had bribed the populace by distributions of money, said that he would use a dagger to cut off the neck of anyone who proposed making peace. (2. 76)

In the event it needed siege, famine, starvation, and assassination before Athens capitulated in May 404.

That was one reaction to Sicily. Another, not surprisingly, was widespread revolt in the Aegean. We know of revolts by Chios, Erythrae, Clazomenae, Lesbos, Miletus, Rhodes, Abydos, and Euboea by summer 411, and soon after of those of Byzantium, Thasos, Cyzicus, and much of the North Aegean seaboard. We can see too that their recovery by Athens needed a fleet on the spot, that some cities, such as Chios, were stubborn, and that Athenian action on reconquest had to be delicate. One document of 408 lays down that:

> [the Athenians are to return] the hostages they hold, and in future are not to take (hostages), and the Selymbrians [have full rights to establish] their constitution [in whatever way] they see fit . . . As for the moneys lost in the war belonging to Athenians or the allies, or if the magistrates exacted any debt due or a deposit from someone who had it, exaction shall not be permitted except in the case of land and house. (ML. 87, lines 8–12 and 18–22)

But a notable degree of loyalty to Athens also emerges. A decree of winter 410–09 enjoins: 'Praise the men of Neopolis-by-Thasos, first because, though being colonists from Thasos and being besieged by them and by Peloponnesians, they did not wish to revolt from the Athenians but showed themselves men true to the expedition and the people of Athens and the allies . . .' (ML 89, lines 6–11). Even after the total Athenian defeat in 405 at Aegospotami had ended her naval resistance, she could still

> praise the Samian envoys, both those who came before and those now here, and the Council and the generals and the other Samians, because they are good men and eager to do what good thing they can . . . In return for the benefits they have conferred on Athens, are now conferring, and are promising, resolved by Council and People, Samians are to be Athenians, managing their own affairs as they wish: in order to make these arrangements most conveniently for both parties, as they themselves say, consult jointly about the other matters when peace is made. The Samians are to use their own laws in full autonomy, and to act in other respects in accordance with the oaths and agreements which subsist between Athenians and Samians . . . (ML 94, lines 7–17)

As these years from 413 to 404 made clear, the Athenian Empire was not just a tyranny. As before and later, so now, there were good intrinsic reasons for the Aegean states to stick together. Not the least of these reasons was Persia's long-term ambition, frustrated since 478, to recover the territories and revenues of the coastal cities of Asia Minor. The ambition became legitimate after Athens had supported a revolt in Caria in 414 against Persia. The ambition became realistic after 413, and was actively pursued thereafter. Two possibilities emerged, between which Persian policy was to oscillate for decades. One was to play the leading Greek powers off against each other. Still in exile in the winter of 412–11, and having attached himself to the new Persian viceroy in Sardis,

Alkibiades . . . advised Tissaphernes not to be in too great a hurry to end the war, or to let himself be persuaded to bring up the Phoenician fleet which he was equipping, or to provide pay for more Greeks, and thus put the power by land and sea into the same hands. Rather, he should leave each of the contending parties in possession of one element, thus enabling the King, when he found one troublesome, to call in the other. For if the command of the sea and the land were united in one hand, he would not know where to turn for help to overthrow the dominant power; unless he at last chose to stand up himself, and go through with the struggle at great expense and hazard. The cheapest plan was to let the Greeks wear each other out, at a small share of the expense and without risk to himself. (Thucydides 8. 46. 1–2)

Not, one imagines, that Tissaphernes could not see this argument for himself, but the other possibility was to reach a firm understanding with Sparta, and, as events proved, this suited both Persia and Sparta.

Spartan reaction to Sicily was to come alive. Thucydides notes how they had had a bad conscience about the outbreak of 431, but felt by 414 'that Athens had now committed the very same offence as they had done, and had become the guilty party: and they began to be full of enthusiasm for the war' (7. 18. 3). The argument was now not about whether to take the initiative, but where. Though her commanders always showed more than their fair share of timidity, incompetence, and brutality, at least till 404

individual and collective ambitions worked well enough together
to give Sparta victory. Those ambitions required an understanding with Persia. Hitherto Sparta had jibbed (see pp. 64 and
121), but 412 saw two treaties made with Persia, each as naive as
the other. As a tougher-minded Spartan envoy said in the winter
of 412–11:

> Neither of the treaties could stand. It was monstrous that the
> King should at this date claim the possession of all the country
> formerly ruled by himself or by his ancestors. Such a
> pretension implicitly put back under the yoke all the islands,
> Thessaly, Locris, and everything as far as Boeotia, and made
> the Spartans give Greece a Persian master instead of freedom.
> He therefore invited Tissaphernes to conclude another and
> better treaty, as they certainly would not recognize those
> existing and did not want any of his pay upon such conditions.
> This offended Tissaphernes so much that he went away in a
> rage without settling anything. (Thucydides 8. 43. 3–4)

However, a 'better treaty' was ultimately made, the nub clause of
which was that 'The land of the King, whatever lies in Asia, shall
be the King's: and concerning his own land the King shall decide
as he pleases' (Thucydides 8. 58. 2). This decision, to acknowledge the coast of Asia Minor as the boundary, became the Greek
'historic compromise'. Tensions remained, between Persian
ambitions and Greek irredentists, or between those Spartans who
cared little for Asia Minor and those Spartans who shared the
Athenian commitment to the Panhellenic ideals of liberation for
all Greek states. Such tensions sometimes surfaced, but cold
prudence largely won. In the short run, the arrangement gave
Sparta what she wanted: the money to build, equip, and pay a
fleet; the confidence to surmount early naval defeats; and the
ability to carry the war into the Aegean against Athens' major
island allies, to attack her corn-route through the Hellespont, and
ultimately to annihilate the Athenian fleet at Aegospotami in 405
and blockade Athens into capitulation. Xenophon and Diodorus
cover these events well enough, but they are less explicit in
tracing the longer-term opportunities and problems which Sparta
faced, so that here we must again find the patterns for ourselves.

Three main patterns emerge. The first hinged on Lysandros, who had commanded the Spartan fleet in 407–6 and again in 405–4 with spectacular success. 'Ambition and the spirit of emulation were firmly implanted in him by his Spartan training, and no great fault should be found with his natural disposition on this account. But he seems to have been naturally subservient to men of power and influence, beyond what was usual in a Spartan. He was content to endure an arrogant authority for the sake of gaining his ends, a trait which some hold to be no small part of political ability', noted Plutarch shrewdly (*Lysandros* 2. 2–3). Able as well as ambitious, Lysandros used all the techniques of self-advancement that were available. The first was to strike up a close friendship with Cyrus. He had been appointed viceroy of Asia Minor by his father, King Darius II, in 408, and saw in Spartans in general, and in Lysandros in particular, allies who would forward both Persian interests and his own. A second technique was to establish his friends in power throughout the Aegean via governmental juntas, often of ten men, 'dekarchies'. He was not very scrupulous about it.

Of such a sort were his dealings with Miletus, according to the record. For when his friends and allies whom he had promised to aid in overthrowing the democracy and expelling their opponents, changed their minds and became reconciled to their foes, openly he pretended to be pleased and to join in the reconciliation; but in secret he reviled and abused them, and incited them to fresh attacks on the many. When he perceived that the uprising had begun, he quickly came up and entered the city, where he angrily rebuked the first conspirators whom he met, and set upon them roughly, as though he were going to punish them, but ordered the rest of the people to be of good cheer and to fear no further evil now that he was with them. But in this he was playing a shifty part, wishing the leading men of the popular party not to fly, but to remain in the city and be slain. This was what actually happened: for all who put their trust in him were slaughtered. (Plutarch, *Lysandros* 8. 1–3)

His third technique was the creation of a remarkable personality cult, no doubt orchestrated by his 'friends', the elements of which ranged from statues and flattering odes to festivals held in his honour. Though our information comes only from the historian Douris (writing after 300), quoted by Plutarch, Lysandros was probably the first Greek to receive cultic honours, as god or hero, in his lifetime. A fourth technique was to collar the wealth of the Aegean. Plutarch and Diodorus speak of 1500 talents sent back to Sparta, Xenophon of another 470 talents which Lysandros took back himself, and Diodorus of his levying a tribute of 1000 talents a year. If this last figure is credible, it compares with that of the Athenian Empire at its most uncompromising. That was the point. Sparta was being offered an overseas empire, wherein the Aegean states contributed the money which financed the ships which protected the garrisons which guaranteed the régimes which ran the states. The price of the offer was to accept, and to institutionalize somehow, Lysandros' own charismatic role as admiral friend of Cyrus, friend of the oligarchs, and major Spartan politician.

It all went wrong. In 402:

Cyrus sent messengers to Sparta and appealed to the Spartans to show themselves as good friends to him as he had been to them in their war against Athens. The ephors regarded this as a perfectly fair request and sent orders to Samios, who was then in command of their fleet, telling him to help Cyrus in any way that was required. Samios on his side was very willing to do what Cyrus asked. He and his fleet sailed with Cyrus' fleet round the coast to Cilicia and and prevented Syennesis, the governor of Cilicia, from employing his land forces against Cyrus while he was marching against the King of Persia. Themistogenes of Syracuse has recorded the story of that campaign – of how Cyrus collected an army and marched inland against his brother, of the battle in which Cyrus was killed and how afterwards the Greeks came safely to the sea.

Thus Xenophon (*Hellenika* 3. 1. 1–2), coyly referring to the account he published pseudonymously, which we have as his *Anabasis*. That the expedition (in 401) was a spectacular military success comes out clearly. The 10,000 Greek mercenaries whom

Cyrus recruited with covert Spartan help defeated Persian forces, surmounted the arrest of their official leaders after Cyrus' death, and survived, virtually intact, their harassed retreat northwards through the Turkish mountains in the winter of 401–0. For ambitious Greeks who had eyes to see, the military weakness of Persia was nakedly exposed. Politically, however, the expedition was a disaster, for Sparta had helped Cyrus enough to curdle relations with his brother for the next eight years.

Again, Lysandros' 'dekarchies' aroused intense hostility. The only case we know much about is, as usual, Athens. Some time in later summer 404 (the date is disputed), he blackmailed the Athenian assembly into voting a junta of thirty men into office, stating 'that the terms of peace had been broken by the Athenians, since, he asserted, they had destroyed the walls later than the days of grace agreed upon' (Diodorus 14. 3. 6). Few episodes in ancient history are better documented, from so many separate traditions, as are the subsequent convulsions in Athens till the Thirty were deposed in early summer 403, the exiled democrats returned in force, and democracy was re-established in October 403. The two leading, and cleverest, politicians of the junta, Theramenes and Plato's uncle Kritias, each saw that the game had to be played Lysandros' way, even though, from their previous careers, both seem to have been inclined by temperament to a wider oligarchy giving participation to all hoplites. Kritias was prepared to play it more ruthlessly than Theramenes, and managed to force the issue with him and to have him executed. What broke Kritias' position and régime was partly the growing opposition to the Thirty in Athens, among the exiles, and from general Greek public opinion, and partly the fact that Lysandros' influence had faded slightly in Sparta by summer 403. Other dekarchies perhaps lasted longer, but they had certainly all vanished by 396, 'dissolved by the ephors, who had proclaimed that all cities should return to their traditional constitutions' (Xenophon, *Hellenika* 3. 4. 2).

Thirdly, as the ephors' act shows, Lysandros' power and ambitions came to be regarded as, and perhaps to be, a threat to traditional Spartan government. In and after 403 his partisans in Sparta were prosecuted, he himself withdrew briefly from politics, and the régime of the Thirty in Athens came to an end because 'the Spartan King Pausanias was jealous of Lysandros and feared that his success in this undertaking would not only win him fame but would also result in his taking Athens as his personal property. He won over three of the (five) ephors, led a field force out of Sparta' (Xenophon, *Hellenika* 2. 4. 29), and superintended the return to democracy. But it was not just that, like any major politician, Lysandros made enemies. Rather, 'love of honour' (see pp. 114–16) challenged established Spartan values, even though it was itself one of those values.

We know a fair amount about Spartan society at this period, partly from Plutarch but mainly from Xenophon, who was a contemporary, lived many years as an exile in Peloponnese, and had close links with Sparta. His *Hellenika*, his *Life of Agesilaos*, and his *Constitution of the Lacedaemonians* give portrayals of Spartan leaders and Spartan society all the more revealing for being sympathetic, because the underlying tensions and contradictions were stark. In theory, as Plutarch said,

> of the descendants of Herakles who united with the Dorians and came down into Peloponnese, there was a numerous and glorious stock flourishing in Sparta. However, not every family belonging to it participated in the royal succession, but the kings were chosen from two houses only, and were called Eurypontidai and Agiadai. The rest had no special privileges in the government because of their high birth, but the honours which result from superior excellence lay open to all who had power and ability. (*Lysandros* 24. 3)

The close comradeship of these 'Equals' was reinforced by a high degree of communal living, by uniform and rigorous military and social training, and by their common interest in keeping land, wealth and power in their own hands. Their cohesion was the greatest strength of Sparta, but it was now being eroded in various ways. Though the prerogatives of the kings had dwindled with time, their paramount and anomalous public position remained (see p. 14). The workings of the inheritance law were making some men wealthy, while others, too poor to remain contributing members of the mess-groups, were disfranchised. The admission of non-Spartiates, and even of enfranchised helots, into the army had created a contradiction between their legal and their functional status, while eroding the legitimacy of the Spartiates' claim to monopolize power. Lastly, now that Sparta controlled Greece, and now that any Spartan who went abroad on public business was a figure of Panhellenic standing and authority, status-envy and competition for power conflicted lethally with traditional solidarity.

Two known episodes illuminate all this. The first involves not Lysandros but one Kinadon,

> a youth in physique and strong in courage, but not one of the 'Equals', who organized a conspiracy (in summer 397). According to the informer who gave him away, Kinadon had taken him to the edge of the market place and then told him to count how many full Spartan citizens were there. 'And I', said the informer, 'counted up the king and the ephors and the members of the Council and about forty others, and then asked him "What was the point, Kinadon, in asking me to make this count?" Then he said, "I want you to consider those men as your enemies and all the others in the market place, who are more than 4000, as your allies" . . . And as for those who happened to be on the full citizens' country estates, he would point out one, the owner, as an enemy, and all the other as allies . . . Kinadon had said that those actually in the plot with himself and the leaders were not very many, though they were trustworthy: it was rather the case, the leaders claimed, that they were in the plot with everyone else – helots, enfranchised helots, 'inferiors', and 'dwellers around' – since all these people showed clearly enough, if there was ever any mention of the full citizens, that they would be glad to eat them up raw'. He was betrayed and arrested, and before he was executed 'the ephors asked him: "But what was it you hoped to achieve by this?" He replied: "To be inferior to nobody in Sparta".' (Xenophon, *Hellenika* 3.3. 5–11)

The second episode does involve Lysandros, but the sources give us irreparably inconsistent information. When King Agis died in Autumn 398, the succession was disputed between his lame brother Agesilaos and his wife's son Leotychidas, who was suspected of being not Agis' son but Alkibiades'. Amid the counter-bidding of gods, oracles, and month-counting

> Lysandros, speaking on behalf of Agesilaos, objected to an oracle warning them 'to beware of the lame kingship'. He said that in his opinion the oracle did not mean that they should beware if some king of theirs pulled a muscle and became lame; what was meant was that they should beware lest someone not of the royal blood should become king. For kingship really would be lame if people other than the descendants of Herakles were to be leaders of the state. After hearing these and similar arguments from both sides, the state chose Agesilaos king. (Xenophon, *Hellenika* 3. 3. 3–4)

Thus say all our sources consistently. However Plutarch, relying (it seems) on Ephoros, also says that after Lysandros' death in battle in 395 papers were found in his house which revealed an elaborate rigmarole of draft speeches, bogus oracles, and manufactured portents. By their means, Plutarch says,

> Lysandros planned to take the government away from the two royal houses, and restore it to all the descendants of Herakles in common, or as some say not to the descendants of Herakles but to the Spartans in general, in order that its high prerogatives might not belong to those only who were descended from Herakles, but to those who, like Herakles, were selected for superior excellence, since it was this which raised him to divine honours. And he hoped that when the kingdom was awarded on this principle, no Spartan would be chosen before himself. (Plutarch, *Lysandros* 24. 4–5)

Lysandros as kingmaker makes good sense within traditional Spartan terms, wherein close personal friendships, often, as here, with a homosexual component, influenced public policy. Lysandros as king may represent more what traditional Sparta feared in him, even posthumously, than what he historically hoped. At all events, whatever challenges he and Kinadon represented to current status rules were beaten off. The Spartan revolution had to wait another 150 years, and even then tradition was upheld and it was led by kings.

As Lysandros' influence waned, a second pattern of public action came to dominate Spartan policy. Here the new initiative was royal. The reaction in Asia Minor to the death of Cyrus had been to ask the Spartans, 'as the leading power in Greece, to take them also, the Greeks of Asia, under their protection, to save their land from being laid waste and to maintain their freedom' (Xenophon, *Hellenika* 3. 1. 3). From autumn 400 onwards Spartan support for them, for dissident satraps and local dynasts, increasingly took on the aspect both of Panhellenic irredentism and of Spartan empire-building. The underlying drive became explicit in spring 396, when Agesilaos' first acts as king were to sacrifice at Aulis in ostentatious imitation of Agamemnon, to announce as his aim 'that the cities in Asia should be as independent as are the cities in our part of Greece' (Xenophon, *Hellenika* 3. 4. 5), and to batter the Persian position in Asia Minor for three campaigning seasons. He did so with such success that his main adversary Tissaphernes, sent by the Persian King Artaxerxes in winter 401–400 to retrieve the situation after Cyrus' death, was executed in 395 for failure. His successor was reduced to offering a compromise: 'The King now thinks it right that you should sail home and that the Greek cities in Asia should be self-governing, and should pay to him the tribute that they used to pay in the past' (Xenophon, *Hellenika* 3. 4. 25). The offer would have reconciled Greek constitutional obsessions with Persian fiscal interests. Yet eight years later the King 'thought right' something very different indeed, for, with Agesilaos as with Lysandros, success was self-destructive.

For once reactions in two regions, the Aegean and Central Greece, moved in step. The Persian fleet, news of the building of which in 397 had prompted Agesilaos' campaign in the first place, was entrusted to an Athenian, Konon, who had (alone among his colleagues) emerged with credit from Aegospotami. Konon had then taken service as a mercenary leader abroad, setting a pattern which was to become common. Konon used his three roles as Persian admiral, mercenary leader, and Athenian politician, to link Athens more closely to Persia, destroy the Spartan fleet off Cnidos in August 394, and begin to re-create the Athenian

Empire in the Aegean. Meanwhile, in Central Greece the
renewed resentments of Corinth and Thebes at having done less
well out of the war than they hoped did not simply estrange them
from Sparta, as in 421–20, but made them willing to make
common cause with Athens and Argos. The 'causes' of the
intricate and superficially amorphous 'Corinthian War' were both
mixed and controversial. 'We all understand, men of Athens, that
you would like to get back the Empire which you used to have',
Xenophon made the Thebans say in summer 395 (*Hellenika* 3. 5.
10) when alliance between them was being made. Consistently, in
the winter of 392–1 an Athenian politician listed as reasons for
going to war 'that our city should be free: that we should be
allowed to build triremes, and keep and equip those we have: that
we should get back the islands, Lemnos, Scyros, and Imbros:
that we should get back Chersonese and the colonies and private
property holdings and overseas debts; till we defeat the Spartans
and their allies' (Andocides 3. 14–15). Xenophon, however,
giving a strongly pro-Spartan and anti-Theban explanation,
singled out Theban provocation of Sparta and the bribery of
Greek politicians by Persian agents. Diodorus claimed 'that it was
(the allies') thought that, since the Spartans were hated by their
allies because of their harsh rule, it would be an easy matter to
overthrow their supremacy' (15. 82. 2). Diodorus' ultimate
source, *Hellenika Oxyrhynchia*, reckoned that in Athens two
politicians

> badly wanted to make Athens hostile, and they held this view
> not because they had spoken to Timokrates (the Persian King's
> agent) and taken the money, but long before then. However,
> some say that the King's money was what caused them to
> move, as well as the people in Boeotia and in the other cities I
> mentioned. This view fails to recognize that all of them had
> long been hostile to the Spartans and had been exploring how
> to make their cities hostile. The Argives and the Boeotians
> hated the Spartans for having their personal enemies among the
> citizens as their friends, while those in Athens wanted to split
> the Athenians away from placidity and peace and lead them
> towards war and ambitious involvement, so that they could
> themselves make profits out of public funds. Those of the

Corinthians who wished to stir things up mostly resembled the Argives and the Boeotians in being hostile to the Spartans: Timolaos alone had had private grounds for becoming hostile, though he had previously been well-disposed and strongly pro-Spartan. (7. 2–3)

Moreover, all the sources underestimate the continuity of issues and configurations from the Peloponnesian War, to which the Corinthian War forms a coda.

The course of the war showed, as always, how decisive Persia and seapower were in Greek affairs. By land it was scrappy and inconclusive, and became mostly a dispute over the possession of the Isthmus, with damaging effects on Corinth herself. As if to emphasize regional links of power or loyalty, the rest of the Peloponnese remained notably loyal to Sparta. By sea, however, the more success Konon had, the more Athenian and Persian interests diverged, and the more Sparta could exploit the gap. By winter 392–1:

the Spartans now heard that Konon was not only rebuilding the walls of Athens with the Persian King's money but was also, from this same source, maintaining his fleet and winning over for Athens the islands and the cities on the coast of Asia Minor. It seemed to them that if they informed Tiribazos, the King's general, of this, they would either bring him over into alliance with them or, at least, stop him from maintaining Konon's fleet. So, when they had reached this conclusion they sent Antialkidas to Tiribazos, instructing him to inform Tiribazos of what was happening and to try to bring about peace between Sparta and the King. The terms were to be 'those which the King had long wanted, that the Spartans should put forward no claim against the King for the Greek cities in Asia, and are content that all the islands and the other cities should be governed according to their own laws'. (Xenophon, *Hellenika* 4. 8. 12 and 14)

Though this initiative failed, the link between Athens and Persia broke when Konon was arrested in spring 391. Thereafter the increasing Athenian tendency to act in terms of continuity with the pre-404 Empire, and the increasing Spartan success in creating havoc with small squadrons, eventually made Persia come down decisively on the Spartan side:

> King Artaxerxes thinks it right that the cities in Asia Minor shall be his, and also the islands of Clazomenae and Cyprus, and that he should leave autonomous all the other Greek cities, both great and small, except Lemnos and Imbros and Scyros, which are to belong to the Athenians as of old. Whosoever do not accept this peace, on them I shall make war in concert with those who wish this peace, by foot and by sea with ships and money. (Xenophon, *Hellenika* 5. 1. 31)

Thus the King's rescript, issued to a conference in winter 387–6. The Athenians, blockaded and again threatened with starvation by a Spartan fleet, had no option, and their other allies had little enthusiasm for war. Sparta, though having lost one Empire in Asia Minor, now stood to gain another in mainland Greece. The peace, variously called the Peace of Antialkidas or the King's Peace, was signed in spring 386. Xenophon goes on to relate how Sparta went on to bludgeon recalcitrant states into line, to garrison Thebes, to break up existing or emerging states, and in general to interpret 'autonomy' in the sense most convenient to herself, while keeping her side of the bargain with Persia by giving no help to the rebellions against Persia in Cyprus and Egypt.

In this way Sparta evolved her third and most successful pattern of foreign policy. It renewed the compromise of 412, and was acquiesced in by all Spartan politicians we know of. For Persia too it was the ideal arrangement, which her generals were still trying to re-establish in 333–2 in the face of Alexander's onslaught. For the other Greeks it, and Spartan action in terms of it, set up a resentment whose effects can be traced till 338 and beyond.

IX

Social Change

THE 380s are a turning point. Till that decade the main lines of
division in Greek society had remained constant for nearly a
century, while the dominant patterns of social articulation had
been stable for nearly 300 years. Thenceforward all the elements in
this picture undergo rapid change. New centres of political and
military force arise and impinge strongly on events: monarchy,
cavalry, and mercenaries all assume far greater importance: and
changed attitudes, beliefs, and tastes substantially modify the
social institutions of the states. After the 330s the pace of change
slowed. Politically, in Greece Macedonian suzerainty, once
created by Philip after 338, survived repeated challenges and gave
Greek politics their basic orientation until Rome replaced
Macedon. In the eastern Mediterranean the collapse of Persia
before Macedonian assault from 334 onwards yielded a new zonal
order, based on the age-old power centres of Egypt, Syria-
Mesopotamia and Western Turkey as well as Macedon, which also
remained stable until the Roman conquest. Culturally, in both
Greece and the soon-to-be-Hellenized eastern Mediterranean the
330s saw the emergence of a new sort of Greek culture, open to all
who wished to speak and to behave as Greeks. It was based on cities
which flourished as cultural and administrative units, abjured the
ambition to become serious power-units, concentrated rather on
securing protection, autonomy and privileges from the suzerain
kings, and managed on the whole to combine formal democracy
with effective oligarchy.

Of course, we must not be too schematic. Hellenistic society was
itself as much a developing thing as was classical Greek society,
while conversely many elements of fifth-century public and private

life survived unchanged to the 330s and beyond. Yet the fact of
drastic transition between the 380s and the 330s remains, and
needs explanation and interpretation. The task is peculiarly
intractable. From the 380s onwards events become harder to
follow, happening in many areas at once with no clear connecting
thread and at dates which are not always determinable with
precision. The impression we get is of confusion, frustration and
stalemate, as initiatives taken by this state or that run into the
sands or arouse fatal internal contradictions. Yet explanations of
the stalemate framed at the level of the individual state merely
prejudge the problem of deciding whether the important shifts
come from within Greek societies or impinge from outside. At the
same time, we must not belittle the creative initiatives repeatedly
taken on the political plane by intelligent men to break the
deadlock.

Even more important, technically and intellectually the fourth
century was a spectacularly creative period in Greek culture.
Admittedly, we can scarcely judge its imaginative literature in
traditional genres, since so little survives. The real explosion is in
serious and scholarly work ranging over virtually every area of
human activity and enquiry. Isokrates and others created a
system of education which satisfied the perceived needs of society
till the end of antiquity and which is still influential. Plato defined
the fundamental problems of philosophy in a way which has
provided the basis for Western philosophy ever since. Ephoros
created the new genre of Universal History, while Philistos and
Theopompos created the genre of histories orientated round men
of force and authority (their *About Dionysios* and *Philippika*
respectively). Natural phenomena, whether in plant biology or
meteorology or animal physiology or geology or medicine, were
classified and analysed, as were political systems. Valid modes of
argument and proof were formulated and applied in geometry and
rhetoric. Intellectual models were formulated to explain and
simplify the phenomena, such as Eudoxos' theory of concentric
spheres, developed to explain the stations and retrogradations of
the planets, or Aristotle's concepts of *telos* ('end' or 'purpose') and
entelecheia ('full realization of potential'), developed to explain
the biological processes of growth and maturation. Rationally
based systems of moral order were created to replace traditional

theologically buttressed systems. Countless handbooks were written to give technical information and advice in all the avocations which were proper for a citizen and a gentleman. Greatest of all was the superhuman achievement of Aristotle in redefining an intellectual and moral world and in systematizing human knowledge in virtually every field. Whatever view we take of these fifty years must take account of this atmosphere of creativity and achievement and should not pose too fierce a contrast between it and political action.

Unfortunately, the sources help less than they should. Athenian speeches and documents give us snapshots of action, but no real narrative and no analysis that goes very far. Of the historians, Xenophon does no more in the later books of his *Hellenika* than narrate in close-up salient events of the 380s, 370s and 360s, ending his narrative after the battle of Mantinea in 362 with the despairing words 'Each side claimed to have won, but neither appeared to have gained any advantage in land, city, or power, than before the battle. There was even more confusion and chaos in Greece after the battle than before it' (7. 5. 27). The *Hellenika* of other writers on the period (Anaximenes, Kallisthenes, etc) are firmly lost, and we have to turn to Diodorus' summary of Ephoros' *Universal History*, which gives us a narrative parallel to Xenophon's till 362 and our only extant narrative of Greek affairs thence till 336. Regrettably, it has failings. When Diodorus' account goes back to a vivid and incisive historian such as Thucydides, *Hellenika Oxyrhynchia*, Philistos, or Hieronymos, some glint of the original's quality always shows through, but here in Books 15 and 16 the narrative is flat and colourless. It reveals instead a rather stuffy myth-bound religiosity, and tends towards moralists' stereotypes of virtue and vice rather than towards political realism or any sense of the dramatic. Worse, since Ephoros 'solved' the problem of describing simultaneous polycentric action by narrating events in one theatre over a longish period until a natural close, the chronology is fuzzy and cross-references to contemporary events elsewhere are not flagged as they should be. Matters might be otherwise if we had better access to the evidently colourful and lively accounts by Philistos and Theopompos, but even so we should have to evolve an interpretation independent of their biographical approach. As it is, we are on our own, with the extant narratives as raw material.

Interpretation needs to begin at the most general level of institutions, values, and ideas. The central institution of the city-state set up a conflict of ideas and ideals. On the one hand it was vital and attractive. The pressures were not to alter or to supersede it as a unit of government, but to emulate it and to participate fully in its corporate life. We can see area after area striving to turn itself from a geographical expression either into some form of federal state, such as Achaea by the mid-fifth century, Boeotia from 446, and Aetolia by 367, or preferably into a cohesive centralized republican state. Equally, the urge to participate was a strong-running current, visible not only in the frustrations of Kinadon at Sparta (see p. 145) but also in the appearance of primary decision-taking assemblies in previously oligarchic states. Reflecting this movement of opinion, Aristotle defined a citizen functionally as 'one who enjoys the freedom to participate in deliberative or judicial office' (*Politics* 1275^b 18) and explicitly denies that rights in private law were enough. The effect of such ideals was to stabilize, and perhaps to ossify, the city-state structure. Fifth-century poets were prepared to use the word 'polis' to denote areas like Peloponnese, or even sprawling monarchies such as Persia, but Aristotle was firm that 'a *polis* could not consist of ten men, and one composed of 100,000 men would no longer be a *polis*'. (*Nikomachean Ethics* 1170^b 31)

However, other ideals and needs pointed in a very different direction. In 388 or 384 the speech-writer Lysias gave a display of oratory at the Olympic Games, and the first part of his speech survives. 'I come', he said, '. . . thinking that the role of a good man and a worthy citizen is to give advice on major issues, when he sees Greece in so shameful a state, with much of her subject to the barbarian and many cities uprooted by tyrants' (Lysias 33. 3). His targets were Persia and Dionysios of Syracuse, against whom (unsuccessfully) he asked Sparta to lead the Greeks. At the same Games in 380, in another display speech which survives in full, another orator, Isokrates of Athens, turned instead on the Spartans themselves:

Who could desire a situation in which pirates occupy the sea and light mercenary troops occupy the cities? Instead of fighting for their land against others, citizens fight each other inside the city walls. More cities have been taken prisoner than before we made the Peace. So frequent are revolutions that men who live in their own cities are more despondent than those punished with exile; the former fear the future, the latter expect to return at any moment. So far are cities from 'freedom' and 'autonomy', that some are under tyrants, others under Spartan governors, others are in ruins, others are under barbarian masters. (Isokrates 4. 115–17)

Both men were articulating a new, fundamental, and far-reaching fact of Greek politics, namely the resentment felt on all sides against this or that city-state subordinating other states to itself and using their resources to further its own quarrels and ambitions. Such resentments had already helped to erode the Athenian Empire. From now on, as the values of autonomy and participation came to be held or aspired to ever more strongly, the formulas for interstate cohesion, or for concentration of resources, employed by Athens and Sparta simply ceased to be viable. It is the retreat from them, and the search for more acceptable modes of formalizing interstate relations, which produce the apparent incoherence of fourth-century politics, since the search took various contradictory forms. Athens, still needing to dominate the Aegean in order to safeguard her food supply, tried (not very successfully) to give imperialism a human face. Interstate diplomacy at the top level ceased to be a matter of bilateral arrangements; instead, all the leading states participated in Congresses and in the multilateral peace treaties of the 370s and 360s which came to be known as Common Peaces. As the weaker states strove to get would-be imperialists off their backs, increasing stress was laid, both in practice and in the political theory of contemporary thinkers, on the political independence and the economic self-sufficiency of the single circumscribed state.

Yet the search itself led to contradiction, for secure independence and self-sufficiency were no more possible in the fourth century than they had been in the fifth. They were ideals attainable only if the integrity of the state could be effectively

defended, if need be by force: but while the ideal of participation
pointed to small units, self-defence pointed either to large units or
to the need to get a guarantee of protection. Yet such guarantees
set up a very ambivalent relationship, which easily became one of
subordination to the protector. Precisely because traditional
republican Greek states found no way of reconciling the
subordination of one state to another with the values which had
come to matter, the monarchs on the fringes of Greek culture
could move in successfully, filling the vacant roles of leader and
guarantor and exploiting them for their own purposes.

Other changes reflected shifts in social values. For example,
Aristophanic comedy made no bones about using coarse and
bawdy language, and fifth-century painters on vases or walls
felt equally free to depict a wide range of heterosexual and
homosexual acts. Such depictions gradually disappear from
comedy and the visual arts after 400. The reasons are complex
and far from clear. One strand may be the decline of Athenian
vase-painting in the fourth century, as it ceased to be able to keep
abreast of innovations by wall and panel painters during their
great period, but even so painted vases did continue to be made
elsewhere, especially in Boeotia and South Italy, and their
preferred themes are caricature or the portrayal of stage per-
formances: we clearly have to do with a shift of taste by painters
and buyers. Again, homosexuality may have been most nearly
institutionalized as a social ritual among aristocrats and their
hangers-on, in the contexts of banquets and drinking parties, of
which the painting from Paestum (FRONT COVER) or Plato's
Symposium give us complementary portraits a century apart.
Athenian speeches of the fourth century reveal that some wealthy
men or groups continued to act as before, but the political or
economic bankruptcy of many of the old aristocratic families in
Athens after 400 may have made such portrayals inappropriate.
So too from the 320s onward Menander's comedies, preoccupied
with wealth, citizen status, romantic love, and the interplay of
character, reflected a wholly different spectrum of obsession and
fantasy from that visible even in the later plays of Aristophanes.
Again, there has been a shift of taste in the audience, though here
the lack of extant comedies between the 380s and the 320s leaves

the change not closely datable. In general, we can see an increasing reticence, applying to heterosexual as well as to homosexual relations, though obviously that does not mean that sexual habits changed in fact.

A second equally complex shift can be seen in attitudes to the past. Late in 348 the Athenian politician Aeschines was trying to rouse Athenian and Greek opinion against Philip, and Demosthenes in 343 described his tactics:

> Who was it who shouted aloud that Philip was seizing control of Greece and Hellespont while you were asleep? Who was it who made those lovely long speeches, and read out the decree of Miltiades and the decree of Themistokles and the oath of the ephebes in the temple of Aglauros? Wasn't it Aeschines? (Demosthenes 19. 303)

Later, in 346, when Aeschines had changed tack and was counselling peace with Philip, the boot was on the other foot:

> The political speakers in serried ranks got up and made no attempt to discuss the safety of the state, but bade you gaze upon the Propylaia of the Akropolis, and to recall the sea-battle at Salamis and the tombs and war-trophies of your ancestors. I said that we should indeed keep all these things in mind, but should imitate the judicious decisions of our forefathers while avoiding their mistakes and inopportune jealousies. I urged that we should imitate the land battle at Plataiai, the contests off Salamis, the battle at Marathon, the sea-battle off Artemision, and the generalship of Tolmides, who marched fearlessly through enemy country, through the middle of Peloponnese, with a thousand picked Athenians: but that we should avoid imitating the Sicilian expedition, which they sent out to help Leontini when the enemy had invaded our land and when Decelea had been fortified against us . . . (Aeschines 2. 74–7)

Aeschines and his contemporaries feel a discontinuity between themselves and the past which is not there in the speeches of the 380s or the 370s. The famous battles and exploits are not theirs but 'their ancestors'', to be used as a standard of emulation or as part of the ammunition of political argument, to be used, turned or countered as convenient.

Another example provides a parallel. We have fragments of a large inscription, set up about 279, which recorded the victors – poets, choregoi and actors – from 502–1 onwards in the contests between poets, tribes and teams of actors which comprised the dramatic festival of the Dionysia at Athens. Two preserved entries tell us that 'In the archonship of Theodotos (387–6) the performers of tragedy first re-staged an old play' and that 'In the archonship of Theophrastos (340–39) the performers of comedy first re-staged an old play' (*IG* ii² 2318, lines 201–3 and 316–18). True, new tragedies went on being written and staged, their poets became famous, and it is dangerous for us to say that because their works have not survived therefore they were less good than those of their fifth-century predecessors. Yet it does seem that the fourth-century poets did not include the best minds of the time, and that the three great poets of the fifth century were increasingly regarded as 'classics', much as we regard Mozart and Beethoven: a process completed in the 330s when the Athenian politician Lykourgos enacted a law:

> that bronze statues of the poets Aeschylus, Sophocles and Euripides be erected, that their tragedies be written out and kept in a public depository, and that the secretary of the City should read them through for comparison to the actors; it should be unlawful to depart from the authorized text in acting. ([Plutarch], *Moralia* 841 F)

Again, a discontinuity needs explanation. It can hardly have been primarily a shift on the part of audiences, for the popularity of tragedy and comedy is apparent from the building of theatres all over Greece in the fourth century. More importantly, the poets met increasing difficulties and temptations, which were themselves part of social change. A man interested in rhetoric could now find more scope in writing for one or other of the three main contexts which fourth-century rhetorical theory recognized – display, the lawcourts, or the political assembly. Again, the fifth-century poets at their best had been moral philosophers and theologians in the mainstream of the intellectual currents of the time. They had been able to read into the stories and legends which gave them their materials the themes which tragedy at its best could tackle supremely well – man's relationship to other humans, to the forces within himself, to the gods, or to the outside world. Yet, such evidence as we have (largely of course the dialogues of Plato) does suggest that the problems which attracted philosophers after Sokrates were hard to fit inside the conventions of tragedy. Epistemology, mathematics and astronomy, the meanings of complex words such as 'virtue', 'happiness' and 'justice', or the creation of proper social and political relationships inside a city of citizens, were not topics which emerged straightforwardly from the myths of Oedipus or Theseus or Agamemnon.

Herein lies the core of the problem: the role and status of myth in current thinking after 400. The problem affected much more than the single art-form of tragedy, or than its relationship to philosophy, but since it may have been first felt there we may begin with it. In the fifth century the convention was only very rarely broken that the proper subject matter for tragedy was the mythic stories set in heroic times before and after the Trojan War. In the fifth century it had proved a constructive constraint, since it allowed distancing and formalization and thereby gave the dramatist a means of control over material which could otherwise be repellent. But the convention could stifle too, as Euripides' occasional lurches into parody and melodrama suggest, and the more so the more drastically the myths needed to be rewritten or reinterpreted if they were to serve their fundamental purpose, of validating or explaining a current state of affairs. It became therefore a stark choice: to stick to the myths at the cost of intellectual content, as the fourth-century poets seem to have done, or, as Plato did, to tackle the philosophical problems nakedly and directly at the cost of ditching the myths.

Elsewhere, too, we can see confusion over the role of myth. For example, till the late fifth century the sculptures on the friezes and pediments of temples usually represented myths or festivals closely linked with the deities whose temples they were, but that was no longer true of the two fourth-century temples whose decoration we know of, that of Asklepios at Epidaurus (built probably in the 370s and 360s) and that of Athene Alea at Tegea (built probably in mid-century). Of the latter we know from Pausanias' description that

> The figures in the front pediment represent the hunting of the Kalydonian boar, with the boar in the middle and on one side Atalante and Meleagros and Theseus, Telamon, Peleus, Polydeukes, Iolaos who shared most of Herakles' labours, Thestios' sons and Althaia's brothers Prothous and Kometes. On the other side of the boar Ankaios already wounded and dropping his axe and held up by Epochos, Kastor beside him, Amphiaraos son of Oikles, Hippothous son of Kerkyon son of Agamedes son of Stymphelos, and last of all Peirithous. The figures on the rear pediment are the battle of Telephos and Achilles in the Kaikos plain. (Pausanias 8. 45. 6–7)

The connection of these legends and heroes with Athene is tenuous at best. The temple has clearly become a context for separate and sculpturally appropriate portrayals, not for a unified assemblage thematically centred on the god.

Another break with traditional myth is visible in education. For the old-fashioned, Homer and Hesiod and the other poets complemented music, dancing and martial exercises in an ensemble of culture which affirmed Pindar's standards (p. 28) but gave little attention to critical or creative thinking. Exponents of newer educational ideas met much abuse and intolerance. Even in his last work, the *Panathenaikos*, written between 342 and 339, Isokrates complained how at some undated moment

> some of my friends met me and said that three or four of the vulgar sophists who claimed to know everything and were always turning up everywhere had been sitting in the Lykeion and had been talking about the poets, especially about the poetry of Homer and Hesiod. They had nothing of their own to say, but recited extracts from the poems and quoted the most brilliant bits from some earlier commentators. When the bystanders applauded their activities, the boldest sophist began to abuse me, alleging that I despised such studies, that I was for throwing out other men's philosophies and systems of

education, and that I said that the only people who did not talk nonsense were my own former pupils: at which point some of those present became very hostile to us. (Isokrates 12. 18–19)

In fact the claim Isokrates was making was larger and less egotistical, deriving from his strongly-held view of the centrality of *logos*, 'rational speech', in culture. As he wrote in 368, and repeated in 353,

In all our other characteristics we are no different from animals: indeed we are inferior to many of them in speed and strength and other faculties. But once we gained the power of persuading one another and of indicating our desires to ourselves, we broke free from savagery, came together and founded cities, created laws, invented skills; *logos* is what has created for us virtually all our inventions. It has given us our laws about just and unjust, shameful and honourable: without their formulation we should be unable to live together . . . By its means we teach the uncultivated and test the wise: for we consider that to speak fittingly is the best proof of being intelligent, and a true *logos* which conforms to law and justice is the image of a healthy and trustworthy soul. With its aid we argue disputed matters and pursue enquiry into the unknown, for the arguments by which we convince others when speaking are the same as we use in abstract thought. To speak of its power in a word, we shall find that nothing done with intelligence is done without *logos*. *Logos* is the guide of all acts and thoughts, and the most sensible people use it most. Men who dare to insult teachers and philosophers should be loathed like sinners against the gods. (Isokrates 3. 5–9 = 15. 253–7)

Implicit in this fundamentally humanist hymn to *logos* is a break with all the older myths which derived human culture from the acts of gods such as Zeus, Prometheus, Athene, Apollo or Asklepios. So too, though for different and much more complicated reasons, Isokrates' main rival in educational theory, Plato, made Sokrates end the discussion on the role of poetry in the ideal city with the traumatic conclusion:

Then, Glaukon, said I, when you meet encomiasts of Homer who tell us that this poet has been the educator of Hellas, and that for the conduct and refinement of human life he is worthy of our study and devotion, and that we should order our entire lives by the guidance of this poet, we must love and salute them as doing the best they can, and concede to them that Homer is the most poetic of poets and the first of tragedians, but we must know the truth, that we can admit no poetry into our city save only hymns to the gods and praises of good men. For if you grant admission to the honeyed Muse in lyric or epic, pleasure and pain will be lords of your city instead of law and that which shall from time to time have approved itself to the general reason as the best. (Plato, *Republic* 10. 606E–7A)

Even so, we cannot speak of a total repudiation of mythic thinking. Politicians of the 370s and 360s are represented in Xenophon and other authors as using arguments drawn from mythology in order to support this or that alignment in foreign policy. According to Diodorus, the Thebans justified their destruction of Orchomenus in 346 by alleging that they had been subject to the Minyans at Orchomenus until Herakles liberated them (see p. 203). Arguments of the 340s between Philip of Macedon and the Athenians as to who had the better claim to the city and territory of Amphipolis in Thrace were conducted as much on the mythic plane as on the legal or political, as when Aeschines in 346 gave 'the facts about our original acquisition both of the district and of the place called Ennea Hodoi, and the story of the sons of Theseus, one of whom, Akamas, is said to have received this district as the dowry of his wife' (2. 31). Isokrates, in the same context, but with opposite purpose, used the Herakles myth to brilliant effect in his *Philippos* in order to establish the legitimacy of Philip's claim, as a descendant of Herakles, to the leadership of Greece. Similarly, he had earlier used the myths surrounding the goddess Demeter and the Eleusinian Mysteries in order to back Athenian claims to primordial dignity among the Greek states. Even Plato himself repeatedly feels the need to buttress the argument of a dialogue by introducing at a late stage a story, located outside the 'real' world but linked with it, which functions as a charter myth for the philosophical view or interpretation he is putting forward. Mostly (it seems) his own creation, they are often of great imaginative and poetic beauty, and show not only how much of a suppressed poet there is in Plato but also how hard he and his contemporaries found the intellectually essential emancipation from myth to be.

Last among the fourth-century changes which can only be noticed briefly come developments in the history of art. Some are changes in technique, either visible from surviving creations and copies or recorded by later art historians, especially the elder Pliny. Among the latter are, e.g. the development of encaustic technique and of still-life painting by Pausias of Sicyon and the exploration by various artists of chiaroscuro painting and later of highlights on dark figures. It is tragic that Greek painting in this, its greatest period, is totally lost to us, so that few of these changes are visible till they begin to be reflected in surviving mosaics (itself a developing art) from Northern Greece, particularly Olynthus and Pella. Matters are a little better with the techniques of foreshortening and perspective, since here the vase-painters could and did try to follow the struggles of the panel-painters to make theory and practice satisfactory. Easier still to trace, naturally enough, are developments in sculpture and architecture. In sculpture we can see changes in theme, such as a growth of interest in depicting the female nude: changes in ideal proportions away from those established by Polykleitos towards figures with longer limbs and smaller heads: and changes in aspect, which broke away at long last from the notion of the statue as a thing meant to be seen only or mainly from the front. All these can without too much violence be regarded as developments internal to the arts and crafts concerned, much as architects were experimenting with the Corinthian capital for columns or were trying out various rearrangements of the internal area within the walls of a temple in order to create a richer sense of space.

However, other changes can most plausibly be put down to the changing tastes and values of patrons. Here art history is also social history. For example, at the very end of our period, about 340, grave-monuments in Athens begin to move away from the restrained and dignified bas-relief which had been the norm for a century (see Plate 6a) in favour of new and more elaborate decoration (see Plate 6b); here above all, where the patron or purchaser will always have been the family of the deceased, we must infer a general change in taste. The same is probably true for the trend towards more realistic portraiture, visible in busts and full-length statues as well as on gravestones. It might amount to little more than the representation of an elderly person as stooping or lined of face, and be thereby a study of old age rather than of appearance and personality (see Plate 7a), but the latter must be uppermost when we hear of the statue of a Corinthian general, Pellichos, by an early fourth-century sculptor, showing him as 'a pot-bellied bald man, wearing his cloak half-naked fashion with some wisps of beard floating in the wind, his veins clearly visible – the spitting image of the man' (Lucian 34. 18). Real portraits of rulers and tyrants, such as Maussollos of Halicarnassus (see Plate 7b) or Aristratos of Sicyon, were an innovation. In some of these cases the literary tradition tells us that the commission came from the ruler himself, the resurgence of monarchy itself affecting artists' activity.

Similarly, the demands of patrons account for certain innovations in architecture. The practice of setting up monumental commemorations, at international shrines such as Delphi or Olympia, of victories or notable events had been common for centuries, but cities rather than individuals had long predominated as commissioning patrons. After 380 the balance changes. The significant precursor was a group of statues at Delphi which commemorated the Spartan victory over Athens at Aegospotami in 405 and had Lysandros both as centrepiece and as dedicator, and three monuments of the 330s encapsulate the change. At Olympia Philip's eventual domination of Greece was reflected in the erection of a circular building, the Philippeion, containing statues of himself, his parents, his wife and son. Also at Olympia a huge square building, probably intended as a guesthouse for distinguished visitors to the sanctuary and the Games, bore the inscription 'Leonides son of Leotes made [and dedicated (this building) to Olympian Zeus]' (*Olympia* V, no. 651): it was known to Pausanias, and hence to us, as the Leonidaion. So too, in about 337 Philip's agent Daochos of Thessaly commemorated his family, their athletic exploits, and his own public position by commissioning a nine-statue monument at Delphi with the inscription 'These gifts were dedicated to Lord Apollo by

Daochos, tetrarch of the Thessalians, Sacred Remembrancer of the Amphiktyons, to vaunt the prowess of his own ancestors, in honour of his family and fatherland, availing himself of an honourable opportunity' (*SIG*³ 274, VIII). We are left in no doubt whom we are meant to admire most. Lastly, in equally pointed reflexion of the resurgence of private wealth and prestige to overshadow public funds and civic dignity, come funeral monuments and private houses. About houses Demosthenes in 352 was explicit:

> Any of you who know which is the house of Themistokles or Miltiades or of the famous men of that time can see that they were no more grandiose than the normal, while the city's own buildings and structures – these Propylaia here, the shipsheds, the colonnades, the Piraeus, and the other constructions with which you see the city furnished – are of such a size and quality that no later generation can surpass them. But nowadays every politician is so well off that some of them have made their own houses more grandiose than many public buildings, while others have bought more land than all of you in this court own put together. As for what you build publicly and slap stucco on, it's a disgrace to say how mean and shabby they are. (23. 207–8)

'Architect-built' houses are even later: if a flatterer in the 320s is the sort of person who says that his patron's 'house has been well architected; his farm has been nicely planted; and his portrait is an excellent likeness' (Theophrastus, *Characters* 2. 12), he is being trendy twice over. As for grave-monuments, those from Athens could be immodest enough, but they were quite over-shadowed by those commissioned from Greek artists by dynasts on the fringe of the Greek world, especially in Asia Minor. The most spectacular of all was the tomb which Maussollos' widow commissioned for him from four or five (our two accounts, in Pliny and Vitruvius, diverge) of the leading Greek sculptors of the 350s: something like 35m × 44m in ground-plan, 41m high, with three friezes, and with sculpture on all four sides, the visual impact of the Maussolleion must have been overwhelming. That Greek artists should work for non-Greeks was itself new, and though the styles of these monuments are Greek the forms are not: different conventions are combining with the ambitions of the men with the money to break away from traditional Greek norms.

We must turn now to another enormous area of change, that of cult and religion. Here, change comprised a mass of separate developments and readjustments, often small or subtle in themselves or seeming to be traditional because they fitted well inside the traditional framework. The reception of new gods is a case in point. The Kabeiroi from the North Aegean island of Samothrace, Ammon from Libya, the goddesses Bendis and Kotys from Thrace, Sabazios and the Great Mother from Phrygia, were all among the foreign deities accorded worship, a cult-spot, or even a temple in one or more Greek cities in the two generations before or after 400. Some, like Bendis or Ammon in Athens, became officially recognized gods of the state, but the majority remained on the fringes, tolerated for that reason, worshipped mainly by the immigrant communities of slaves, freedmen, or itinerant traders, and glanced at rather rudely by fourth-century orators and comic poets.

Equally, new cults could be home-made creations, as three curious early fourth-century inscriptions from the Bay of Phaleron near Athens show. One is a base, inscribed 'Kephiso-dotos son of Demogenes of the deme Boutadai founded the altar too' and surmounted by a stele, carved front and back, representing various deities and reading respectively 'Hermes: Echelos: [B]asile' and 'To Hermes and the Nymphs Alexo [dedicated this]'. The second is an altar, dedicated 'To Hestia, Kephisos, Pythian Apollo, Leto, Artemis Lochia, Eileithyia, Acheloos, Kallirhoe, the Geraistian Nymphs of the family, and Rhapso'. The third runs: 'Xenokrateia daughter and mother of Xeniades of Cholleidai, founded the altar for the sake of instruction, for anyone who wishes to sacrifice over good things achieved' (*IG* ii² 4546–8). Scholars are far from sure exactly what is going on, or why the various deities named should be linked together, but the core must be the foundation of cults of the river-god Kephisos and of the Nymphs.

Other new cults involved new gods of a different kind. Greeks had long tended to supplement the worship of local or Olympian gods by that of abstractions: cults of the Graces, or of the Winds, were well established by 400. Yet it seems to have been in the fourth century that the need for such personifications seems to have been felt most strongly. Cults and iconographical representations of Peace, Wealth, Fortune, Love, Desire, Persuasion, People, Democracy, and Opportunity spread steadily and suggest by the 330s a cultic atmosphere very different from that current a century earlier. So too do changes in the 'profile' of traditional gods. When Aristophanes in spring 423 makes a character describe the old systems of education as 'Old-fashioned and Diipolieia-ish, full of cockroaches and Kekeides and Bull-Slaughterings' (*Clouds* 984-5), he is referring to a ritual, at a festival of Zeus in Athens, which was rapidly becoming a museum-piece whose meaning was (and remains) a matter of guesswork. Conversely, it is not till 390 that we hear of 'Zeus the Saviour' or of his festival in Piraeus in early July which had become a major occasion by the Hellenistic period. It may even be a new cult, introduced to commemorate the salvation of Athens and of her democracy in 403 by the 'men of Piraeus'. Most striking of all, it has long been seen that the 'Zeus of Friendship' who is first attested in the 420s is very nearly an abstraction of the same type as Peace or Wealth, and a fourth-century dedication from Athens takes us to the limit: 'Aristomache, Theoris, and Olympiodoros dedicated to Zeus All-Powerful, of Friendship, and to Friendship the mother of the god and to Good Fortune the wife of the god' (*IG* ii² 4627). Here a whole new divine family has been created, which is composed entirely of abstractions and cuts straight across the traditional 'Homeric' family relationships of Zeus.

Another kind of new god is more disconcerting:

Lysandros was the first Greek to whom, as Douris relates, the cities erected altars and made sacrifices as if to a god. He was also the first to whom paians were sung. The start of one of them they recall as follows:

> 'The general of noble Greece
> Who came from wide-dancing Sparta
> We shall hymn. O ie paian!'

The Samians also voted to call their festival of Hera the Lysandreia. (Plutarch, *Lysandros* 18. 3)

Douris' report, in a context of summer 404, has been doubted, but is now confirmed by a near-contemporary inscription. So far as we know, too, his claim that Lysandros was the first living man to be thus honoured is correct. It is startling, and we must make distinctions. For a man to receive honours as a hero after his death was not unexampled. The tyrants Gelon and Hieron of Syracuse were both thus honoured, but the most famous example is the general Brasidas. After his death outside Amphipolis in late summer 422,

> all the allies followed in arms and buried him at public expense within the city in front of what is now the agora. The Amphipolitans placed a boundary wall round his tomb and ever since then sacrifice to him as a hero and have given him the honours of games and annual sacrifices. They dedicated the colony to him as their Founder, pulled down the buildings named after their Athenian founder Hagnon, obliterated everything whose survival could remind them of his role in the foundation, and considered that Brasidas had been their Saviour. (Thucydides 5. 11. 1)

All the same, to heroize the dead is one thing, to deify the living is quite another. Lysandros' statues had been accorded him by grateful oligarchs, who owed to him their restored power on Samos. It needed time and opportunity for the mental structures involved to take root elsewhere, and it was not until Alexander and his successors that the practice became common. It came to express (as at Samos) a relationship of gratitude to a powerful figure for services rendered or benefits conferred. As such its core was political, but the religious implications take us well outside traditional beliefs and practices and could even challenge them.

There were other challenges, too, which cannot well be classified in terms of individual gods or groups of gods and which present problems of their own. For example, the curse-tablet quoted on page 7 exemplifies a class of document, from Athens and elsewhere, which is very rare in the fifth century but numerous in the fourth century. The problem is whether their emergence reflects a change in belief, or increased literacy, or greater tension in the social contexts from which they stem. Or again, we can see a slight loosening of attitude towards temple treasures. During the Peloponnesian War Sparta had refrained from touching the dedications at Olympia or Delphi, while Athens borrowed money from Athene, reckoned the interest scrupulously, and began to repay the principal and interest after 421. In contrast, as we know from Xenophon's detailed narrative, after the Arcadians had captured Olympia in 365 and had run the Games of 364 in the teeth of a counter-attack from Elis, they began to use the sacred moneys of Olympia to maintain their mercenary force. It took a protest by Mantinea before 'others too began to say in the Assembly of Ten Thousand that the sacred treasure ought not to be touched and that it was wrong to leave to their children for ever afterwards such an act which would merit the anger of the god. And so a resolution was passed in the Arcadian Assembly forbidding the further use of the sacred treasure' (Xenophon, *Hellenika* 7. 4. 34), but even then civil war was only narrowly averted.

In general one gets the impression, not that Greek society in general was moving towards new religions or towards agnosticism, but that the spectrum of attitudes was gradually and confusedly widening. At one end lay, as always, obsessive religiosity, visible in superstition or in an edginess about behaviour deemed to be offensive to the gods. Theophrastus' portrait of the 'superstitious man' shows, among much else, how,

if a weasel crosses his path, he will not go a step further until someone else has overtaken him, or until he has thrown three stones across the road. Should he see a snake in his house, if it's a harmless one he invokes Sabazios: but if it's a venomous one he immediately builds a shrine to Herakles on the very spot . . . If, when walking, he hears owls hoot, he is alarmed, and will only go on when he has pronounced the words 'Athene is greater' . . . If ever he catches sight of cross-road offerings to Hekate wreathed in garlic, he goes away and washes his head thoroughly, and calls in some wise women and gets them to purify him by walking round him with a lily-bulb or a puppy for sacrifice. If he sees a madman or an epileptic he shivers, and spits into the fold of his gown. (Theophrastus, *Characters* 16)

So too, when in 399 the Athenian politician Andocides was indicted on various charges of impiety, one of his prosecutors urged the jury to

Concentrate your attention, and let you mind's eye seem to see what this man did, and you will be the better judges. He donned the sacred robe of the hierophant, parodied the ceremonies and revealed them to the uninitiated, and uttered with his voice the forbidden words: he mutilated the images of the gods in whom we believe, and to whom we sacrifice and pray in a spirit of worship and purity. Wherefore the priests and priestesses stood facing the west, shook their purple robes and cursed him according to the old and archaic usage. And he admitted his guilt. What is more, he broke the law you made, that he should be barred from sacred ceremonies as a sacral sinner. In defiance of all this he has entered our city, sacrificed on the altars which were forbidden to him, presented himself at the ceremonies which he profaned, entered the Eleusinian shrine, and washed himself with the holy water. Who can tolerate this? Which friend, which relative, which juryman can extend to him a secret favour at the cost of attracting the open hatred of the gods? You must rather take the view that by punishing and removing Andocides you are purifying the city and releasing it from sin and expelling the carrier of evil and removing a sacral sinner, for he is one of them. (Lysias 6. 50–3)

From the same real convictions, but less stridently and no doubt called forth by the innovations of which we have seen the symptoms, come complaints against change. As Isokrates put it in about 355 with historically unscrupulous sentimentality,

Our ancestors did not hold a procession of 300 bulls, when they felt like it, while suspending the ancestral sacrifices arbitrarily: nor did they conduct with great éclat the supplementary festivals, to which some feasting was attached, while entrusting to the revenues from rents the holiest of the sacred sacrifices.

Rather, they were concerned with one thing, that they should neither abolish any of the ancestral observances nor add anything which was not traditional. They did not think that piety consisted in vast expenses but in changing nothing of what they had inherited from their forefathers. (Isokrates 7. 29-30)

Less loaded and more informative, but just as concerned with preserving traditional rituals, are the 'sacred calendars', a series of documents from Athens later imitated elsewhere. These documents lay down in remorseless detail which sacrifices are to be made (and their costs) through the year by this or that community, be it the state or a tribe or a phratry or a deme or group of demes. The purpose of these documents is usually implicit, but one of them does spell it out. In 363-2 the Salaminioi, a large Athenian cult-group which was evidently being torn in two by quarrels, asked arbitrators to settle their differences for them. To the arbitration, set out on the stone in 67 lines of detailed specifications, an amendment was added:

Archeleos moved: in order that the Salaminioi may ever sacrifice to the gods and heroes according to ancestral custom, and that effect may be given to the terms on which the mediators adjusted the differences between the two groups and to which the persons chosen took the oath, be it decreed by the Salaminioi that the archon Aristarchos inscribe all the sacrifices and the stipends of the priests on the stele on which are the terms of settlement, so that the archons succeeding one another in office for both parties from time to time may know the amount of money each party must contribute for all the sacrifices from the rental of the land at the Herakleion. (*Hesperia* 7 (1938) 1, no. 1, lines 80-5)

It is a fair guess that for most people most of the time such rituals and sacrifices formed the central core of religious observance, unaffected by the meanings of myths, the complications of a polytheistic theology, or the awkward challenges of rationalism and scepticism.

Yet there were doubts. Protagoras began his book *On the Gods* by saying 'Concerning the gods, I am unable to discover whether they exist or not, or what they are like in form: for there are many hindrances to knowledge, the obscurity of the subject and the brevity of human life' (Protagoras, DK 80 B 4). Kritias makes a character in his play *Sisyphos* say, among much else, that:

> When the laws prevented men from open deeds of violence, but they continued to commit them in secret, I believe that a man of shrewd and subtle mind invented for men the fear of the gods, so that there might be something to frighten the wicked even if they had acted, spoken, or thought in secret. From this motive he introduced the conception of divinity. There is, he said, a spirit enjoying endless life, hearing and seeing with his mind, exceedingly wise and all-observing, bearer of a divine nature. He will hear everything spoken among men and can see everything that is done. If you are silently plotting evil, it will not be hidden from the gods, so clever are they. With this story he presented the most seductive of teachings, concealing the truth with lying words . . . (Kritias, DK 88 B 25, lines 9–26)

Such formulations came mostly from intellectuals working in Athens, and had made considerable impact by the end of the fifth century. Protagoras and Kritias, or the three or four men by then spoken of as 'atheists', challenged the ontological status of gods. Others, such as Euripides in play after play, equally subversively challenged the role imputed to the gods in upholding a moral order. Those involved were a tiny, unorganized, argumentative group of men, whose comments on religion were only a small part of their thinking, and whose lasting importance in the history of ideas can very easily lead us to overestimate their immediate influence on contemporary society. Yet they do seem to have been thought important or dangerous enough for some of the people concerned to be arraigned on charges of impiety. Not all the reports of such charges in the sources are trustworthy, but we do know for certain the formal charge in the other and more famous impiety trial of 399, in which Sokrates was accused 'of refusing to recognize the gods recognized by the State and introducing other new divinities. He is also guilty of corrupting the youth. The penalty deemed is death' (Xenophon, *Memorabilia* 1. 1. 1.). To the explicit charge has to be added the implicit charge, formally unspecifiable because of the amnesty of 403, that Sokrates' teaching had been responsible for the misdeeds of Alkibiades and for the horrors of the oligarchies of 411 and 404. As the orator Aeschines put it 50 years later, 'you executed Sokrates the sophist, men of Athens, because he was shown to have educated Kritias' (Aeschines 1. 173). Rightly or wrongly, philosophers were thought to influence society as a whole. To trace how and why will need a fresh start, which will also bring us back into the sphere of political action.

X

Philosophers, Mercenaries and Monarchs

THE PHILOSOPHERS bring us to an area of social change best explored in terms of the new or changed roles which certain individuals or groups came to play in Greek society. This chapter singles out three such roles. They illustrate no one tidy pattern, for the pressures which produced them were very diverse. However, once emerged, they were all important enough to become defining features of fourth-century Greek society. Moreover, each poses a similar interpretative problem, that of deciding whether their emergence is best understood in terms of the ambitions, skills and opportunism of individuals or in terms of the needs and gaps felt by Greek society as a whole.

At first sight, the philosophers and intellectuals scarcely comprise a group. Quarrelsome and individualistic, they showed little sign of cohesion, and were socially diverse and geographically scattered. Yet they came to be denoted by labels such as 'sophist' or 'philosopher' which imputed some unity of role or status to them, and they came in fact to fulfil two functions of basic importance. First and foremost, they were teachers. Beyond elementary instruction in schools or by private tutors in reading and writing, music and dance, fighting and athletics, which was well established in the fifth century, lay, as we have seen (see p. 99), the need to acquire the more complex skills appropriate for participating in public life. Not everyone thought they could be 'learnt' in the same way, and the claim that they could sometimes provoked hostility or the sort of derision which is exemplified in Aristophanes' *Clouds*. That play also depicts Sokrates' *Phrontisterion,* or 'thinking-shop', as a home of arcane learning, 'which it is not proper to speak of save to disciples' (*Clouds* 140), but that was gross caricature, for what came to prevail, among those who set themselves up as teachers, were various more or less open forms of teaching. In the fifth century the first two generations of such men, called 'sophists' in a way which became increasingly sour, taught above all by means of public lectures, for which some of them charged exorbitant fees. In contrast, Sokrates 'taught' for nothing and far less formally, by conversation in public or private with whoever chose to listen and participate. By the late 390s the pattern was changing in favour of more formal 'schools' which took paying pupils of undergraduate age or over. We know of Isokrates' school from about 390, Plato's Academy from about the mid-380s and Aristotle's Lykeion from about 335 in Athens (to be joined later by Epicurus' Garden in 306 and Zeno's Stoa in 301−300). There were others, less well-attested, in Elis, Eretria, Megara and Cyrene.

For most of these men their writing was closely linked with their teaching, especially for Aristotle, whose surviving writings are really the notes for his lecture courses, and show all the signs of telegraphic abbreviation and of second and third thoughts. However, there were others, such as Demokritos of Abdera, who wrote rather than taught, and still others such as Parmenides and his pupil Zeno of Elea in Italy, or Empedokles of Acragas in Sicily, whose influence was concentrated on one or two direct pupils but otherwise spread diffusely through knowledge of their writings. Furthermore, as a tiny group of men who all knew each other in person or by repute, who mostly travelled readily if not incessantly and who mostly were or became wealthy men (here too Sokrates was the exception), much of their activity lay in public conversation and argument. The classic portrayal of such occasions is by Plato in his *mis-en-scène* of the *Protagoras*:

When we found ourselves in the doorway, we stood there and continued a discussion which had arisen between us on the way. So that we might not leave it unfinished, but have it out before we went in, we were standing in the doorway talking until we should reach agreement. I believe the porter, a eunuch, overheard us, and it seems likely that the crowd of Sophists had put him in a bad temper with visitors. At any rate when we knocked at the door he opened it, saw us and said, Ha, Sophists! He's busy. And thereupon he slammed the door as hard as he could with both hands. We knocked again, and he answered through the closed door, Didn't you hear me say he's busy?

My good man, I said, we have not come to see Kallias and we are not Sophists. Cheer up. It is Protagoras we want to see, so announce us. So at last the fellow reluctantly opened the door to us.

When we were inside, we came upon Protagoras walking in the portico, and walking with him in a long line were, on one side Kallias, son of Hipponikos; his stepbrother Paralos, the son of Perikles; and Charmides, son of Glaukon; and on the other side Perikles' other son, Xanthippos; Philippides, son of Philomelos; and Antimoiros of Mende, the most eminent of Protagoras' pupils, who is studying professionally, to become a Sophist. Those who followed behind listening to their conversation seemed to be for the most part foreigners – Protagoras draws them from every city that he passes through, charming them with his voice like Orpheus, and they follow spellbound – but there were some Athenians in the band as well. As I looked at the party I was delighted to notice what special care they took never to get in front or to be in Protagoras' way. When he and those with him turned round, the listeners divided this way and that in perfect order, and executing a circular movement took their places each time in the rear. It was beautiful.

'After that I recognized,' as Homer says, Hippias of Elis, sitting on a seat of honour in the opposite portico, and around him were seated on benches Eryximachos, son of Akoumenos, and Phaedros of Myrrhinous and Andron, son of Androtion, with some fellow citizens of his and other foreigners. They appeared to be asking him questions on natural science, particularly astronomy, while he gave each his explanation *ex cathedra* and held forth on their problems.

'And there too spied I Tantalos' – for Prodikos of Ceos was also in town, and was occupying a room which Hipponikos used to use for storage, but now owing to the number of people staying in the house Kallias had cleared it out and made it into a guest room. Prodikos was still in bed, wrapped up in rugs and blankets, and plenty of them as far as one could see . . . But what they were talking about I couldn't discover from outside, although I was very keen to hear Prodikos, whom I regard as a man of inspired genius. You see, he has such a deep voice that there was a kind of booming noise in the room which drowned the words. (Plato, *Protagoras* 314b–16a)

Of course, Plato is being malicious, and is concentrating his prima donnas in a chronologically unlikely way, but such occasions did occur and did help to give these men a common role or status in society.

To describe what they taught is superficially easy: everything. Gorgias claimed to be able to answer any question he was asked, and Plato makes him reply, when challenged about it, 'That is the very claim I made just now, and I assure you that nobody has asked me a new question these many years' (Plato, *Gorgias* 448a). Hippias, whom we saw above discoursing on astronomy, also wrote or lectured on poetry, arithmetic, geometry, music, the properties of letters and syllables, rhythm and harmony, ethnography, genealogy and antiquarian studies in general, besides writing speeches, poetry and dialogues himself, compiling a list of Olympic victors which became the basis of later chronography, serving as ambassador for Elis repeatedly, and weaving his own clothes: apart from intelligence and ambition, the tradition gives him what he must indeed have had, a flypaper memory and uncrushable self-admiration. Another major fifth-century figure, Demokritos, is credited with some 61 titles, which later scholars grouped under the headings Ethics, Physics, Mathematics, Music, Technics and 'unclassified'. Plato's dialogues, reflecting his teaching, touch on, and show thorough knowledge of, virtually every topic that was then a subject for rational enquiry, while Aristotle's surviving works range over formal logic, modes of argument, the nature of the physical world and the processes within it, meteorology and cosmology, psychology and sense perception, animal biology and the problem of growth and decay, ethics, metaphysics, politics, rhetoric and constitutional history. True, it was in reaction to the pretentious claims of Gorgias and Hippias that Sokrates used 'to ask questions but not to give answers, for he confessed that he did not know' (Aristotle, *Refutations of the Sophists* 183^b 7–8), but the Sophists and their fourth-century successors did give their hearers, readers and pupils increasingly detailed, systematic and accurate information about the world they lived in, their own past, and the constituent elements of their culture. Pupils could emerge as educated men, in a sense wholly new not just in Greece but in human history.

They could also emerge as effective men. As Hippias was made to put it in some irritation after having been gently taken apart by Sokrates,

> But I must ask you, Sokrates, what do you suppose is the upshot of all this? As I said a little while ago, it is the scrapings and shavings of arguments, cut up into little bits. What is both beautiful and most precious is the ability to produce an eloquent and beautiful speech to a law court or a council meeting or any other official body whom you are addressing, to convince your audience, and to depart with the greatest of all prizes, your own salvation and that of your friends and property. These then are the things to which a man should hold fast, abandoning these pettifogging arguments of yours, unless he wishes to be accounted a complete fool because he occupies himself, as we are now doing, with trumpery nonsense. ([Plato], *Hippias Major* 304a–b)

To teach pupils how to speak well and act effectively in public life became a major component of this educational movement. Much of the impetus must have come from potential pupils, who saw in what the intellectuals could offer not just an education but a route to power and influence. In this sense, once teaching oratorical and intellectual skills for payment had become the norm, the long-term effect of this educational movement was deeply conservative, since it strengthened the hands of those who could afford to pay.

All the same, the intellectuals were not just teachers of disconnected topics, whether practical skills like rhetoric or 'academic' disciplines such as astronomy. They had another, more complex role, at once subversive and creative. It emerged in part from the same dissatisfaction with poetic myths and formulations about the world which was noticed above (see p. 159). By the late sixth century Ionian philosophers, trying to provide more naturalistic explanations of the existence, make-up and characteristics of the external world, had formulated various theories. Trying, it seems, to answer the question 'What came first?', Thales answered 'Water', Anaximandros more elaborately that 'the Boundless held the whole responsibiity for the growth and decay of everything: . . . at the birth of this world a seed of Hot and Cold was separated off from the Boundless, and from this a sphere of fire grew round the air surrounding the earth, just as bark grows round a tree' (DK 12 A 10), and Anaximenes that 'Air was the beginning of all things: this was boundless in magnitude but bounded by the qualities about it: all things came into being through a condensation of it and conversely through refraction, while motion was eternal' (DK 13 A 6). Such theorizing was brought up short by the poem 'Way of Truth' of Parmenides: we do not know its date, but between 480 and 460 may be about right. Three fragments probably give us the core.

Come now, I will tell . . . the only ways of enquiry that are to be thought of. The one, that it is and that it is impossible for it not to be, is the path of Persuasion (for she attends upon truth). The other, that it is not, and that it must necessarily not be, that I declare is a wholly indiscernible track: for thou couldst not know what is not – that is impossible – nor declare it, for it is the same thing that can be thought and can be. (DK 28 B 2–3)

One way alone is yet left to tell of, namely that 'It is'. On this way are marks in plenty that since it exists it is unborn and imperishable, whole, unique, immovable and without end. It *was* not in the past, nor yet *shall* it be, since it now *is*, all together, one and continuous. For what birth of it wilt thou seek? How and from what did it grow? I shall not allow thee to say or think 'from what is not', for it is not to be said or thought that 'it is not'. And what need would have prompted it to grow later or sooner, beginning from nothing? Thus it must either fully be or else not be.

Nor will the force of evidence suffer anything besides itself to arise from what is not. Therefore justice does not relax with her fetters and allow it to come into being or perish, but holds it fast.

The verdict on this lies fast: It is or it is not. But this verdict has already been given, as it had to be, that the one path should be left alone as unthinkable, unnamed, for it is no true path, and that the other exists and is real. How could what is afterwards perish? And how could it come into being? For if it came into being, it *is* not, nor yet if it is going to be at some future time. Thus becoming is extinguished, and perishing not to be heard of. (DK 28 B 8)

The argument seemed inescapable: no unity could generate a plurality, so the problem of change was insoluble; and if what really existed was eternal, then the external perceptible world of growth and decay had no secure ontological (or indeed moral) status whatever.

It is not too much to say that much of Greek philosophy during the period covered by this book has a unity of theme, as successive thinkers made the most ferocious efforts either to escape from Parmenides' unwelcome logic or to incorporate it in an intellectual model of the world which accommodated the phenomena. The spectrum of solutions was wide and confusing. One could simply agree with Parmenides and try to buttress his argument, as his pupil Zeno did with his paradoxes about Achilles and the tortoise, etc. Or one could postulate a plurality of original elements, as Empedokles did in his poem *Purifications*, written about the middle of the fifth century, by positing Fire, Water, Earth and Air as the uncreated, equal and coeval elements which produce the external world by the processes of Love and Strife, or mingling and separation. Or, as the atomists Leukippos and Demokritos did, one could postulate an infinite number of constituent elements, which 'act and are acted upon as they happen to touch (for in this way they are not one) and generate by coming together and interlocking' (thus Aristotle, *On Coming to be and Passing away* 325a 33–5, summarizing their views). Or one could single out a directive force or principle, Mind or Intelligence.

These theories could sound pretty silly in themselves, and were duly caricatured by Aristophanes, but they were real efforts to solve the crisis. So also, with more sophistication and success, was Plato's theory of Forms, which sought to reconcile the relentless otherworldliness of Parmenides with the external world by distinguishing between the 'Forms' (ideas or concepts), which were timeless and perceptible only by the mind, and the time-bound copies of them which comprised the external world and were perceived (at a lower level of perception) by the senses. So too was the far more detailed and systematic exploration by Plato himself and by Aristotle of the use of verbs of cognition and reference. Aristotle's fundamental perception that ' "Being" is a word used in several senses' (*Metaphysics* 1028ᵃ 10) was part of this process; combined with the formal logic it has produced, it is probably the most promising way to cope with Parmenides. In this way, Parmenides' challenge provoked a century of intellectual speculation of the utmost generality and abstractness. The paradox is that increasingly precise observation of the external world went forward at the same time, often conducted by the same people, with results of permanent value especially in biology, astronomy and medicine. Yet at least in part the objective was that scholars and thinkers should know precisely what the phenomena in the external world were which their cosmological theories would be called upon to explain.

There was also another objective. Greeks were no strangers to the perennial practical insight that to take no account of the realities of the world in choosing one's pattern of living is a recipe for disaster. Earlier generations had interpreted 'realities' theologically, by thinking of the gods as beings whose will could be divined by signs, dreams, or oracles, and should be obeyed by a prudent man. Protection of the moral order was therefore imputed to them, especially to Zeus. That view encountered the problem met by many theologies, that of reconciling the existence of evil with the hypothesis of an all-powerful, all-just god. It was also vulnerable to the criticisms which could justly be levelled at the behaviour of the gods, including Zeus himself, in myth after myth: 'Both Homer and Hesiod have attributed to the gods all things that are shameful and a reproach among mankind: theft, adultery and mutual deception' (Xenophanes, DK 21 B 11). Herein, in the need to secularize morality and to find a more rational basis for moral behaviour, lay a further impetus to a precise understanding of the world. It became common ground among moral philosophers that one needed to know what the make-up and principles of action of the world were in order to be able to act appropriately.

Such knowledge, of course, did not have to be systematic. Hardly surprisingly, much of it lay at the level of shrewd common sense, as exemplified by proverbs or by the train of totally untheistic unmythical observations which survive to us from Demokritos: 'One must either be good, or imitate a good man'; 'He who tries to give intelligent advice to one who thinks he has intelligence, is wasting his time'; or 'It is unreasonableness not to submit to the necessary conditions of life' (DK 68 B 39, 52, 289). However, such aphorisms are by their nature fragmentary, amount to no coherent system, and are therefore vulnerable to individual attack, whereas moral codes that looked to a single principle would at least be coherent, however pretentious and peculiar. The bias of moral thinkers inclined strongly in this latter direction. Thus, for example, at one extreme cosmological theories of Strife, when combined with observation of the relativities of moral codes (see p. 32), could yield deeply brutal interpretations of the need to live in accordance with nature (*cf.* Kallikles' outburst, p. 108). At the other extreme the notion of living in harmony with reality became more than a metaphor with the exploration of the nature of numbers and their interrelations, which tradition associated with the sixth-century figure Pythagoras and his followers: 'they supposed the elements of numbers to be the elements of all things and the whole heaven to be a *harmonia* and a number' (Aristotle, *Metaphysics* 968a 1). In consequence, as Aristotle's pupil Aristoxenos reported of them, 'Every distinction they lay down as to what should be done or not done aims at conformity with the divine. This is their starting-point: their whole life is ordered with a view to following God, and it is the governing principle of their philosophy' (in Iamblichus, *Life of Pythagoras* 137).

We are here very close to what becomes in both Plato and Aristotle a major element in their moral systems, the view that the way in which some modes of behaving were more valuable than others was parallel to, and backed up by, the varying way in which phenomena participated in reality. To think (about the world perceptible only by thought) was better than to act (in the world perceptible by the senses): and,

If happiness is activity in accordance with virtue, it is reasonable that it should be in accordance with the highest virtue; and this will be that of the best thing in us . . . That this activity is contemplative we have already said. Now this would seem to be in agreement both with what we said before and with the truth. For, firstly this activity is the best (since not only is reason the best thing in us, but the objects of reason are the best of knowable objects): and, secondly, it is the most continuous, since we can contemplate truth more continuously than we can do anything. And we think happiness has pleasure mingled with it, but the activity of philosophic wisdom is admittedly the pleasantness of virtuous activities; at all events the pursuit of it is thought to offer pleasures marvellous for their purity and their enduringness, and it is to be expected that those who know will pass their time more pleasantly than those who inquire. And the self-sufficiency that is spoken of must belong most to the contemplative activity. And this activity alone would seem to be loved for its own sake; for nothing arises from it apart from the contemplating, while from practical activities we gain more or less apart from the action. And happiness is thought to depend on leisure; for we are busy that we may have leisure, and make war that we may live in peace. Now the activity of the practical virtues is exhibited in political or military affairs, but the actions concerned with these seem to be unleisurely . . . So if among virtuous actions political and military actions are distinguished by nobility and greatness, and these are unleisurely and aim at an end and are not desirable for their own sake, but the activity of reason, which is contemplative, seems both to be superior in serious worth and to aim at no end beyond itself, and to have its pleasure proper to itself (and this augments the activity), and the self-sufficiency, leisureliness, unweariedness (so far as this is possible for man), and all the other attributes ascribed to the supremely happy man are evidently those connected with this activity, it follows that this will be the complete happiness of man, if it be allowed a complete term of life (for none of the attributes of happiness is incomplete). (Aristotle, *Nikomachean Ethics* 1177ᵃ12–1177ᵇ26)

At this point the social role of the philosophers comes into the open. We have seen very briefly their two main substantive preoccupations, 'What are the constituents and the principles of action in the natural world?' and 'What is the proper way to live?' To them we must add two preoccupations of method, 'What counts as a good argument?' and 'How do we know what we think we know?' The matrix formed by these four preoccupations generates all of what we know as Greek philosophy, and the activity of its practitioners mattered for fourth-century Greek society in two main ways. Firstly, they supplemented or even replaced the poets in their role as articulators of what Greek society was and should be about. Secondly, and more specifically, they provided not just an education for those who could read their works or afford to be their pupils, but also ideologies of ideal behaviour, which differed in detail but largely shared a distaste for activity, democracy and politics, and a strong bias towards the life of the cultured, leisured intellectual in a well-ordered conservative society. The strength of the new sort of élite culture which they created was that it was more rationally based than poet-based education and was not limited to Greece, ethnically defined, but came to be accessible to all the other élites which were attracted by it. Its weakness was that by eroding the links between religion and high culture, and between intellectual and political activity, it helped to fragment the cohesion of traditional society in the individual states.

So, far more violently, did mercenaries. Mercenary service was nothing new in itself. Greek soldiers had been serving Near Eastern rulers for payment since the eighth century, and had served fifth-century Persian satraps as bodyguards. The fifth-century Athenian navy depended at least in part on mercenary rowers (see p. 79), and the practice went on in the fourth century (see p. 20). Yet at least they came largely from the Empire itself, and did not replace, but merely supplemented, the services of Athenian residents, while the core of fifth-century armies everywhere was the citizen hoplite. Yet between 399 and 375 there were never fewer than 25,000 mercenaries in service, and often more; by the 360s even Sparta was employing mercenaries in Peloponnese itself, and equipment and tactics had changed visibly; and by the 350s virtually every state was using mercenaries as the core of its land forces, even though this floating population was causing serious alarm. Since the erosion of the role of the citizen-soldier helped directly to erode the viability of the city-state as a power unit, the phenomenon needs explanation.

To do so is complex, since three separate developments are involved, each of which spread out from a separate problem in widely separated regions. The first involves Persia. Cyrus' employment of the Ten Thousand (see pp. 142–3) used one opportunity – the end of major fighting in Greece in 404 – in order to exploit another, the dynastic tensions at the Persian court after the death of Darius II in spring 404. Xenophon is explicit about the Greeks' motives:

> Most of the soldiers had not sailed out to take this paid service because they had no livelihood, but because they heard of the nobility of Cyrus. Some actually brought servants along, others had even spent money beforehand. Some of these had run away from their parents, others had even left children in the hope that they would come back with money for them, having heard that the other mercenaries with Cyrus were active and prosperous. (*Anabasis* 6. 4. 8)

From the Persian side, the visible proof in this campaign that Greek hoplites could demolish a Persian army even on its home ground was exploited by Persia's opponents in the 390s in Cyprus and Egypt. Ultimately, in self-defence the Persian King accepted the military realities and employed Greeks himself, probably soon after 386, for his campaign against Euagoras, the tyrant or king of Salamis on Cyprus. It may even be that one motive for his enforcing the King's Peace of 386 was in order to make mercenaries available. It was certainly so ten years later, when 'Artaxerxes King of Persia, intending to make war against Egypt and intent on gathering together a considerable mercenary force, decided to bring the wars in Greece to an end. He much hoped that if they were freed in this way from their own wars the Greeks would be more willing to enter mercenary service. So he sent envoys to Greece to urge the cities to make a Common Peace'

(Diodorus 15. 38. 1). Fifteen years later, *c*. 360, Xenophon could write 'Since the Persians themselves recognize the parlous state of their own forces, they give up, and no one makes war without Greeks any more, either when they fight each other or when Greeks make war upon them. They have decided to use Greeks even in order to fight Greeks' (*Education of Cyrus* 8. 8. 26): a statement which went on being true till the end of the Persian Empire.

The second region involved was mainland Greece, where after 404, and even more after 386, the predominance of Sparta's full-time professional soldiers needed soldiers of the same calibre to challenge it. Either a state raised the standard of its own citizen-soldiers, or it sought innovations, or it bought professionals. Thebes did the former, by creating in 378, as the 'Sacred Band', an élite force of 300 men who combined full-time training with homosexual pair-bonding and with the idealistic emotional cohesion of a secret society. The Band won Leuctra in 371 and Mantinea in 362 for Thebes, and was copied by Arcadia and later by Philip, but it was not by itself a viable solution. It was too small to transform a large army, as became clear at Chaeronea in 338, but a normal state's resources were too limited to maintain a larger standing force. In contrast, the professionals offered something more valuable. First, they could be disciplined properly. 'At Corinth (in the late 390s) Iphikrates commanded his army (of light-armed troops from Thrace) with such strictness that no troops in Greece were ever better trained or more obedient to their leader's command. He instilled into them the habit of falling into line, when the commander gave the signal for battle, so precisely without any order on the general's part that they looked as if they had been individually stationed by an expert commander' (Nepos, *Iphikrates* 2. 1–2). Secondly, an experienced commander could innovate.

> Iphikrates . . . acquired long experience of military matters in the Persian War and made many inventions useful for war, paying especial attention to weaponry. Whereas the Greeks were using large shields and were therefore slow to move, he made their shields smaller, and provided suitable 'peltai' instead. He succeeded in both objectives, to protect the body

adequately, and to let the users of the 'pelta' be completely free in their movements because of its light weight . . . He made the contrary alterations as regards spear and sword. He increased the length of spears by half as much again, and made swords almost twice the length . . . He made soldiers' boots light and easy to untie, and to this day they are called 'Iphikratids' after him. (Diodorus 15. 44)

Diodorus' account, placed in 374–3, may be misdated, and may be confusing a change in equipment with a change in tactics, but the basic fact is clear: the light-armed soldier, the 'peltast', has come in from the social fringe (previously he was the poor relation of the hoplite) and from the geographical fringe (the equipment and techniques were traditionally thought to be Thracian in origin). These innovations worked. It was a peltast army that cut down a Spartan regiment near Corinth in 390, and another peltast army, defending Thebes against Spartan attack in summer 378, to which 'Chabrias and Gorgidas gave the order not to charge, but to stay firm, point their spears forward, and rest their shields on their knees. Agesilaos was taken aback by the immovable format of the battle-line and retreated, thinking it tactically wise to beware of the strength of his opponents' (Polyaenus, *Stratagems* 2. 1. 2). However, they worked only at a price. States whose citizens had previously formed a seasonal unpaid army were dragged willy-nilly into a more monetary public economy and into endemic financial crisis (cf. Arcadia in 365–4, p. 169). Groups of unpaid mercenaries became private armies or (like Xenophon's Ten Thousand) potential cities in themselves.

In this way mercenary service emerged as a social role, precipitated both by the poverty, skill and ambition of individuals and by the needs of governments. If we turn now to Sicily, the third region which helped to mould the new pattern of mercenary service, we can see the next stage, in which a mercenary commander who could dominate his troops could emancipate himself from his city and move towards becoming 'general with full powers', tyrant, and hereditary dynast.

We saw in Chapter Seven how Syracuse lost her predominant

position after 465 and how first the diplomatic, and then the military intrusion of Athens had polarized affairs in the island between her and Syracuse. After Athens' withdrawal in 413 old patterns quickly reappeared, both in Sicily and in Syracuse herself. In Sicily (see Map 4) three entities mattered: Syracuse with Acragas and Gela in the south-east; the Carthaginians in the west; and the amorphous mass of non-Dorian or non-Greek cities and communities in the centre and north of the island. The power-politics of the island were moulded by the states of this third group. They had little cohesion in themselves, but whichever power could command their allegiance and their resources had a decisive advantage. For most of the fourth century that power was Syracuse, for straightforward reasons. In 409 the Carthaginians moved in, exploiting the gap which Athenian withdrawal had left. They captured and sacked Selinus and Himera in summer 408, Acragas in December 406, and Gela and Camerina in summer 405. Those menaced turned to Syracuse as the only city with the resources and the moral authority to lead a resistance, and this opportunity was exploited by an upper-class Syracusan, Dionysios. As a cavalry commander and an effective demagogue, he was in a position to get himself elected as 'general with full powers' shortly after the fall of Acragas. As such, he used the Carthaginian threat to build up an army which gave him a power base independent of the city. As its commander he dealt adequately enough with the Carthaginians. As 'national leader' against them he used, and could justify, the expedients of alliances, transfers of population, repression, pillage and exaction on such a scale as to bring virtually all the Greek-speaking states of the west (in Italy as well as Sicily) under his control by the early 380s. He held his empire till his death in 366, and passed on to his son Dionysios II what was far and away the strongest military monarchy that the Greek world had yet seen.

Our information about him and about Sicily after 413 comes almost entirely from Diodorus, whose narrative, detailed till 383–2 though skimpy thereafter, is good enough to give Syra-cusan society and politics some depth. His ultimate source was the *Sikelika* of Philistos, Dionysios' wealthy associate, adviser and admiral, who seems to have given a sympathetic portrait of Dionysios and to have followed Thucydides in his style and interests. The technical writers record a few of Dionysios' military and money-raising 'stratagems', and a little more information, much less favourable to Dionysios, comes from Plutarch's life of Dion, another of Dionysios' associates, and from the Seventh and Eighth Letters of Plato, written to Dion's 'friends and associates' after Dion's death in 356. Even so, the themes relevant to interpreting Dionysios and Syracuse are largely chosen for us by Philistos through Diodorus. Fortunately, they give us a credible picture.

The first theme is naturally the wars against Carthage. The first war, which brought Dionysios to power, ended late in 405 with a treaty which gave the Carthaginians most of the island: 'Under the Carthaginians are to be the Elymians and Sicans along with their original settlers. The men of Selinus, Acragas, Himera, Gela and Camarina are to live in unfortified cities and are to pay tribute to Carthage. The men of Leontini and Messene and all the Sicels are to be autonomous. The Syracusans are to be subject to Dionysios. Prisoners and ships are to be returned to their own sides' (Diodorus 13. 114. 1). The second war, begun by Dionysios as a war of revanche in 398, oscillated wildly from the Greek capture of Motye in 398 to a siege of Syracuse in 397–6, but ended in 392 rather more favourably for the Greeks: 'The terms were similar to those of the earlier treaty, but the Sicels were to be subject to Dionysios, and he was to take possession of Tauromenium' (Diodorus 14. 96. 4). A third war began in 382 with a spectacular success for Dionysios, but his proffered peace terms, 'that the Carthaginians should evacuate the cities of Sicily and repay the incurred costs of the war' (Diodorus 15. 15. 4), were not surprisingly unacceptable, and the war seems to have gone on till 374. Ignominiously 'each side was to keep what it previously possessed, with the exception that the Carthaginians took possession of the city and territory of Selinus and of the territory of Acragas as far as the River Halykos. Dionysios paid the Carthaginians 1000 talents' (Diodorus 15. 17. 5). A brief fourth war began in 367, but was ended by Dionysios II soon after his father's death.

The wars then merely confirmed the status quo, at the cost of much death, destruction and suffering. One asks what the instigators hoped to gain. Diodorus sketches Carthaginian motives for the first war: as the result of a land dispute between Selinus and Segesta, the latter asked Carthage for help:

> and the Carthaginians were in a quandary. They wanted to get hold of a well-placed city, but they feared Syracuse because they had seen the total destruction of the Athenian forces. However, since their leading politician was also urging them to take over Segesta, they told the envoys that they would send help. To superintend the expedition, should the need for fighting arise, they appointed Hannibal as general, who was the constitutionally elected king at the time. He was the grandson of the Hamilcar who had fought Gelon [in 480] and had died at Himera, and was the son of Gescon, who had been exiled after his father's defeat and had passed his life in Selinus. Hannibal therefore inherently hated the Greeks, wished to put right the dishonour suffered by his family, and was ambitious to perform something useful to his country on his own account. (Diodorus 13. 43. 4–6)

This Hannibal may be an ancestor of the Hannibal who fought Rome 200 years later. The description of his private and public ambitions recalls Thucydides' comments on Alkibiades (see p. 127), as may have been Philistos' intention, but need not be wrong for all that. However, the other three wars were blatantly provoked by Dionysios, and we can only guess why. One motive may be fiscal: though we do not know its amount, the 'tribute' to be paid to Carthage by the western Greek cities from 405 on could have been well worth fighting for, especially since we know Dionysios was perennially short of money. Another motive may have been legitimation: to be intermittently fighting the 'national enemy' justified not only his own existence and powers but also the existence and the financial burden of his mercenary army.

However, a third motive may have been to legitimate, and to exploit, his growing control of the other communities in Sicily and South Italy. His actions here are not easy to grasp, since the sources give us little guidance about motive and fail to set his acts against the longer-term geopolitical configuration of the area. The historian is therefore again on his own, and must begin with the narrative of military action in Diodorus. In 403 (all the dates that follow are approximate) he captured Aetna, Enna, and Catane, captured and destroyed Naxos utterly, and forcibly united Leontini to Syracuse. He founded Hadranon in 400, and in 394 planted his mercenaries in Leontini (see p. 193) and refounded Messene, which had been totally destroyed by the Carthaginians in 396. In 394 an invasion by Rhegium was beaten off, and continued warfare between 390 and 387 ended with the capture of Rhegium and the destruction of Caulonia and Hipponion, their populations being transferred to Syracuse. The mid-390s saw intervention further afield, colonies being planted on various sites in the Adriatic and an alliance being made with the Illyrians, but we hear little thereafter, since Diodorus' record of western Greece between 383 and 359 is miserably skimpy.

This activity was much less arbitrary than it looks. It emerged naturally from the traditions and ambitions of Syracuse in the previous century (see pp. 130–1), from existing tensions elsewhere, and from certain slow shifts in Italian society. To take the last aspect first, the decline of the Etruscans as a western Mediterranean power, for reasons which cannot be explored here, helped to explain why they and the Romans had been unable to stop the Gallic invasion of Italy in 387: Dionysios was clearly exploiting the subsequent disruption by his attacks on Etruscan interests and by his occupation of the South Adriatic. More relevantly still, from the 440s onwards the Greek states of South Italy came under pressure from the southward drift of Italic-speaking tribes along the Apennine ridge to threaten the fertile valleys and plains. Lucania was mostly in their hands by the 430s, Cyme north of Naples fell to them in 421–20, Naples kept herself Greek only thanks to help from Tarentum and Rome, and Croton, Sybaris, and Caulonia joined forces about 420 to ward them off. Other cities joined them in 393–2, but the result was merely to ally Dionysios with the Italic Lucanians in a wider polarization. A second tension which could be exploited was that between Rhegium and Locris for control of the toe of Italy. Just as relations between Dorian Locris and Dorian Syracuse had been close for generations, so too throughout the fifth century Ionian Rhegium had sought support from Carthage or Athens to protect her independence from

Syracuse. Again, Dionysios acted along the existing lines of force, marrying a Locrian aristocrat (appropriately called Doris) in 398, settling Locrians in Messene in 394, and in 390 starting his first attack on Rhegium from Locrian territory.

This all tells us how, but not why. To call him 'desirous of nothing else except perpetual one-man rule' (Nepos, *Lives* 21. 2), in a way typical of the literary tradition, underestimates the extent to which Dionysios, as the government of Syracuse, inherited traditional Syracusan ambitions and preoccupations, and neglects what we have to imagine for ourselves, the deep shock inflicted on his generation by the aggressions of Athens in 415–13 and of Carthage in 409–5. To copy Gelon, tyrant of Syracuse in the 480s, and shift populations wholesale to Syracuse was the only way to get the manpower both to man the ships she needed and to build the massive fortifications needed to make her impregnable (as they did till her capture by Rome in 212). To eliminate Rhegium, Leontini, and the other power centres of north-eastern Sicily was the only way of denying an invader (Carthage, Athens or another) a base from which to attack Syracuse. To control the straits of Messene was the only way to prevent hostile fleets from Carthage or Etruria from sailing through and blockading Syracuse herself. To obliterate the separate city-states as political entities was the only way of eliminating the quarrels which, as his first father-in-law Hermokrates had said in a famous speech in 424, 'are so fatal to communities generally and will be equally so to Sicily if we, its inhabitants, absorbed in our local quarrels, neglect the common enemy' (Thucydides 4. 61. 1). To extend the Empire far up the coasts of Italy was the only way to ensure the supplies of the primary resources – tin, copper, iron, silver, wood – which a major naval power needed.

The logic is very like that which fuelled the Athenian Empire of the fifth and fourth centuries. Naturally, it was not a logic which appealed to the town-halls of Sicily and South Italy, any more than it did in the Aegean, and its execution in practice had caused much dislocation, violence and human suffering. By 389, however, it had largely run its course, and had created an empire which was to be stable for over twenty years.

It remains to see how that stability was sustained. In terms of power its basis was quite nakedly Dionysios' mercenary army.

It was recruited from all directions – men from Sicily itself and mainland Greece, especially Peloponnese, Campanians and Ligurians from Central and North Italy, and Iberians from Spain. It was commanded partly by his friends and relations, partly by professional officers from elsewhere, and was mainly stationed in the fortress which Dionysios had built in 405–4. Moreover, the army was backed by the resources of a huge arsenal of arms, the creation of which in 399 Diodorus describes in one of his more vivid passages:

> He collected many skilled workmen, split them up according to their various skills, and assigned them to the supervision of the leading citizens, promising large gifts for those who created weapons. He distributed among them an example of each kind of armour, because the mercenaries had been recruited from many nations. He was anxious that each soldier should be equipped with his own national arms, expecting that in this way the army would cause much consternation and that all who fought with him in battle would use best the armour they were most used to. The Syracusans supported Dionysios' policy with enthusiasm, and there was much rivalry over the manufacture of the arms. Not only was every space full of men at work, in the entrances and back rooms of temples, in the gymnastic schools and the colonnades of the market, but even apart from public places an immense quantity of arms were being made in the best private houses. (Diodorus 14. 41. 4–6)

The army thus created had various functions. It acted as Dionysios' bodyguard, protecting him from attempted coups d'état on several occasions. It also served as the field army of the city, once he had disarmed the citizen population, and provided the garrisons for the towns he annexed to his empire. It also functioned on occasion as the source of Athenian-style kleruchs. In 396, on the arrest of their commander, 'the main body of the mercenaries assembled under arms and demanded their pay rather bitterly. Dionysios . . . offered them (who were about 10,000) the city and territory of Leontini in lieu of salary. They happily agreed because of the fertility of the land, cut it up into allotments, and went to live in Leontini, while Dionysios collected another force of mercenaries and entrusted power to them and to his freedmen' (Diodorus 14. 78. 1–3).

Visible here are the financial pressures attendant on keeping a large mercenary army. Not surprisingly, we hear a good deal about money-raising in the sources. We hear of a property-tax, of confiscations and of various financial dodges. A treatise on finance ascribed to Aristotle describes how 'being short of money, Dionysios minted some tin coins, summoned an Assembly, and sang the praises of the coinage he had minted. The citizens voted, though unwillingly, to treat whatever they received as silver and not as tin' ([Aristotle], *Oikonomikos* 2. 20c). Or again, in 384:

> he sailed to Etruria with 100 ships, and took from the temple of Leukothea a large quantity of gold and silver and many other ornaments. He knew that the sailors had taken a lot too, so he announced that they were each to bring him half of what they had and keep the other half, under pain of death for not doing so. The sailors assumed that by bringing half they could keep the rest, so they brought in their booty without fear, but once Dionysios had taken possession of it, he ordered them to bring the other half too. (*ibid* 2. 20i)

In more need, and with fewer scruples, than the mainland Greeks (see p. 169), Dionysios comprehensively broke old taboos, but died in his bed nonetheless, unharmed by the thunderbolts of Zeus.

All the same, the régime was not just an oppressive military tyranny. As the rearmament programme (see p. 193) shows, he had some support in the upper class, and had a firm ally in the Spartans, who made commanders available to him and allowed him to recruit mercenaries from Peloponnese. Again, at least after the first turmoil he refrained from 'tyrannical' acts of violence against citizens, deliberately seeking their goodwill instead: naming his daughters Justice, Self-control and Virtue may have been an embarrassment to them but need not have been hypocrisy on his part. In a sense he did remain a citizen. Two of his wives were citizens, the first being the daughter of the Hermokrates who had led the political defence against Athens in 425–4 and the military defence in 415–13. Against the label of 'tyrant' have to be set the dinner-parties he gave, the presents he conferred, and his willingness in 401 to help build the city wall with his own hands. Aristocrat that he was, he wrote poems and tragedies (in bad verse, tradition has it: too little survives to judge), acted as patron to poets and philosophers (though he and Plato got on each other's nerves), competed in the chariot-races at Olympia, and financed or instigated grandiose public works ranging from the city walls, the fortress on Epipolai, and the dockyards to temples and gymnasia. Moreover, as the episode of the tin coinage (see p. 194) shows, political institutions and public opinion did matter. The city's coinage shows no sign of his existence, carrying the legend 'Of the Syracusans' throughout, and he never seems to have claimed any title save that of 'general with full powers'. A treaty which Athens made with him just before he died in 367 shows that though he made the treaty, those who were to swear to it were 'Dionysios and the archons and the Council of Syracusans and the generals and the trierarchs' (Tod 136, lines 35ff.), and refers to him accurately as 'Ruler of Sicily'.

Yet he was also visibly a man apart. This was so physically:

> He was so distrustful and suspicious towards everyone, and so much on his guard for fear, that he would not even have his hair cut with barber's scissors, but a hairdresser would come and singe his locks with a live coal. Neither his brother nor his son could visit him in his apartment wearing any clothes they pleased, but everyone had to take off his own clothing before entering and put on another set, after he had been seen naked by the guards. Once, when his brother Leptines was describing to him the nature of a place, and drew the plan of it on the ground with a spear which he took from one of his bodyguards, Dionysios was extremely angry with him, and had the man who gave him the spear put to death. (Plutarch, *Dion* 9. 3–5)

The portrayal comes from a hostile tradition, but must be substantially true. Yet it was not just fear, for there was symbolic distancing too. There is some evidence that on occasions he adopted what later became symbols of monarchy – purple dress, a golden crown, a span of four white horses, and others, some of which may reflect the dress conventions for kings in tragedy. The

hint is important. It was in Dionysios' generation that some
philosophers of politics were moving away from the Herodotean
stereotype of king-as-tyrant and began to create a theory of
monarchy. They focused on the monarchs ruling on the fringes of
Greece, in Macedon, Persia and Cyprus. The earliest surviving
reflexion of these treatises 'On Kingship' comes in the imaginary
speech which Isokrates wrote for Nikokles of Cyprus about 368:

> Oligarchies and democracies seek equalities among those who
> participate in the state, and what is approved of in them is that
> nobody should have more than others – which suits bad men.
> Monarchies give most to the best, next most to the next best
> . . . and so on . . . What sensible man would not rather participate
> in a régime where he will not be ignored if he is virtuous, than
> be carried along with the crowd as a non-entity? . . . We shall
> best see how much better monarchies are at deliberation and
> action, if we juxtapose the main activities and try to compare
> them. Men who hold office for a year become private citizens
> again before understanding public affairs and gaining experi-
> ence of them, while men permanently in charge are much
> better than others by experience even if less well-endowed by
> nature. The former ignore many matters and pass the buck to
> others, while monarchs neglect nothing because they know that
> the responsibility for everything lies with them. Again, in
> oligarchies and democracies men damage the public interest
> through their private rivalries, while the subjects of a monarch
> have no object of envy and therefore do the best they can.
> Again, the former miss opportunities; they spend most of their
> time on private affairs, so when they sit in council one would
> see them argue more than deliberate in common, while
> monarchs have no councils and fixed dates, attend to business
> night and day and do not miss opportunities, but do everything
> in due time. The former are jealous, and would like their
> predecessors and successors in office to be totally incompetent
> so that they themselves can gain the most glory: while
> monarchs, in charge for life, keep goodwill for life too . . .
> Monarchies are not just better at ordinary everyday affairs, but
> encompass every superiority in war. Tyrannies are better than
> republics at gathering forces, deploying them to deceive or get

there first, using persuasion or force, buying men's services and bringing them over by other modes of flattery. (Isokrates 3. 15–22)

Much here is unctuous or disingenuous, of course, for Nikokles was even more of a thug than Dionysios, and the anti-tyrant case was argued with ferocity by Lysias and in the most lurid colours by Plato in the *Republic*, with explicit or implicit reference to Dionysios. Yet having created a new monarchic entity which fitted no traditional pattern and which Greeks therefore found very hard to understand or to describe objectively, Dionysios did make a serious attempt to legitimize his positions and some of his actions both reflected and contributed to the theory of monarchy. It remained to be seen in 380 whether the product of his unscrupulous political creativity would last, and be copied elsewhere, or not.

XI

Athens and Thebes after 380

ISOKRATES' PUBLIC letter of 380 (see p. 154) suggested that the Greeks should suspend their differences and mount a crusade against the real enemy, Persia. The leader he envisaged in 380 was Athens, but in later pamphlets which reiterated the suggestion he looked to individual rulers, such as Dionysios or King Archidamos of Sparta, before finally, in his *Philippos* of 346, reorientating the crusade round Philip of Macedon. Other constant themes in the pamphlets were the need for Greek unity; the need for a leader; and the need to control such threats to the social order as mercenaries and democracy presented. They mirror the shifting balance of political power in Greece so accurately that some scholars have seen them as true blueprints for action, whether stimulating the renewed Athenian League of 378 or encouraging the subjugation of Greece by Philip in 338. Others differ, noting Isokrates' lack of sympathy for Thebes as a major Greek power, the inordinate time he took to write each pamphlet, and his capacity for burying the realities of interstate conflict under cloudy myths of past or future harmony. Yet he did offer a rationale for conquest, unification and eastward aggression, attuned to traditional Greek fears and ambitions and available to any Greek power which needed or wanted it. That the traditional powers did not or could not exploit it, intent instead for good reasons on just those interstate realities, left a gap which was to prove important.

Resentment against Sparta erupted into action very soon after the Olympia of 380. In mid-winter 379–8, a conspiracy at Thebes slaughtered the pro-Spartan government and expelled the Spartan garrison. A rapprochement between Thebes and Athens, tentative at first, gathered force when a Spartan attempt in spring 378 to preempt Athenian action by seizing Piraeus failed miserably but was not repudiated by Sparta. By March 377 Athens had added Thebes to her existing Aegean allies (Chios, Lesbos, Rhodes and Byzantium), and created a confederacy to accommodate them. She issued a manifesto to the rest of the Greek world to join them:

> in order that the Spartans may allow the Greeks to be at peace in freedom and autonomy, possessing all their lands in security, and in order that the common peace which the Greeks and the King swore may be valid and may continue in accordance with the agreements. (Tod, *GHI* 123, lines 9–15)

Defeats of the Spartan army in 376 and 375, and energetic expeditions by Athenian commanders in the Aegean and North-West Greece, pushed the membership up to about seventy states. The allies extracted from Sparta a promise that all the cities should be autonomous and free from garrisons when hostilities were briefly ended late in 375 by a renewal of the King's Peace. This peace in turn broke down some eighteen months later, while relations between the major allies became increasingly strained, as Thebes devoted her energies to re-establishing her control over Boeotia. Peace was again made with Sparta in spring 371, it seems on Athenian initiative because of her financial straits. However, resentment against Thebes may have contributed too, for the terms of the Peace contained a clause that:

> the Spartans were to withdraw their garrison-commanders, and were to demobilize their forces by land and by sea, and were to leave the cities autonomous. If anyone contravenes these terms, anyone who wishes may come to the aid of the wronged cities, but for those who do not wish it is not obligatory to fight on behalf of the injured parties. (Xenophon, *Hellenika* 6. 3. 18)

The clause reflected the Athenian wish not to be dragged into the showdown, which by now looked inevitable, between Sparta and Thebes. The Theban claim to represent newly unified Boeotia conflicted head-on with the interpretation of the autonomy-clause which the Spartans had given it in their own interest since 386.

Since the Thebans refused to give way, and since Agesilaos as presiding officer of the conference thereupon forced the issue by excluding them from the treaty, the showdown duly came a few weeks later. The outcome threw Greek history out of gear for a generation. In stunned silence the Athenian Council heard Theban envoys announce that the Spartan army under Kleombrotos had been totally routed at Leuctra and had lost nearly 1000 men.

> At the same time they asked the Athenians for help, saying that now they had the chance to take revenge on the Spartans for all the Spartans had done to them. The Athenian Council happened to be in session on the Akropolis. When they heard the news, it was clear to everyone that they were greatly annoyed. They did not even invite the herald to dinner, and made no reply to the request for help. (Xenophon, *Hellenika*, 6. 4. 19)

As for Sparta herself,

> The man who brought news of the disaster to Sparta arrived on the last day of the Gymnopaidia festival, while the men's chorus was in the middle of performing. When they heard of the disaster the ephors were grief-stricken (they could hardly not have been, I think). However, they did not bring the chorus away, but let it finish the performance. They notified the relatives of the names of each of the dead, and instructed the women not to lament but to bear the disaster in silence. On the next day the bereaved could be seen going round in public radiant and bright, while of the relatives of the survivors there were few to be seen, and those who were seen went round scowling and humiliated. (Xenophon, *Hellenika* 6. 4. 16)

Turning-points in history are rarely as dramatic as this, but Leuctra did upset everything overnight. It was the end of the gigantic Spartan confidence trick, by which they had controlled Greek affairs for a generation while allowing their population of adult male full citizens to sink to fewer than 1000. As the Theban démarche to Athens indicated, the only question was how much would be dismantled, by whom, and to whose benefit.

Thebes moved first. She achieved great success in two regions of Greece and had some impact even at East Mediterranean level. Her interventions in Peloponnese are the easiest to follow, since Xenophon's *Hellenika* concentrates on the area in the 360s. Here the Thebans moved into a power vacuum which their victory created. They acted out a role, as guarantor of freedom from Spartan domination, which the Athenians declined and the Thebans therefore made their own. Invasions of Peloponnese in winter 370–69, summer 369, late 367, and the summers of 364, 362, 361 and 352 detached Messene from Spartan control and re-created it as a separate state (369); re-founded the Arcadian League (369); founded Megalopolis in Southern Arcadia (369); smashed the Spartan army yet again at Mantinea (362); and protected Megalopolis against renascent Spartan power (361 and 352).

In Central and Northern Greece her impact, though brief, was even greater (see Map 3). By the end of 370 all of Boeotia was under Theban control, and her allies included Phocis, Euboea, Locris, Acarnania, Aetolia, the Malian gulf states, and some Thessalians. By 367 Sicyon, Megara and Corinth were virtually client states, and Thebes had taken a major role in abortive negotiations with King Artaxerxes to renew the King's Peace. By 364 Orchomenus was destroyed and Thebes had a fleet in the Aegean. In 354 she even emulated the Spartan action of nearly fifty years before by sending forces to assist a revolt against Artaxerxes in Asia Minor. Yet in 357 she lost control of Euboea, other allies dropped away, and from 356 she embroiled herself in a war with Phocis whose course had brought her by 348 to a very precarious position indeed. As Isokrates put it in 346,

> Instead of taking the cities of Phocis she has lost her own, and her invasions of enemy land do them less harm than she suffers on the return: in Phocis they kill some mercenaries who value death more than life, and on the retreat they lose their most notable citizens. (5. 54)

Even in 352, though they were able to send a force of 4500 men to help Megalopolis against Sparta, they had declined so much that in a debate on the subject at Athens much of Demosthenes' extant speech could turn on how 'it is in Athens' interest that both the Spartans and the Thebans should be weak' (16. 4).

Thebes' rise and fall in power-politics has therefore to be explained, and this choice of levels of explanation reveals a historian's values and assumptions. One explanation must be in terms of personalities. Her two leading politicians, Epameinondas and Pelopidas, both had exceptional military and diplomatic abilities. They had what was rare among Greek politicians, a warm and close working relationship, and they stand out so sharply in the tradition from their less sensible or able rivals that Theban predominance has long been called a two-man band. Thebes' treatment of Orchomenus illustrates. In 370:

> the Thebans attacked Orchomenus with a large force. Their aim was to enslave the city, but they changed their minds when spameinondas advised them that men who aimed to lead Greece had to keep by generosity what they had gained by military valour. So they enrolled Orchomenus in among the land of their allies (Diodorus 15. 57. 1)

However, in 364, while Epameinondas was in the Aegean and Pelopidas in Thessaly, they adopted the final solution:

> They decided to attack Orchomenus for the following reasons. Some exiles who wished to change the Theban régime into an aristocracy persuaded the cavalry of Orchomenus, three hundred in all, to join the plot. The cavalrymen used to meet those from Thebes on a fixed day for training, and agreed to make the attack on that day. Along with many others who joined the plot and added their efforts, they met at the time fixed. However the initiators of the affair changed their minds, betrayed their fellows, and revealed the plot to the Boeotarchs. By this service they saved their own lives. The authorities arrested the cavalrymen of Orchomenus and brought them before the assembly. The people voted to kill them, to enslave the Orchomenians and to raze the city. The Thebans had been hostile to them from time immemorial, since they had paid

tribute to the Minyans at Orchomenus in the heroic period but
had later been liberated by Herakles. So the Thebans thought
they had a good opportunity and plausible pretexts for
punishing them, and attacked Orchomenus. They captured the
city, killed the men, and enslaved the women and children.
(Diodorus 15. 79. 3–6)

Secondly, one could emphasize the motif noted by Isokrates (see
p. 201). Theban resources of available citizen manpower were
limited, and unlike Athens she had no internal supply of gold or
silver with which to pay mercenaries. Her military impact was
therefore mainly a matter of innovative generalship and competent
training, which had their limits.

Thirdly, one could detect a double contradiction. Theban
action in Boeotia made them vulnerable to Isokrates' angry
editorial comments in 371:

They accused the Spartans of occupying the Kadmeia and
garrisoning the cities. Yet when they themselves, instead of
installing garrisons, destroy the walls of some cities and totally
exterminate others, they think they are doing nothing wrong.
They are so shameless that they call upon all their allies to
protect them while they put themselves in a position to enslave
others. (14. 19)

However, the legitimating rhetoric of such action was libertarian
and legalistic. Isokrates here admits as much, their démarche to
Athens in 371 confirms it (see p. 200), and Plutarch analyses
Pelopidas' intervention in Thessaly in much the same way:

What especially spurred him on was the glory of the act. At a
time when the Spartans were sending generals and garrison-
commanders to help Dionysios the tyrant of Sicily, and the
Athenians were receiving pay from Alexandros the tyrant of
Pherae and had erected a statue of him as their benefactor, he
was ambitiously desirous to show Greece that the Thebans
were the only people who marched to the relief of those
oppressed by tyranny or who overthrew those régimes in Greece
which rested on illegality and violence. (*Pelopidas* 31. 4)

Yet the more success such a programme enjoyed, the less it could be sustained. States once 'liberated' required either repeated intervention (as in Thessaly) or a protective organization. In Peloponnese in the 360s Xenophon records treaties 'to be allies and to follow wherever the Thebans may lead' (*Hellenika* 7. 1. 42). Military control involved Theban garrisons and commanders, whom Xenophon describes with the Spartan word 'harmost'. There were even some steps towards integration. When some exiles killed the tyrant of Sicyon at Thebes in 365 and were put on trial there, Xenophon makes them say in their defence, 'You Thebans voted that exiles should be extraditable from all the allied cities. Could anyone say that it is unjust to kill an exile who returns to his city without waiting for a collective decree of the allies?' (*Hellenika* 7. 3. 11). We are not very far from Athenian-style hegemony.

Fourthly, one could think geopolitically, in terms of settlement patterns and political cohesion. Athens, Sparta, Corinth or Elis were 'city-states' in the extreme sense. The political centre was also by far the largest population centre, and the area united under its control and participating in its government could be called by the name of that centre. It is very easy to see this not just as the predominant pattern but as the norm (see p. 13ff.). Such a view is strongly reinforced by surviving Greek political philosophy (Plato's *Republic* and *Laws*: Aristotle's *Politics*), for which the problems of power are exclusively those thrown up by the centralized city-state. North and west of Mt Cithaeron the pattern ceased to hold. Moreover, if one approaches this cultural divide from the north rather than from the south, it is the city-state which is the anomaly. The cantonal, tribal, or monarchic areas to the north are far more typical of the dry-farming areas of Europe and Asia Minor in the Iron Age. That the centralized city-state should spread northwards was therefore not a foregone conclusion, perhaps not even a natural process. Much of the history of Central and Northern Greece reflects the tensions which its attractions imposed upon what was local and organic but incohesive.

Nowhere was the tension stronger than in Boeotia. By the time of the Persian Wars there were national institutions: a common festival, the Pamboeotia at Coronea; a coinage which shared

common symbols since its inception in the sixth century; and a
college of national magistrates, the Boeotarchs, whom Herodotus
mentions in a context of 479. But national unity was pretty feeble.
Till the fourth century such public documents as we have were
set up by individual cities, not by the larger entity, and one of *c*.
550–25, 'The Orchomenians dedicated to Olympian Zeus booty
from Coronea' (*SEG* XI 1208), reveals that intra-Boeotian
conflicts were still worth boasting about at Olympia. Similarly in
519 Thebes attempted to coerce Plataea into the larger entity, but
was told by Corinthian arbitrators 'that the Thebans should leave
in peace those of the Boeotians who do not wish to participate in
Boeotia' (Herodotus 6. 108. 5). In 480 the basic decision whether
to submit to Persia or not was taken separately by the individual
cities. Such disunity allowed Boeotia to be overrun and controlled
by Athens between 457 and 446.

The trouble was, however, not that there was no leading city
but that there were two, Thebes and Orchomenus. While neither
had the strength to dominate the smaller cities of Tanagra,
Plataea and Thespiae completely, let alone each other, both had
the ambition to do so. There were two possible solutions. One
was to devise a political system which acknowledged these
realities, guaranteed local autonomies, and gave a fair chance of
power to all. In and after 446 this was done, by the creation of a
federal constitution of which we know the salient features from a
sketch of it as it functioned in 395.

The situation in Boeotia at that time was as follows: there
were four councils (Boulai) then in each of the cities; not all the
citizens were entitled to membership, but only those who
owned a certain amount of property; each Boule in turn met
before the main session, and held a preliminary discussion,
after which they put proposals about the matters under
consideration to the other three. Decisions approved by all four
became valid. Such was the form of local government in each
town, but the affairs of Boeotia as a whole were handled as
follows. All the population was divided into eleven wards, and
each one provided one Boeotarch in the following way: the
Thebans contributed four, two for the city and two for Plataea,
Skolos, Erythrae and Skaphae with the other territories which

had formerly been politically united with those cities but were then subject to Thebes. The men of Orchomenus and Hysiae provided two, as did those of Thespiae together with Eutresis and Thisbae. Tanagra produced one, and another came from Haliartos, Lebadaea and Coronea, and the last from Akraphion, Copae and Chaeronea: in the last two cases each of the three cities provided the Boeotarch in turn. The wards provided the magistrates in this way, and together with each Boeotarch they supplied sixty members of the central Boule, and paid their expenses themselves. Each had the duty of providing about 1000 hoplites and 100 cavalry. In general terms, in the same proportions as the distribution of magistrates were the benefits they received from the central treasury and the contributions they made to it, the jurors they supplied, and the extent of their share of everything in the state, good and bad. Such was the political organization of the people as a whole; the Boulai and Assemblies of the Boeotians used to meet on the Kadmeia. (*Hellenika Oxyrhynchia* 11. 2–4)

The whole is a monument of fifth-century oligarchic theory. It imitated contemporary Athenian institutions, and perhaps Spartan ones as well, but it transformed them by inserting a low property qualification for active citizenship and by suppressing the primary assembly in favour of a large representative Council of 660 men. Nor was the intellectual traffic one way, for it was itself imitated in the draft constitutions of the Athenian oligarchs in 411.

Yet, though Boeotia ended the Peloponnesian War a far stronger power than she had been in 446, it is fair to say that that strength was achieved not because of the constitution but in spite of it. Thebes made a determined effort to transform Boeotia into a unitary state centred on Thebes, and it was this second solution which won in the end. In eastern Boeotia slippage towards Athens by democratically minded towns such as Plataea and Thespiae was used through the Peloponnesian War and later as an excuse for attack and siege in time of peace (Plataea in 431), for dismantling walls (Thespiae in 423), for the annexation of territory (Plataea in 373), for the transfer of populations to Thebes (implied by Xenophon for 371) and for outright destruction (Plataea in 427 and 373; Thespiae in 373). In the west, the more power concentrated at Thebes, the more restive Orchomenus became. As soon as effective Spartan protection was forthcoming in 395, she left the League, and kept her independence till Leuctra made it impossible. What matters here is not so much that Theban politicians, in their haste to emulate the cohesion, and to overhaul the power, of the major states, adopted highly Bismarckian tactics which lost them sympathy elsewhere. Most states had similar skeletons in their cupboards, and the sort of sympathy which Isokrates expressed for the Plataeans in his *Plataikos* of 371 was no more disinterested than the help which Athens and Sparta gave to Orchomenus. More important, such acts expended much political and military energy which would otherwise have been available for use outside Boeotia. Even worse, they did not work. Demosthenes' speech 16, already quoted, shows that Orchomenus, Plataea and Thespiae had been refounded by then, and Boeotia never did become a unitary state like Athens or Corinth. The city-state was simply an inappropriate pattern of cohesion.

The second centre of post-Leuctra politics, Athens, followed a comparable pattern, being active in all directions but successful in none. Her first initiative was in Peloponnese, all the states of which, except Elis, made a defensive alliance with her in 370. They swore: 'I shall be faithful to the agreements which the Persian King sent down and to the decrees of the Athenians and their allies. If anybody attacks one of the cities which swore this oath, I shall help with all my forces' (Xenophon, *Hellenika* 6. 5. 2). Not six months later, in the winter of 370–69, this treaty involved Athens in sending an expedition in full force to defend Sparta's existence against the first Theban invasion. Thereafter Athenian land forces, especially her cavalry, were active in Peloponnese, with varying allies but always in opposition to Thebes, nearly every year till 362. Otherwise, apart from desultory attempts to stop Theban efforts in Thessaly and to destabilize the Macedonian monarchy, her main effort was in the Aegean. Here, from 368 onwards, her leading generals actively sought to re-establish an Athenian presence on a fifth-century scale. Substantial conquests were made, from Samos in 365, towns in Chersonese from 365 onwards, much of Chalcidice in 364, to Euboea in 357. Admittedly, her attempts to recover her position at Amphipolis and in Thrace from 368 onwards ruined the careers and reputations of successive generals and gained little but paper treaties with unreliable dynasts, and there was spasmodic discontent in the Aegean throughout, but the impression is of gradually intensifying Athenian control. She seems to have been totally taken by surprise when in winter 357–6 her major allies Chios, Rhodes, Byzantium, and Cos allied with Maussollos, nominally satrap of Caria, revolted from Athens, and defeated the Athenian navy in battles off Chios in 356 and 355. When an attempt to play a rival satrap against Maussollos and the allies merely served to bring the Persian King back into Aegean affairs against her, Athens had willy-nilly to acknowledge her allies' seccession in 355–4. For the next few years she concentrated on what most mattered, the corn-route from the Black Sea, amid temporary bankruptcy, the prosecution, disgrace, or death of many leading figures, and a major though subtle shift in public opinion away from the heroics of power.

Again, we have a problem of explanation. One explanation sees a decline in patriotism and moral fibre. Such explanations have perennial appeal anyway as a substitute for analysis, and they do echo contemporary utterance. An unwillingness to fight or to row seems to emerge, for example, from Apollodoros' struggles to get and keep a crew in 362–60, in spite of conscription (see p. 20), or from Demosthenes' exhortations from 351 onwards to 'serve yourself' in the army and not rely on mercenaries. Likewise, other themes in the oratory of the 350s, 340s and 330s contrasted the simplicity, altruism, energy, democratic vigilance, and/or aristo-cratic self-control, of earlier generations with the sloth, decadence, venality and greed of the present. It is very easy to take all this at face value and to seek no further for the causes of Athenian or of general Greek decline. Yet contemporary rhetoric, whether tuned to exhortation in immediate public contexts (thus Demosthenes) or to the reinforcement of long-term attitudes (thus Isokrates), can be misleading and self-contradictory. Quietism, for example, could be seen by Demosthenes in 349 as a contrast to the altruism and idealism of the past:

What astonishes me, men of Athens, is that you once took up arms against the Spartans in defence of Greek rights. You could often have drawn much private profit for yourselves, but you refused; instead you expended your own property in war tax, went on campaigns and confronted danger in order that others should attain their rights. But now you are slow to go on campaign, you are dilatory about paying war tax in defence of your own possessions. You have often saved other Greeks, collectively and separately, and now, after losing your own possessions, you just sit there! (Demosthenes 2. 24)

Yet by Isokrates in 354 it could be seen rather as a repudiation of those who 'are implanting the expectation that we shall get back our possessions in the Aegean cities and shall recover the power which we once had' (8. 6). Moreover, the historical bases of such rhetoric were very shaky. Bribery was not exactly unknown in the fifth century and earlier; Athens used mercenaries in the fifth century; and reluctance to serve, in the 360s and later, is better seen as a reluctance to serve without being paid regularly and properly.

Other reasons have more force. Some lay outside Athens' power. At least some of the hinterland states of the Aegean were better organized, wealthier, or had access to better weaponry, than a century previously during Athens' first buildup. In particular, even though the satraps of Asia Minor were at odds with the King and in intermittent revolt from *c.* 366 onwards, Persia's position was entrenched. The Athenian League of 378–7 explicitly rested in part on the King's Peace of 387–6 (see p. 199), under which the cities of the Asia Minor coast were recognized as belonging to the King. Whereas in the 430s, as the Tribute Lists show, they contributed well over 100 talents to the 400 talents or so of actual tribute revenue, from 386 on they and the cities on the Asian shore of the Propontis area were formally out of bounds. In any case, tribute and other features of the fifth-century Empire had been so widely seen as tools of subjection that Athens in 377 had to promise to behave. Any potential allied state 'is to be free and autonomous, having whatever constitution it pleases, and is not to have any garrison, governor, or tribute imposed upon it'. The Athenians themselves 'would resign the ownership of all properties which may be owned privately or publicly by Athenians in the territory of those entering the alliance'. In future 'it is to be illegal for any Athenian privately or publicly to possess house or land in the territories of the allies, whether by purchase or by security or in any other way' (Tod 123, lines 20–3, 27–30 and 36–44). Tribute was in fact reintroduced, delicately renamed 'assessments', by or in the late 370s, but the embargo on property-owning, though diplomatically essential, was crippling. Kleruchies for the poor, and widesprea landholding overseas for the propertied class as absentee landlords, had given all classes before 404 a very strong vested interest in maintaining the Empire and the fleet. Without that interest, fainéant quietism among the upper class had more scope after 378, and was increasingly reflected in lawcourt speeches and Isokrates' pamphlets. Tepidity or veto on the part of the rich would not have mattered had there been a substantial reserve available to finance campaigns, but the booty from hostile action against non-Greeks which had formed the core of the fifth-century reserve was accessible only at the cost of active war with Persia or Thrace. To take booty from Greeks who were political allies was diplomatically suicidal. We can see in inventories and decrees of the 370s and 360s some attempt to turn the treasures of Athene into a reserve, but windfalls from dedications were too rare, and the melting down of such cups and crowns too much a last resort, for them to serve adequately as the reserve of ready money which Athens needed.

Even so, Athens could have made some choices differently. Within Athens there was certainly much slackness in the administration of the navy, and some bad will among the rich men appointed to commission and command the warships. The problems which Apollodoros said he encountered in 362–60 (see p. 20) were evidently not peculiar to him, and another speech describes the emergency of 356 by saying that 'A fleet was being sent out, and reinforcements were being despatched in all haste. There was no equipment for the ships in the dockyard, because trierarchs who had borrowed it had kept it and had not returned it. What was more, there was not even enough sail cloth, hemp, or rope to commission the ships to be bought in Piraeus' (Demosthenes 47. 20). We know of various laws and expedients adopted to remedy the situation, but they were not effective at the right moment.

Moreover, in both the regions of Greece wherein they were militarily active in the 360s and 350s, the Athenians acted with growing insensitivity. In Peloponnese they made what hindsight can only call a fundamental blunder, by backing Sparta against Thebes from 369 onwards. Granted, there were good reasons, even apart from the treaty obligations of 370 (see p. 207). Thebes was close, powerful, and brutal towards Boeotian communities which had traditionally looked to Athens. Sparta was remote anyway, and romantically attractive now she was crippled. During the crucial debate in Athens the Spartan envoys

described how many good things existed, when the two powers acted in concert; they recalled how they had jointly repulsed the Persians, and how the Athenians had been chosen by the Greeks as leaders of the fleet and guardians of the common moneys, with Spartan assent, while the Spartans themselves had been selected unanimously by all the Greeks as leaders by land, again with Athenian assent. (Xenophon, *Hellenika* 6. 5. 34)

The claim by another envoy, Prokles of Phleious, that 'Some god has given you the chance of having the Spartans as unhesitating friends for all time, if you help them in their need' (*ibid* 6. 5. 41), though proved pitifully false in the event, evidently appealed strongly to those, especially conservatives and oligarchs, who knew of the Kimonian tradition: it is no accident that the Athenian forces active on Sparta's behalf in the 360s comprised largely the upper-class cavalry. There were more hard-headed reasons, too. Prokles' statement 'I imagine it is clear to everyone that if they could get rid of the Spartans, the Thebans would attack you next' (*ibid* 6. 5. 38) was plausible. To back Arcadians or Argives against Sparta had always been fatal in the past, and now ran the risk of throwing Sparta and Thebes together against Athens. There was even the chance of a major quid pro quo, recognition by Sparta and others of Athens' claim to Amphipolis in Thrace. All the same it was a disastrous decision. Militarily, operations in Peloponnese and against Amphipolis diverted resources of men and money which needed to be concentrated on the Aegean. Politically, it was a sell-out. Till now the manifesto of

March 377 (see p. 199), directed against Sparta in the name of autonomy, had legitimated Athenian activities. To abandon that manifesto meant that her moral authority vanished, along with the raison d'être of the League, and that Thebes could walk into the role of guarantor of autonomy and democracy which Athens had abdicated.

In spite of all this Athenian action in the Aegean became more exposed and risky. The creation of kleruchies of Athenian citizens from 365 onwards came close to breaking the promises of 377 (see p. 210). Sharp practice by Athenian generals exhausted what goodwill there was, and phrases from two other documents of 357–6 show how Athenian protection and control were undermining allies' autonomies. In the wake of the Athenian reconquest of Euboea in 357, a decree of autumn 357 stipulated that:

> [if] anyone else in future invad[es Ere]tria or any of the other alli[ed cities, whether he be an Athe]nian or from the allies of the Athen[ians, he] is to be condemned [to death] and his property is to be c[onfiscated,] a tenth being dedicated to the goddess Athene. [His property is] to be recoverable from all the [allied cities, and if] any city withholds it, that city is to owe [it to the common fund of] the allies (Tod 154, lines 9–17).

Similarly, in May 356,

> Hegesandros moved; so that Andros may be safe for the people of Athens and the people of Andros, and so that the garrison on Andros may receive its wages out of the assessments in accordance with the resolutions of the allies, and the safeguard may not be broken off: choose a general out of those who have been elected, the chosen man to be responsible for Andros. Also, Archedemos is to exact the moneys owed from the islands to the soldiers on Andros and hand them over to the governor on Andros, so that the soldiers may have wages. (Tod 156, lines 7ff.)

We can understand why in 351–50 Demosthenes said 'The Chians and the Byzantines and the Rhod ans accused us of plotting against them, and that was why they started this recent war against us' (Demosthenes 15. 3). However, he also brings in the opportunism of 'the person who instigated and persuaded them of this'. That person was Maussollos of Caria, whose regime and society, like those of other rulers and would-be rulers on the fringes of Greece, contrasted sharply with those of Athens. To survey Athenian society and administration now at closer range will help us both to grasp the size of that contrast and to help us to understand why the dynasts succeeded in eroding the position of the traditional powers and in creating new patterns in their stead.

XII

Athenian Society in the Fourth Century

NO ONE THEME or quotation or set of documents can encapsulate the complex reality of fourth century Athenian society. At one end of the range of evidence stands the single gravestone or building or item of silver plate, at the other the philosophical theories and technical essays of systemization of knowledge by Plato and Aristotle and their lesser colleagues which are the foundations of our own culture and its 'sciences' (see p. 174). One of those essays will concern us particularly here, the *Athenian Constitution* written in Aristotle's school in the 320s, while some of the remainder are invaluable for the (often very peculiar) light which they throw on their authors' society. Other 'literary' works are disappointingly absent, for the tragedies and comedies which continued to be written for production at Athenian and other festivals (see p. 158) survive only in fragments and quotations until we begin to have Menander's comedies of manners from the late 320s onwards. No other poetry worth notice survives, while we lack even the historian's first basic resource, a respectable year-by-year narrative of events. There were such narratives, whether those created within a specifically Athenian context by the successive generations of Athenian local historians (the Atthidographers) or those which in effect continued Xenophon's general Greek history after it ended in 362, but none of this material survives save in fragments or in the summary and sloppy survey of Diodoros' books 15 and 16 (see p. 153).

What we do have, and in exceptional quantity, are the documents and the speeches. The documents on stone have been briefly noticed already (pp. 16, 63, 99), but it is especially in this context of mid-fourth century Athens that they come into their own and set the framework of interpretation of a society in a way wholly new for Greece. The first and basic way to approach them is via a classification of types and sub-types. One major class comprises dedications to the Gods made by private individuals such as those quoted above (see pp. 180–1). They show us directly which gods, which aspects or titles of gods and which sanctuaries were attracting the attention and the piety of those able and willing to afford the cost and anxious to have their piety publicly known. A second very numerous class is of inscriptions on gravestones and grave monuments. For centuries it had been the norm for a grave not simply to be marked with a stone pillar or a vase but also (if resources allowed) for the stone to be decorated, or provided with a bas-relief representation of the deceased, or even at the extreme to form a large ostentatious monument – to the extent indeed that on several occasions in Athenian history legal restrictions were placed on the nature, size, or cost of the monuments. The fourth century was a period in which the fashion for such ostentation was increasing, as was the expectation that grave markers would carry the name of the deceased. Though in this way secondary to the grave marker itself, inscriptions qualitatively alter the level of our information. Even single names such as Kallimache (*IG* ii^2 11778) begin to create a personality, especially when the monument carries a representation of the deceased, while those which record the father's name and name of the deceased, and perhaps name relatives as well, hint at family and affective relationships. A complex such example is the gravestone of 'Dikaiogenes son of Menexenos of Kydathenaion. Menexenos son of Dikaiogenes of Kydathenaion. Eukoline daughter of Aristogeiton of Aphidna, wife of Dikaiogenes' (*IG* ii^2 6569). Like dedications, such inscriptions have significance beyond the immediate message: surviving in their hundreds from the fourth century, each class of document reveals not only attitudes towards family posterity and the divine but also expectations about widespread literacy and a passion for the written record.

That passion extended equally into the public domain, where the fourth century, and particularly the period from 360 to 320, offers numerous transcripts onto stone of official documents of state. The main groups are (again) dedications, but this time offered to the gods by the state, its public bodies and its magistrates: lists of the officials holding a particular post, especially those who served as councillors on the council of 500: accounts of transactions of various administrative boards: inventories, especially of objects dedicated to Athene on the Akropolis and in the shrines of the other gods: and laws and decrees approved by demes or tribes or cult bodies, or by the Assembly itself. Again, we are speaking of hundreds of documents, long or short, broken or complete, a number which is slowly but continually increasing as new finds are made. Hard to read though many of them are, because of the small, cramped lettering, they were meant to be read. Publicity for public acts, accountability to society for what this or that Board of public officials had done, and the determination to have a publicly accessible record of decisions of state all emerge vividly from the stones themselves via the transcripts, editions, and translations which scholars have made.

There remain finally the speeches, which have already been briefly noticed (p. 16) and intermittently quoted. About 80 of the 145 surviving speeches date from the years 360–20. Their survival, and the particular light which they throw on Athens, have helped to define that period as 'the age of Demosthenes' or 'the age of the orators'. As evidence they are fundamental, but hard to use. Two extended examples may serve both to illustrate that fact and to introduce the themes of this chapter.

The first, [Demosthenes] 59 *Against Neaira*, is well known. It is certainly not by Demosthenes but by a contemporary and associate, Apollodoros, whose style can be detected in seven speeches placed by scholars of antiquity among Demosthenes' own. Its date is the late 340s. The first fifteen sections were delivered by one Theomnestos, who explains that Apollodoros had married his sister and had given a daughter of that marriage to Theomnestos (her uncle) as wife – a practice legal and not uncommon at Athens in order to cement a relationship (as here) or to keep property within the family. He also explains that Apollodoros as councillor in 349–8 had carried a motion to use the balance of the theatre-ticket subsidy fund for war purposes but had been successfully prosecuted for 'illegal proposal' by a politician of some standing, Stephanos, and that Stephanos had tried again but failed with a murder charge against Apollodoros (9–10). Those grievances were openly admitted by Theomnestos as their reasons for the present prosecutions of Stephanos' partner, Neaira, on a writ of 'foreignness' (*xenia*), and of Stephanos himself for collusion.

Apollodoros begins his, the major part of the speech (16–126), by quoting the relevant law, and then narrates Neaira's life and circumstances at length. She had begun, he says, as a child prostitute, one of a group selected for their looks and trained by a madam, Nikarete of Elis. Apollodoros calls witnesses (some reluctant, it seems) to attest that they knew her at work as a *hetaira* in the wealthy circles of Athens, Corinth, and Megara in the 370s, moving by purchase from one lover to another but being at some stage nominally manumitted from slavery. The next section (37–49) describes how Stephanos encountered her in Megara in 371–0, brought her and her three children to Athens to set up household together, and how, when Phrynion, a previous lover/owner of hers, sought to snatch her, 'Stephanos claimed her away from him as free according to the law, and provided pledge for her (as a non-citizen) before the polemarch' (40), until an official arbitration judged that Stephanos and Phrynion should share her favours equally. Next comes a description of three of Stephanos' attempts to infiltrate his new family as Athenians, each exploiting one of Neaira's daughters. A first step was to marry her off, as if his own and as if of citizen status, with a large dowry to a poor citizen peasant. That ploy failed when her husband's kin-groups refused to acknowledge the legitimacy of his child by her. A second step was to prosecute as a 'seducer' (i.e. of a citizen woman) a man of Andros, a former lover of Neaira, who had turned his attentions to her daughter. The case had to be withdrawn, according to Apollodoros, but yielded a tidy sum via arbitration 'towards her giving-away' (71). That encouraged a third and bolder step, to marry her to no less a person than the Archon Basileus, Theogenes. He, as it happened, was a poor man inexperienced in public affairs for whom Stephanos was conveniently acting as Assessor and who needed a wife to perform the public rituals of state incumbent upon the Basilinna. In an attempt to milk this 'scandal' for all it was worth, Apollodoros first relates with unctuous glee how Theogenes was carpeted by the Areiopagos as a result and had to apologize and to divorce his 'wife'. He then contrasts the circumstances with Athens' normal extreme caution in conferring citizenship on non-citizens: a theme which leads him to show off his antiquarian and legal knowledge about the office of Archon Basileus and about the generous Athenian treatment of the Plataians after the Theban-Spartan capture of their town in 427. He ends in textbook style by asking the jurors to imagine how angry their wives will be if their husbands come home to report an acquittal, by emphasizing how bad a signal to civic society an acquittal would be (and against recent precedent, too), by refuting some of the likely defence arguments, and by interpreting Stephanos' refusal to release Neaira's slave servants for torture as a lack of confidence in the defence case.

In this and similar speeches there is almost more information than we can cope with. It will be helpful to use once more the themes of Chapter VI – people, money, and power – in order to gauge the effects of an eventful century on Athenian society, and to use the speech primarily for the light which it throws on people. Apollodoros himself, son of a rich ex-slave banker, is a complex enough figure on his own, but his knowledge of law and legal process, his use of history as signals for the present, his oratorical skills, and his obsessions were not peculiar to him but were shared within the world of free men which he portrays. As in most male societies, it matters who you know: the clubbiness of male Athenian society is palpable throughout the speech, even though there is a clear gulf between the comfortably off (sources of income are not mentioned) and the poor man such as Phrastor, 'a working man who had painstakingly put his livelihood together' (50). So too the portrait of Stephanos as the outsider, the struggling young politician who 'was not yet gaining much from politics, and was not yet a *rhetor*, but was still a *sykophantes*, one of those who shout their support near the platform (of the Assembly) and bring writs and denunciations for money and add their names to other people's motions till he became a fawning supporter of Kallistratos of Aphidna' (43), would have a wide application. All the same it gives the impression, confirmed in other speeches, of being one world, wherein distinctions of wealth or nationality exist but are easily permeable socially.

Conspicuously, that is not true for the worlds of women, which this speech illustrates better than any one other. Apollodoros is crudely explicit: 'that is what "to live together" is, when one makes children and introduces the sons to the phratry members and to the demesmen, and gives the daughters as one's own to husbands. We have *hetairai* for the sake of pleasure, bedmates (*pallakai*) for the daily care of the body, and wives for making children genuinely and for having a trusty guardian of things within (the house)' (122). As with virtually all our evidence about women, his remarks were written by a man and reflect male perceptions of male interests – sexual, social, and economic – in separating women's worlds from each other. The household world is the best attested, not just because it accorded with male values and met economic needs but also because it was the predominant environment for most women most of the time. A late work by Xenophon, his *Oikcnomikos* or *Household Manager*, adds more details. Through the mouth of Ischomachos, Sokrates' interlocutor and himself a classic portrait of an Athenian landed gentleman, he presents a picture of Ischomachos' young wife as (after training by her husband) the ideal housekeeper, discreet, active in the 'covered' areas of household and estate life, and managing the servants and resources of the household. It is unbearably patronising and repressive, but is more complex than it looks. For Xenophon's Ischomachos, 'discretion both in a man and a woman means acting in such a way as to keep their existing possessions in the best possible state and to secure the greatest possible increase, accruing by fair and honourable means' (*Oik*. vii 15). It is an odd way to define discretion, but the emphasis on collaboration in an economic enterprise and on maximising returns portrays women as managers, producers, and trainers in a far more positive and realistic way than much previous Greek writing had done. Nor was even this world one of total social invisibility. Women attended family occasions and some festivals (though perhaps more by social expectation than through real autonomy of conduct), some of the latter on their own, while the convention that deities had servants of their own sex gave some few women high and visible public status as priestesses of Athene.

All the same, one should not claim too much. The higher the

social status of the household, the greater the emphasis which was laid on women as the transmitters of status and property rather than as beneficial owners. Heiresses to an estate therefore had to be married to the nearest male relative (on occasion against the wishes of both parties) in order to discourage fortune hunting and the concentration of estates in fewer hands: the chastity of women had to be guarded so that the legitimacy, and therefore the citizen status, of her children could be vouched for: and so on. Indeed, for women, as not for men, status and autonomy stood in inverse ratio. For example, another speech of the 340s shows us a man threatened with disfranchisement for having a foreign mother. His opponent, he says,

> said too about my mother that she had been a wet-nurse. But we do not deny that, when the city was in difficulties and everyone was doing badly, this happened; I shall explain clearly how, and for what reasons, she was a wet-nurse. I hope that none of you will be offended, Athenians: you will find today many female citizens working as wet-nurses, and I will mention them by name if you wish. If we had been rich, we would not have sold ribbons, nor been in any way in difficulties. But what has this to do with my descent? Nothing, I think. Do not, members of the jury, please, dishonour the poor – their poverty is sufficient hardship – nor those who choose to work and make a living by just means. ([Demosthenes] 57, 35–6)

For once, though it is filtered by the need to temper the prejudices of the speaker's male citizen audience, we can see the more 'open' and less status-defined world of employment and small-scale trade in the *agora*. More open still, in a sense, was Neaira's environment. The arbitration judgement which resolved the quarrel between Stephanos and Neaira's former lover/owner described her, very significantly, as being 'free and her own mistress' ([Dem.] 59.46) – i.e. she had no male validator (*kyrios*) of her acts. The contrast with the world of the citizen family is profound.

In the last few pages the subject of citizen status has arisen repeatedly – with good reason, for it aroused acute sensitivities.

That had been so ever since the reforms of *c.* 460 (Chapter IV above) had given Athenian citizens collectively and individually more power, and ever since the citizenship law of Perikles in 451/0 had turned the Athenian citizen body into a closed corporation, recruited only by descent from citizen father and citizen mother duly pledged. The law had been relaxed somewhat after the Sicilian disaster of 413, and had been totally superseded during the civil war of 404–3, which had in fact been to a considerable degree a conflict within Athenian society about who should be a citizen. In that war violently reactionary measures disfranchised about ninety per cent of the pre-404 citizen body, and were followed, after the democratic restoration of autumn 403, by proposals to enfranchise some free men who had never been citizens, together with some who were said to be 'clearly slaves'. None of these proposals was acceptable, and the upshot was to reaffirm and to clarify the status quo of Perikles' law.

The result was a growing internal contradiction. To the state as a whole and its segmental bodies, as to jurors sworn to uphold the law, its reinforcement clearly mattered: there was even a general scrutiny of deme membership lists in 346/5. Yet to individuals the boundary could mean frustration, anxiety and unhappiness. Those outside the boundary largely stayed outside, however loyal or deserving: refugees from civil wars remained Plataian or Olynthian, rich metics might at best become *isoteleis*, 'paying the same taxes' as Athenians, and only a handful of men (mostly bankers and captains of mercenaries) gained entry. As a result, men whose activities in Athens were indistinguishable from each other, such as those concerned with financing and running the merchant ships of the Aegean, or the members of the scholarly and educational intelligentsia, had wholly different levels of access to lawcourts, landowning or the political process. Correspondingly, those within the boundary were vulnerable to gossip or to malicious accusations of not being proper Athenians. When Aeschines alleged that Demosthenes' 'own descent comes on your mother's side from the nomads of Scythia' (2.78), or when Demosthenes reminded Aeschines of 'the fact that your father Tromes was a slave in the service of Elpias, the schoolmaster who taught by the Theseion' (18.129), they were not just trading ritual insults but were each seeking quite literally to delegitimate the other's position in civic life. Most intractable of all, for those within or without, was the illegality of marrying across the boundary. Menander in play after play from the 320s onwards might create rosy fantasies and mind-numbing coincidences in order to ensure that young man and young woman would turn out in the end to be both of citizen families of good standing and thereby able to marry; the reality, as Stephanos and Neaira knew all too well, was very different.

The second theme, money, calls for a sharp distinction between public revenues and expenditure and private monies. The former were a perpetual anxiety till the 330s. Since the recurrent costs of the democratic administration and of the popular courts could normally be met, the system could clearly survive the absence of revenues from an empire. What it could not do, for all the fiscal ingenuity of its politicians and the intermittently brutal heavy-handedness of its military men, was to amass a reserve sufficient to finance the sorts of military action which Athenian foreign policy needed to be able to threaten and to carry out effectively. As a result wars, especially wars by sea, repeatedly left Athens fiscally penniless, tempted by expedients such as prosecuting the wealthy on dubious charges for the sake of confiscating their property (as in 390–87), or of suspending the lawcourts (as in the late 360s and in 348), or of levying money directly from the wealthier landowners as a forced public loan (as in 362). To be fair, one should add that such pressures also had more positive effects, in the shape of more sophisticated financial systems, of the development of officials who were Finance Ministers in fact and eventually in name, and of the evolution of something close to a recognizable annual budget. A pamphlet of Xenophon's old age (his *Revenues* of *c.* 355) even suggested measures to stimulate trade and attract non-citizen residents back to Athens which look positively Keynesian (and were to some degree acted on). Yet it was not really till after the disaster of 338 at Chaironeia and Athens' enforced withdrawal thereafter from most naval activity that public revenues recovered enough to create a surplus. Even then, though the size of the public projects put Perikles' building programme in the shade, they were significantly accompanied in the 330s and 320s by the private financing of public works – bridges, temples, city gates etc. – in a way which Athens had not seen for over a century.

The getting and spending of resources in private hands which such behaviour exemplifies can be usefully analysed in the light of a single document. It is quoted in a speech of the 340s, [Demosthenes 35] *Against Lakritos*, where the speaker Androkles says he was persuaded by two prominent politicians to put up some money for a shipping loan. Uniquely in Athenian speeches, we are given the text of the ensuing written agreement *verbatim*:

Androkles of Sphettos and Nausikrates of Karystos lent to Artemon and Apollodoros of Phaselis 3000 drachmai of silver [for a voyage] from Athens to Mende or Skione, and thence to Bosporos, and if they wish along the left-hand coast as far as Borysthenes and back to Athens, [the interest being] at 225 per 1000, and if they sail out from the Black Sea to Hieron after the rising of Arcturus, at 330 per 1000, lent on the security of 3000 amphorai of Mende, which will sail from Mende or Skione in the twenty-oar ship which Hyblesios commands. They lay these sums under pledge, not owing besides these sums any money to anyone, nor will they raise an extra loan. They will bring back from the Black Sea to Athens all the goods taken on board in exchange in the same vessel. Once the goods have reached Athens safely, the borrowers will give back to the lenders the money accruing according to the agreement in twenty days from when they reach Athens, intact save for jettison which the fellow-voyagers may throw overboard after voting in common, or if they pay any ransom to enemies, but intact of all other things. They will provide for the lenders to have the pledge at their free disposition until they give back the money accruing according to the agreement. If they do not give the money back in the stated time, it is open to the lenders to pawn the pledge and to sell it for the established price; and if there is any shortfall in the money which is due to the lenders according to the agreement, the lenders (either one of them or both of them) may distrain upon Artemon and Apollodoros and from their possessions, landed and maritime, everywhere where they may be, as if they had lost a lawsuit and were overdue to pay. If they do not enter (the Black Sea), after remaining ten days in Hellespont at the time of the Dog Star, unloading wherever there are no rights of seizure against Athenians, and sailing thence back to Athens, they are to pay the interests specified last year in the agreement. If the ship in which the cargo is sailing suffers a disaster but the goods subject to pledge are saved, the goods saved shall be for the lenders in common. Nothing is to be more valid in these matters than the agreement.

Witnesses: Phormion of Peiraieus, Kephisodotos of Boiotia, Heliodoros of Pitheis ([Demosthenes] 35. 10–13)

The suit arose because, according to Androkles, Artemon and his brother Lakritos had set up a large-scale fraud: they took away much less cargo than was specified, raised other loans on the same security, and claimed on their return that the ship had been wrecked with its cargo in the Black Sea, so that they came back to Athens on a different ship, financed by a different loan from a man of Kition in Cyprus. The details do not matter here, though they are highly entertaining, for on following them through it is hard to resist the impression that all concerned were sharks of the first water. More important is the economic pattern which such loans represent. They have two aspects, the systemic and the individual. Systemically they were a mechanism whereby capital could be raised and concentrated in sufficient quantity to finance an essential trading activity, which could be very profitable but (as the rates of interest show) would also be very risky. As the agreement itself also shows, the basic structure was a triangle. Ships left Athens largely in ballast but carrying the entrepreneurs with the money they had raised on the Athenian market. They bought wine or other foodstuffs from the towns of the North Aegean seaboard, took that cargo into the Dardanelles or into the Black Sea and exchanged it for corn from the Ukrainian seaboard or from the Crimea region, which was brought back to Athens. Other similar triangles involved Egypt and Rhodes or the Asia Minor ports such as Phaselis (the home town of Artemon and Apollodoros), and no doubt involved other commodities such as timber and textiles.

Such networks had of course been in place for centuries, while Athens' place in them had been predominant for a century or more. Whether the state of their financing and management which we see in this agreement can be called capitalist is debated, for it meets some of the pre-conditions for capitalism but not others. What is certain is that Athens was a major source of money for such loans, for what was needed was actual cash in good coin, which could be treated as pure silver and reckoned by weight. Athens' good fortune in having an accessible supply of such silver in the mines at Laureion in south-east Attika must therefore be central to that role, even though the ways in which what was mined or refined in the (still visible) installations there became silver coin in private possession remain surprisingly obscure. However, the effect is clear. Such bullion supplemented the income in cash which a well-off man would receive from other sources such as rents from houses or multiple dwellings, political monies such as those which Stephanos acquired as a *rhetor* (p. 218 above), or the 'rent' of one obol per day (1/6 of a drachma) which any slave 'living apart' from his owner and earning his own living had to pay to his owner.

For the creditors, such loans stood at the extreme profit-seeking end of a range of ways of deploying resources. Other ways, such as interest-free loans to friends or freedmen, were more socially embedded or had more to do with status enhancement and conspicuous consumption. Horseflesh, expensive mistresses such as Neaira, houses of some elegance and luxury, or the taste for fine food which was already making the cook a significant society figure in Menander's comedies, were obvious opportunities, not to mention the jewellery or silver plate or ostentatious grave monuments of which some examples still survive. Also socially embedded, and yet also investments of a different kind, were public gifts such as this one saluted in a deme decree:

Gods. Theodelos moved; resolved by the Sounians, with good fortune, whereas Leukios is giving to the demesmen (the means) to make an *agora* (assembly-market place), choose at once three men, who will define the space of the *agora* with Leukios at not less than two *plethra* in one direction, or than one *plethron* in the other direction, so that there shall be plenty of room for the Sounians and anyone else who wishes to use the *agora*, since the present one has become crowded. To build over it is not permitted, neither for the demarch nor for anyone else within the markers. The demarch is to inscribe this decree on a stone pillar, in collaboration with Leukios, and set it up in the *agora*. (*IG* ii² 1180)

Generosity such as Leukios's had a name of its own – *philotimia* or 'love of honour' – and had long been to some degree codified and channelled officially into the system of liturgies, whereby the richest citizens were expected to meet the costs of commissioning and commanding a warship for a year, or those of producing a play or training a team for a dramatic or athletic or musical contest at a festival such as the Dionysia or the Lenaia (see p. 97 above). In the absence of any preponderant or reliable public reserve of money, amassed from subject allies or from booty, these roles, and the need which they reflected to tap private wealth, gave the wealthy rather greater political and social power than they had had in the second half of the fifth century. It was a diffused power – one should not readily invoke theories of a conspiracy of the rich against the poor or against the state – but just for that reason it was hard for the state as such to neutralize it or to concentrate and mobilize resources independently.

Such considerations bring us to the third theme of this chapter, that of power. The fifth century had seen a concentration of power, within the Aegean context at Athens, within Athens in the Assembly and its feeder institutions, and within the Assembly with the orators and the populist politicians. By the mid-fourth century its location has to be analysed slightly differently, not because of the erosion of empire, but as a result of internal processes.

Those processes stemmed essentially from the traumatic events of 404/3, which had left Athenians determined not to allow anyone to exercise concentrated non-accountable power as the Thirty Tyrants had done. A thoroughgoing revision of the lawcode in 403/399 had been the first consequence, designed among other things to ensure that the powers and duties of magistrates were clearly specified. A second move was to extend the principle of pay for performing public duties to attendance at the Assembly, in order presumably to ensure that attendance would be high enough to discourage political ambushes or nominally legal *coups d'etat*. A third, more long-term consequence, visible throughout the fourth century, was a subtle change in the relationship between Assembly and lawcourts. It came to be as much in the lawcourts as in the Assembly that quarrels between politicians, and even debates over national policy and direction, were acted out. Apollodoros' battles with Stephanos, noted above (p. 217), are minor examples among many others known, while the two great set-piece confrontations between Aeschines and Demosthenes in 343 (Demosthenes 19 vs Aeschines 2, *On the False Embassy*) and in 330 (Demosthenes 18 *On the Crown* vs Aischines 3, *Against Ktesiphon*) probably survived just because they showed how decisive for the reputation and authority of politicians such contests within the framework of a court hearing could be.

However, the prominence of such cases has aroused scholarly debate. The argument has been whether they reflected a deliberately enhanced role for the courts at the expense of the Assembly, and if so whether they indicated a movement away from the views of a (radical?) Assembly towards those of older (thirty was the minimum age) and perhaps more conservative juries. The idea is tempting but should probably be resisted. There was nothing very new in such cases, for fifth-century Athenian history is littered with court cases involving senior politicians. Nor do surviving speeches in court cases suggest any difference in tone when compared with surviving Assembly speeches, so the supposed greater conservatism of juries is probably imaginary. What is true is that in private as in public cases juries were judges of persons as well as of facts. Their oath might indeed run

> I will cast my vote in consonance with the laws and with the decrees passed by the Assembly and by the Council, but, if there is no law, in consonance with my sense of what is most

just, without favour or enmity. I will vote only on the matters
raised in the charge, and I will listen impartially to assusers and
defenders alike.

(summary from Demosthenes 24. 149–151 and other sources)

However, surviving speeches make it clear that litigants did
appeal to prejudice and did cite their own civic virtues and
their opponents' vices, while jurors were correspondingly swayed
by considerations of public policy and affected in their verdicts
the relative status in society of the litigants appearing before
them. The safest view is to see Assembly and courts after 403
not as rivals but as Siamese twins, used as the joint conduits
of public opinion, reinforcing each other and defending each
other's powers and integrity against real or imagined encroach-
ment.

Even so, such developments help to reveal the basic underlying
process: power was being diffused more broadly through the
political system. Three further phenomena may serve to illustrate
it. The first of them is the re-emergence from the late 350s
onwards of the council of ex-archons, the Areiopagos, from
obscurity to become a significant presence in politics, invoked and
respected in a way it had not been for a hundred years (see
Chapter IV). Historians have found its re-emergence very hard
to explain. The impetus behind it may have been conservative,
articulated by one of Isokrates' pamphlets a few years before, but
its effect was not noticeably so, but rather to create a third focus
for civic opinion and thereby to assist the process of diffusion of
power.

The second aspect of diffusion was the reluctance of the citizen
body to accord to any single politician the sort of authority which
a Kimon or a Perikles or even a Kleon had had. It was not for
lack of ability or ambition, for Athenian politics engendered an
endless series of skilled and ruthless professionals. In part,
admittedly, their own competitiveness and sporting tactics played
a part, for they repeatedly prosecuted each other, in person or
through agents, on charges which could, and sometimes did, lead
to exile or a swingeing fine on conviction. In part, too, their
corruptibility encouraged distrust, for few of them resisted the
opportunities for bribery or embezzlement. More important,

however, was a growing specialization, which by 360 had made it rare for an orator to be elected as general or for a military man to be in the first rank of Assembly-based politicians. The partnerships between a general and a politician which can occasionally be detected were a way of overcoming that split, but they rendered each partner that much less a commanding figure on his own. In any case a politician's prestige was precarious. He might attract younger associates to devil for him, as Stephanos did for Kallistratos in the 360s (p. 218 above), but they could be fairweather friends in a climate where a politician was only as influential as his most recent speech and where there were no parties or ministerial teams to tide him over a bad patch.

To this picture there is one major apparent exception. Part of the reaction to Athens' defeat in the Social War (p. 208 above) in 355 and to an accompanying collapse in public revenues was to concentrate more power over financial administration in a single office. At first an expedient, run (bizarrely) from the margin by those responsible for using surplus revenue to subsidize the cost of theatre tickets, but after 337/6 turned into a long-term office, the 'Person in charge of the (financial) administration', it gave at least some of the politicians involved – Diophantos, Euboulos, Lykourgos – some real continuity in office and a corresponding influence. Nonetheless, public wariness could lead to such power being dismantled, as the first version was by a law of 337/6. Paradoxically, therefore, the chief effect of the emergence of this 'Finance Minister' role was to create yet another separate power-focus and thereby to diffuse authority even more widely.

To broach such changes in offices and their powers is to broach the third, most pervasive, and deepest-rooted of the three phenomena of diffusion, namely the multiplicity of officials and magistrates. Here above all the information provided by the *Athenian Constitution* is seminal, for in its second half its author gives us a catalogue of public officials and their responsibilities. He begins with the registration and training of citizens (ch. 42), and then describes the Council of 500 (43–9), the officials appointed annually by lot (50–4), the Archons proper (55–9), the athlothetai and the military officials (60–1), before describing in detail the manning and working of the jury-courts (63–9). It is not a complete survey, and it has its oddities, such as the lack of any sections specifically on the Assembly or the Areiopagos. However, by combining its information with that of contemporary inscriptions and speeches and with some knowledge preserved in later antiquarian writing, something approaching a complete list of Athenian magistrates and other public offices in the period 350–320 can be created. What follows is that list. It looks remorseless, and the faint-hearted reader may skip it, but at the cost of ignoring something unique in classical antiquity and of losing the detailed picture of what Athenians of that epoch thought required public administration and control.

The biggest single group were the five hundred Members of Council, holding office (like nearly all others to be mentioned) for an Athenian year running from July to July. Besides them stood the more specialized officials. Financial and administrative posts included the Sellers (10), the Receivers (10), the Cavalry Registrars (10), the Auditors (10), the Auditors' Advocates (10), the Superintendents of the Mint (10), the debt-extractors (10?), those in charge of the theatre-ticket monies (perhaps 10, later 1), the treasurers of the military fund (1), of the Council (1), and of the People (1), the secretaries for the prytany (1), for the laws (1), for the decrees (1), and of the Assembly (1), two other secretaries called the Anagrapheus and the Antigrapheus (2), the archon to Salamis and the demarch to Peiraieus (2): total for this sector at least 91. Public utilities and amenities required the City-wardens (10, 5 for Peiraieus, 5 for Athens City), the Market-wardens (again 5+5), the Measures-wardens (again 5 + 5), the Corn-wardens (10), later raised to 35 during the corn shortage of the 320s), the Overseers of the (corn-)exchange (at Peiraieus) (10), the road-builders (5), and the Overseer of springs (1): total 56, later 82. Legal officials included the Forty (local judges) (40), the Eleven (gaolers/executioners) (11), the Archons and Secretary (10), the Maritime judges (10), the Introducers (of Lawsuits) (5), and the Guardians of the Laws (7 or 11): total over 80.

The administration of shrines and festivals was another heavily manned area. We know of the Treasurers of the Sacred Objects of Athene (10), the Treasurers of the Other Gods (10, a separate office only from 386/5 till 347/6 in the fourth century), the Repairers of shrines (10), the Hieropoioi in charge of expiatory sacrifices (10), the Festival-organizing Hieropoioi (10), the Overseers of the

Dionysia festival (10), the athlothetai for the Panathenaia festival (10), the Overseers of the shrine of Amphiaraos (10), the Hieropoioi for the Panathenaia (number unknown), the Superintendents from the Brauron shrine (3 or more), from the Eleusis shrine (7), of the shrine of Asklepios (number unknown), and of the shrine of Good Fortune (number unknown), the Amphictyones sent to Delos (5), the Overseers for the Mysteries (4), the Hieropoioi for the Dread Goddesses (the Eumenides) (3, later 10), the Buyers of sacrificial animals (number unknown), the Treasurers for the Two Goddesses (Demeter and Persephone) (2), and the Holy Remembrancer (delegate to the Amphictyonic Council at Anthela or Delphi) (1): total at least 105.

Lastly, the military officials, who included the Generals (10), the tribal regimental commanders (10) who appointed the company commanders (number unknown, but presumably a multiple of 10), the overseers of the dockyards (10), the cavalry commanders (2), the cavalry squadron commanders (10), the cavalry commander for Lemnos (1), the treasurers for the dockyards (1), of riggings (1), and of the trireme-builders (1), the stewards of the State galleys *Paralos* and *Ammon* (2), and the officers of the cadet force (at least 13): total probably *c.* 100.

The total so far is some 832, but we cannot stop there. The 6000 jurors enrolled each year were filling another sort of office, paid from public funds like most of those listed above. Local government will have added at least another 200, for each of the over 150 demes had a demarch, and many are known to have had other officials as well, while the ten tribes each had three overseers. Then there were the priests and priestesses (some of whom were publicly appointed officials), the heralds, the arbitrators, the trierarchs, and the choregoi, not to mention *ad hoc* appointees such as wall-builders, delegates for temple-building in Delphi or Delos, or envoys, who were all publicly appointed and accountable. Granted, there will have been some overlaps, though there were rules against holding two posts at national level at once: some boards of ten did not always have a full membership: and some of the boards or posts may have been subgroups of Council rather than independent appointments. As against which, other sets of officials may yet emerge from inscriptions which await discovery. All in all, it is impossible to avoid the conclusion that in any one year in the mid-fourth century BC 6000 Athenians were serving as jurors and over a thousand others were holding an accountable public post of some kind – altogether about one-third of the citizen body. Aristotle's definition of 'the virtue of a citizen of repute' as 'just this – to be able to rule and be ruled well' (*Politics* iii 4) reflected the reality of active participation in government at this stupendous level.

Even if we leave the six thousand jurors aside, the extreme fragmentation of the political and administrative process is palpable. One asks why. In a sense it made for efficiency, for though all concerned were answerable to Council and Assembly, or ultimately to the courts, practicality dictated a devolution to bodies with much day to day autonomy. Moreover, though change and reform did occur, the system was largely stable, so that people knew by custom and practice what the jobs involved before they took them on. As an exasperated Demosthenes asked the Assembly in 352/1,

> Yet why is it, do you suppose, that the festivals of the Panathenaea and the Dionysia always take place at the correct time, whether the task of managing them is allotted to experts or laymen – and these are things which run into greater expense than any military expedition, and probably demand greater trouble and preparation than anything else at all – whereas our expeditions are invariably too late, like the ones to Methone or Pagasae or Potidaea? The reason is that the festivals are regulated by law. Everyone knows long beforehand who is to head the tribe in the theatre or the games, and when he is to receive what from whom, and what he is to do. Nothing is left vague and unspecified there. But in the military field and in preparation for it there is no order, no organization, no precise control. (Demosthenes 4. 35–36)

Perhaps deliberately, Demosthenes misses the point. The object of the system was not so much efficient government as to pare back to an irreducible minimum the power of the individual magistrate – a power which was seen as essentially oligarchic. For a century and more the impetus had been to replace single posts by committees, to break power down into small circumscribed components, to create groups with overlapping responsibilities so that they could check each other (so that it is very hard to work out, for example, who exactly ran the Panathenaia), and to subordinate them all firmly to Council and Assembly. The cost, inevitably, was a risk of rigidity, of slowness to adapt, and of compartmentalization.

The literal cost was also relevant, for many if not most of these posts – though not, significantly, the military commands – were paid, at varying daily rates. Guesstimates that Council, Assembly, jurors, and paid officials together cost c. 100 talents annually are at least of the right order, though precision is out of reach. As in the fifth century, such public pay had two main objectives. It allowed the poor to participate in executive power without loss of earnings and, even more important, it went some way to preventing patronage relationships reasserting themselves and forcing the poor to become the clients or even the debtbondsmen of the rich. Once again, the purpose was social rather than administrative, negative as much as positive, conservative rather than radical.

For all these reasons, it would be misleading to see the shape and evolution of the fourth-century Athenian polity as a movement away from the fifth-century ideal of the sovereignty of the people. On the contrary, its main feature aimed to preserve it against what was most feared: by diffusing power among several collective institutions and numerous administrative boards, in order to minimize its concentration in any individual's hands; by enforcing accountability for his acts from anyone holding an executive or administrative or financial role; by allowing 'anyone who wishes' to challenge an act of a public entity or an individual in post or even the mover of an Assembly motion; and by reasserting the primacy of publicly displayed statute law while discouraging its alteration. In these ways Athenians sought to protect constitutional stability while not precluding essential innovation.

The objectives were achieved, but at a price. By trimming the claims of any one body to be 'the government', they made it harder to evolve continuous policy in the way a government could do. By eroding the stability of any individual's influence, they hampered any style of proactive leadership from re-emerging. By protecting the existing boundaries of the citizen society, they ruled out amalgamation, or the demographically significant incorporation of non-citizens, as possible expedients to strengthen Athens' position in the international power game. Yet, particularly after the collapse of Sparta in the 360s and the eclipse of Thebes in the 350s, Athens became by default the one mainland state large enough and powerful enough to continue as a real potential power centre. It was Athens' singular misfortune to have rebuilt the defences of her political society after 403 so as to face in what proved to be the wrong direction. The real disruptive threat came not from a potential tyrant within but from actual rulers without – opportunists like Mausollos of Karia, 'the person who instigated and persuaded' Athens' Aegean allies to revolt (Demosthenes 15.3). His role, and that of other rulers and would-be rulers on the fringes of Greece, in eroding the position of the traditional powers and in creating new patterns in their stead, now needs to be traced in more detail.

XIII

The Opportunists

GREEK HISTORY from 360 till 336 is often seen in terms of Philip of Macedon and written round him. There is reason in this, for from the late 350s onwards he became a central figure, politics in the 340s did polarize round him, and in 338 he did forcibly bring mainland Greece under his control in a way which his heirs and successors and Macedonian kings managed to maintain till the early second century BC. However, others too as monarchs or quasi-monarchs used the techniques pioneered by Dionysios to move opportunistically into the gaps left by the interaction, spoiling, and internal contradictions of the major powers (including Persia) and to create principalities for themselves. Their ambitions varied, as did their abilities and circumstances, but their basic family likeness justifies treating them as a group and treating Philip as one of them. The major problem of interpretation is to explain why Philip was the most successful of them.

We must begin in Thessaly (Map 5), which nearly became a major power in the 370s and 360s. To trace and explain how is not easy, for virtually all who wrote about Thessalian affairs were outsiders, inscriptions are few and terse, and the biographical tradition gives us only some anecdotes about the military men in Polyaenus' *Stratagems* and a lurid description of the tyrants of Pherae in Plutarch's *Pelopidas*. The only other useful document is a pamphlet of some seven pages. *On the Constitution*, preserved to us as the work of a millionaire Sophist in Athens in the second century AD but generally agreed to have written in fact in 401 BC for a political crisis in the city of Larisa. As so often, the material is enough to suggest the general lines of events without much precision or analysis.

In the sixth century BC Thessaly as a cohesive unit had been the major power of Northern Greece, controlling Phocis and part of Boeotia, ally of Athens, and powerful at Delphi. The instruments of cohesion consisted of an elective king, the *Tagos*, of a formalized division of the country into four regions, or Tetrarchies, and of some sort of national military levy. The system was conceived in terms of an aristocracy owning vast landed estates, able to call upon the agricultural and military services of serfs, and electing to the kingship from among themselves. The last known *Tagos*, Daochos I of Pharsalus, held office during the Peloponnesian War. He kept his country out of the war, and was commemorated by his grandson Daochos II at Delphi with a statue and the epigram 'I am Daochos son of Hagias of Pharsalus, I ruled all of Thessaly for twenty-seven years, not by force but by law, and Thessaly teemed with much peace and wealth of produce' (*SIG* 273, no. 6). However, our other evidence suggests that Thessaly was breaking apart. Rivalry among the great families played some part, as did the attractions of the city-state pattern farther south, which pointed towards political units much smaller than the geographical expression which Thessaly was becoming. Still another factor must have been external inter-ference. Larisa in the north, with its noble family the Aleuadai, always looked to Macedon for help in time of trouble, and the pamphlet *On the Constitution* tells us that by 401 King Archelaos of Macedon had become a citizen, imposed a garrison, taken hostages, and controlled the mountain border zone of Perrhaebia to the north. Correspondingly Pharsalus in the south tended to look towards Athens for much of the fifth century, though intermittent Athenian diplomacy and expeditions achieved little. However, from the 420s onwards the main external influence was Sparta. Her foundation of Heraclea in 426 gave her effective control of the Spercheios valley to the south. The gist of the pamphlet *On the Constitution* is the need to accept a Spartan offer to expel Archelaos from Larisa. Pharsalus had a Spartan garrison by 395. Lykophron, the dynast of the third major town, Pherae, by the turn of the century seems to have followed a pro-Spartan line. Thessalian cavalry willingly joined a Spartan expedition against Olynthus in May 381.

By 375, however, Spartan influence was being challenged by

one Iason, the son and successor of Lykophron as tyrant
of Pherae. He emerges without warning in the narrative of
Xenophon, who makes a rival pro-Spartan politician, Polydamas
of Pharsalus, go to Sparta in 375 and ask for help against Iason.
According to Polydamas, Iason had said to him

'Polydamas, whether your city liked it or not, I could still bring
it over to my side, as you can see for yourself, if you look at
these facts. I have as my allies most of the cities of Thessaly and
these include the most powerful ones . . . You know too, I
imagine, that I have a foreign mercenary army of up to 6,000
men. In my opinion there is no city which would find it at all
easy to face this army in battle . . . No one serves in my
mercenary army unless he can stand physical hardship as well
as I can myself.' And he himself – for I must tell you the truth –
not only has a magnificent physique but enjoys putting it to the
test. In fact, he tries out his own men every day, marching at
their head in full armour whether on the parade ground or on a
campaign. Any mercenary troops of his whom he finds slack,
he gets rid of, but when he sees men who are fond of hardship
and fond of the dangers of war, he rewards and honours them,
doubling, trebling and quadrupling their pay, giving them
special gifts, and also medical attention when they are ill and
every mark of distinction when they are buried. The result is
that all the mercenaries in his service know that good conduct
in war will guarantee them a life full of honour in which they
will lack for nothing. 'And so,' he said, 'what have I to fear? . . .
Indeed, people who do not know me might reasonably wonder
why I am not marching against Pharsalus at this moment. The
reason of course, is that I think it is in every way better to have
your voluntary, rather than forced, cooperation. If I were
joined by Pharsalus and all the cities dependent upon you, I
should have no difficulty in becoming *Tagos* of all Thessaly;
also, when there is a *Tagos* of Thessaly, he can call on a cavalry
force of 6,000 and a hoplite army of more than 10,000. And
when I see the physique of these men and their fine spirit, I
think that, if these men were properly led, there is no race on
earth to whom the Thessalians would think it right to defer . . .
It is from Macedonia that the Athenians get their timber, and,

with Macedonia under our control, we shall clearly be able to build many more ships than they can. And as for manning these ships, it seems reasonable to suppose that here, too, we, with our large population of first-rate serfs, will be in a better position than the Athenians. The same is true with regard to supplying the crews. Is it not likely that we, who have so much corn that we export it abroad, shall be better able to do this than the Athenians, who have not even enough for themselves unless they buy it elsewhere? Financially, too, it seems clear that we shall be in the stronger position; we do not look to wretched little islands for our revenues but can draw upon the races of a continent; for, once there is a *Tagos* of Thessaly, all the peoples around us pay tribute. And I am sure you know that the reason why the king of Persia is the richest man on earth is that he gets his revenue from a continent and not from islands. Yet I think that it would be easier to subdue him than to subdue Greece. For I know that in Persia everybody except for one man is educated to be a slave rather than to stand up for himself, and I know to what extremities the King was brought by comparatively small forces – the one that marched with Cyrus and the one with Agesilaos.'

Polydamas ended by warning the Spartans that Iason's generalship

is of the highest quality – one who, whether his methods are those of plain force, of working in the dark, or of seizing an unexpected advantage, very seldom fails to achieve his objects. He can use the night-time as well as the day-time and when he wants to move fast, he will put breakfast and dinner into one meal so as not to interrupt his work. He will not think it right to rest until he has reached the point for which he set out and done all that had to be done. And he has trained his men to behave in the same way, although he also knows how to gratify the feelings of his soldiers when they have won some success as the results of extra hard work. So all who follow him have learned this too – that one can have a good time also, if one works for it. Then, too, he is more self-controlled than any man I know with regard to all bodily pleasures. These never take up his time and prevent him from doing what has to be done. Now, then, I ask you to consider this question and to tell me, as is your duty, both what you will be able to do and what you intend to do. (Xenophon, *Hellenika* 6. 1. 4–16, with omissions)

The Spartans did not help Polydamas, Iason became *Tagos*, reunified Thessaly, organized a national army, and allied with Athens (probably) and Thebes (certainly). After Leuctra the Thebans asked for his help against Sparta, but by choosing rather to counsel both sides in their own (and his) best interests, he emerged as the potential arbiter of Greece. In winter 371–70 'because of his superior shrewdness as a general and his bringing many of the dwellers-round into alliance, he persuaded the Thessalians to bid for the leadership of Greece; for this was a sort of prize for valour open to those able to contend for it. The Spartans had met a great disaster at Leuctra, the Athenians only claimed leadership at sea, the Thebans did not deserve a leading position, and the Argives had been brought down by internal conflicts and civil wars' (Diodorus 15. 60. 1–2). Xenophon tells us more:

Now when the time of the Pythian festival (of 370) was approaching Iason sent round to his cities orders for them to produce cattle, sheep, coats and swine for the sacrifice. It is said that the contributions required of each city were very moderate, and yet that no less than 1000 cattle and more than 10,000 of the other animals were brought in. He also proclaimed an offer of a crown of gold as prize to the city which raised the finest bull to lead the procession in honour of the god. And he ordered the Thessalians to be ready to take the field at the time of the Pythian festival. His intention, so they say, was to take personal charge both of the religious assembly and of the games. However, to this day no one knows what his intentions were with regard to the sacred treasure. It is said that when the people of Delphi asked the god what they should do if he tried to take any of this treasure, Apollo answered that he would look after that matter himself. (*Hellenika* 6. 4. 29–30)

The two authors here have different approaches and different information, but the underlying pattern, Iason's cool and determined opportunism, is unmistakable.

It got no further because he was murdered. Macedon moved in from the north, the Thebans from the south, and under Theban influence constitutional government was largely re-established. All the same, Iason's aborted essay in nation-building is important. Xenophon's portrait shows us a charismatic mercenary leader, energetic in public business and self-restrained in private life, altogether very like Dionysios. Yet whereas Dionysios had started as a leader of citizen troops, only to dispense with them in favour of mercenaries as soon as possible, Iason on the contrary, as his preparations for the Pythia show, was moving towards creating a national citizen army. He could move that way because Thessalian society had what Syracusan society did not, a monarchic role recognized and sanctioned by custom, tradition and national mythology. His death, and the honouring of his murderers as tyrannicides, left it quite unclear whether such a role could be modernized and its potential realized, or whether straight reliance on mercenaries was enough by itself.

In the eastern end of the Greek world Dionysios-style dynasts multiplied after the 380s. Their emergence is readily explained. After 387–6 the terms of the King's Peace (p. 150 above) precluded Athens from re-establishing such stability as her fifth-century presence had afforded: Persian control over the coast and hinterland of Asia Minor fragmented in the 370s (see p. 243 below): and centuries of external domination of the coastal cities – by Lydia, Persia, Athens, Sparta, then Persia again – had left them ill-equipped, in terms of military punch or social cohesion, to fend for themselves. Such a power-vacuum created opportunities.

The tensions are illustrated by the tyranny we know most about in the area, at Heraclea on the southern coast of the Black Sea (see Map 2). Our information comes from two main sources. One is a summary, made by one Justin in the third century AD of a world history, the *Philippic Histories* written in the Augustan period by a Romanized Gaul Pompeius Trogus. Trogus devoted part of his Book 16 to the first tyrant, Klearchos, from his *coup d'état* in 364–3, and Justin gives us the gist in three pages. The second

source is also a summary, made by the Patriarch Photius shortly
before AD 858, of a history of Heraclea written by a local man,
Memnon, at an unknown date after 83 BC: by good fortune what
survived for Photius to boil down took up the story more or less
where Trogus' Book 16 ended. Justin gives Trogus' narrative of
the coup in 364–3 thus:

Among many other misfortunes they also suffered a tyranny.
The people were violently demanding a remission of debts and
the redistribution of the lands of the rich. The matter was long
debated in the Council but no solution was found. At length,
faced with a populace petulant with excessive leisure, the
councillors sought help from the Athenian and Theban
generals Timotheos and Epameinondas. Since both refused,
they had recourse to Klearchos, whom they had themselves
exiled; the crisis was so pressing that they called on a man to
protect the country which they had denied him. However, exile
had made Klearchos readier to commit evil. Taking civil war as
an opportunity to establish a tyranny, he first negotiated
secretly with Mithridates, the city's enemy, and agreed to
betray the city to him after his own return and hold power as
Mithridates' agent. Afterwards, however, he used against
Mithridates the trap he had made for the citizens. When he had
come back from exile as the arbitrator of the civil war, he
agreed a time at which he was to surrender the city to
Mithridates, but then took him and his friends prisoner,
releasing them for a vast ransom. Just as he had been ally
turned enemy to Mithridates, so from being protector of the
councillors' interests he suddenly came out as patron of the
people. Not only did he rouse the people against those who had
given him his power, recalled him, and installed him on the
Akropolis, but he also practised the most unspeakable kind of
tyrannical cruelty. He summoned the people to Assembly and
said he would no longer support a Council which acted against
the people, and would stop it if its members continued their
original savagery. If they, the people, reckoned themselves to
be as brutal as the councillors, he would leave with his soldiers
and withdraw from the civil war. If however they distrusted
their own resources, he would not fail to champion the people.

They should decide for themselves whether to tell him to go or, if they preferred, to have him stay as ally of the people's cause. Roused by his speech, the people conferred full powers on him and in their anger against the power of the Council put themselves and their wives and children under the yoke of a tyrant's domination. Klearchos arrested and imprisoned sixty of the Council (the others had fled). The people were delighted to see the Council destroyed by the Council's general, the instrument of the Council's protection turned round to attack it. The people threatened all the councillors with death. This raised their price, for Klearchos took vast bribes, as if for removing them secretly from the people's threats, stripped them of their property and then of their lives. (Justin, *Epitome of Trogus* 16. 4. 1–20)

The value of this narrative is partly historiographical, because Trogus/Justin and Memnon/Photius between them give us the only surviving example of the genre of local histories of particular towns or regions, which formed a major component of Greek historical writing at all periods. Mainly, though, its value is to show us, informatively enough in spite of the rhetoric and the upper-class anti-tyrant bias, the ingredients of turmoil and revolution: an intransigent upper class entrenched in power and landownership but militarily helpless; popular demands for lands, power and revenge; the inability of Thebes or Athens to intervene; the availability of a man whom we know from other references to have been already an experienced mercenary leader; his willingness to exploit the opportunity by double-crossing both ally and employers and to appeal for a 'popular mandate'; and his readiness to extort the money he needed to pay his troops. Klearchos lasted ten years. A pupil of Plato murdered him in 353–2, which was futile, for his dynasty lasted till 289–8. With him the inheritance from Dionysios was explicit. He called one of his sons Dionysios (the other, equally pointedly, Timotheos); in public 'a gold eagle was carried in front of him as a sign of rank, he wore the purple robe and buskins of kings in tragedy along with a golden crown' (Justin, *Epitome of Trogus*, 16. 5. 9–10) (cf. p. 195 above). He trumped Dionysios by calling himself son of Zeus and giving his son Zeus' title Thunderbolt. He had been a pupil of

Plato, and of Isokrates for four years: Isokrates was rather ashamed of him.

Farther south, in Caria and Lycia (Map 6), a principality of a rather different type emerged. It was nominally a satrapy, or province, of the Persian Empire, but the 370s, 360s and 350s saw the western provinces of the Empire involved in a series of disorders known collectively as the satraps' revolt. Few movements of Mediterranean history have been so important, but so badly documented. We know about it only from Plutarch's biography of King Artaxerxes II, from the brief biography by Cicero's contemporary Nepos of one of the chief participants, Datames, and from some brief references in Greek historians to individual incidents. The material does not even give us a chronology, much less a narrative or an analysis; all we can divine are the main structural features. In part it was a succession crisis, for Artaxerxes II was 94 when he died, late in 359, and rivalries within and outside the royal house were blatant and brutal. In part it was a military crisis, for the recruitment of effective troops to the armies which had built the Empire had broken down, for reasons still far from clear, and Greek troops were expensive. It may also have been a crisis of nationalisms, as some of the various erstwhile states or ethnic groupings submerged within the Empire, such as Egypt or the Kurds, strove to recover their independence.

However, we cannot certainly detect this last element in Caria, even though the satrapy was held by successive members of a local family from its creation in the 390s till Alexander's conquest. What we can see, rather, are their answers to the challenge of the satraps' revolt (Do we join?) and to the opportunity (How do we exploit it?). Their response to the former cannot be traced in detail, but seems to have amounted to doing the minimum necessary to stay on the winning side. The second question is easier to tackle, because the evidence goes well beyond the miserable literary record to include over 30 inscriptions (some very informative), coins, and a major programme of buildings of all kinds. Some of these last consisted of temples, gateways, houses, statues, etc., in local sanctuaries, transforming them into complexes of recognizably Greek style and proclaiming the satraps' names via dedicatory inscriptions in Greek. Other surviving ruins scattered through Caria are of town fortifications, many of them uniform in style. They are not all closely datable in the fourth century, but it does look as if they reflect a deliberate plan to create in Caria a network of small urbanized communities, Greek in outward appearance. Confirmation comes if we regard as the complement of this plan the creation of a capital, and that at least can be dated. 'Of the eight cities (on the peninsula of Halicarnassus) Maussollos united six into one city, Halicarnassus, as Kallisthenes tells us, but kept Syangela and Myndos as they were' (Strabo, *Geography* 13. 1. 59). We are in the 360s or the 350s, the Maussolleion (p. 165 above) is this ruler's monument, and he himself is the central figure of the dynasty. Within Caria itself the documents show him reorganizing festivals, getting the communities under his control to honour some men, and to punish others for revolting against him. Further afield he makes treaties, bribes Greek politicians, foments revolts against Athens (p. 213 above), extends control over nearby islands, and casts eyes over Crete:

> Resolved by Maussollos and Artemisie: whereas the men of Cnossos both privately and publicly always are good men concerning Maussollos and Maussollos' affairs, they are to be *proxenoi* and benefactors for ever. They are also to have immunity from taxation in whatever lands Maussollos rules, and the right of entering and leaving ports inviolably and without truce. If anyone does wrong to Cnossians, Maussollos and Artemisie are to see to it that they shall not suffer wrong, so far as is in their power. (J. Crampa, *Labraunda* III, 2: *The Greek Inscriptions* no. 40)

This document, standard in it phraseology, shows him and his sister/wife behaving as a one-household Greek city. However, another startling document, recently discovered at Xanthos in Lycia, gives a different slant. It is in three languages, Greek, Lycian, and Aramaic. The Greek text runs:

> Whereas Pixodaros son of Hekatomnos has become satrap of Lycia, he appointed as rulers of Lycia Hieron and Apollodotos,

and as governor of Xanthos Artemelis. The Xanthians and the dwellers-round resolved to set up an altar to the Kaunian King and to Arkesimas and chose as priest Simias son of Kondorasis and whoever may be closest (by birth) to Simias for ever, and they gave him exemption from taxes for his property, and the city gave the land which Kesindelis and Pigres worked, and what is next to the land, and the habitations, to belong to the Kaunian King and to Arkesimas, and three half-mnai are to be given each year from the city's funds, and all who become freedmen are to pay two drachmai to the god, and all that has been inscribed on the pillar has been consecrated to belong to the Kaunian King and Arkesimas, and (from) whatever produce there may be from this a sheep is to be sacrificed every new moon and an ox every year; and the Xanthians and the dwellers-round swore oaths to perform all that is inscribed on the pillar for these gods and the priest, and not to alter anything or to permit it to another; and if anyone should alter it, let him be a sinner before these gods and Leto, her children, and the Nymphs. Let Pixotaros have the power to enforce. (*SEG XXVII* 942).

The Lycian text is virtually identical, but the Aramaic text is not:

In the month Siwan of year One of King Artaxerxes, in the citadel of Orna, Pixodara son of Katomno, the satrap who is in Karka and Termila, has spoken: The citizens of Orna have proposed to establish a cult in honour of the Lord the God Kaunos and of R[–]. And they have made priest Simias son of Koddorasi. And there is a tract of land which the citizens of Orna have given to the Lord the God. And year by year on the city's part is paid in silver a mna and a half. The said priest sacrifices a sheep at the start of the month to the Lord the God and to R[–], and year by year an ox. And the said land is left as his property.

This law (Pixodara) has written up to be observed (?). And if anyone removes (a provision) sworn to the Lord the God or to the priest in office may he be destroyed by the Lord the God of Kaunos and by Tehom! And may the guilty man be destroyed by the God and by Lato and by Artemis and by Hsatrapati and others! And may those gods demand (expiation) from him! (*ibid* p. 136–7).

The facts and problems, many as yet unsolved, presented by this document reinforce the impression that something new is being created, both as a culture and as a political entity, which is Greek in apparatus but owes nothing whatever to the republican rigmaroles of mainstream Greek political thinking. As satraps, Maussollos and his family filled a traditional role recognized by Greeks as well as by the other nations in the Persian Empire. He could therefore exploit the role's ambiguities and open-endedness. Only in respect of his behaviour *vis-à-vis* the Crown could he be accused of exceeding the powers and prerogatives of a satrap, and there he and his family were very careful indeed. Like Klearchos and unlike Iason, their ambitions seem to have been limited; cautiously but successfully they created a principality.

The opposite happened in Sicily, where Dionysios' empire disintegrated after his death in 367. The catalyst was Dion, a wealthy Syracusan aristocrat who had been both his brother-in-law and his son-in-law via a multiple relationship not uncommon among wealthy Greek families who wanted or needed to keep power and property inside the family circle. Exiled in 366 by Dionysios' son and successor Dionysios II, Dion collected a force of 800 mercenaries from Greece in 357 and after protracted conflict expelled Dionysios II in summer 356. However, by then the conflict had already become three-sided. Dion, now himself 'general with full powers' and backed by mercenaries, is presented as having the confidence especially of the noble and rich and as intending 'to put a curb upon unrestrained democracy, which he did not regard as a constitution at all, but rather as a kind of supermarket of constitutions – to use Plato's phrase – and to introduce a blend of democracy and monarchy on the Spartan and Cretan model. According to this system it is an oligarchy which is in control of affairs and decides the most important issues' (Plutarch, *Dion* 53. 4). Against them and him, popular agitation was pressing for the redistribution of land and houses, while Dionysios II and his brothers and lieutenants made strenuous efforts to recover their position. After Dion's murder in

June 354 a succession of *coups d'état* by the Dionysians and others led by 344 to the break-up of the Empire and to the reassertion of the older patterns of Sicilian disunity (pp. 131ff. and 188 above). Nearly all the Greek cities of Sicily had made themselves independent of Syracuse under mercenary-backed tyrants. At this point

> the Carthaginians appeared with a powerful fleet and hovered off the coasts of Sicily, awaiting their opportunity to invade the island. Their approach struck terror into the Sicilians, and they resolved to send a delegation to Greece and appeal for help to Corinth. This was not only on account of their kinship with the Corinthians and of the many services they had received from them in the past, but because they knew that Corinth had always upheld the cause of freedom, that she detested tyranny, and that she had fought most of her wars – and the greatest ones at that – not to acquire an empire or make herself more powerful, but to defend the liberty of Greece. (Plutarch, *Timoleon* 2. 1–2)

Corinth responded by sending an elderly nonentity, Timoleon, with a force of some 700 men. In autumn 344 he inflicted on Dionysios II what proved to be his final expulsion from Sicily. In the next six years Timoleon managed to depose all the minor tyrants, to inflict a heavy defeat on a much larger Carthaginian army at the River Krimisos in June of (probably) 341, and to re-create Syracuse. The city with a new constitution re-emerged at the head of an alliance of all the Sicilian Greek cities, a massive influx of new colonists repopulated the cities and areas left deserted or underpopulated since the Carthaginian invasions of the 400s, and after Timoleon died, honoured by the Syracusans as their second founder, his settlement and the new prosperity of Greek Sicily continued for nearly a generation.

This bare outline is clear enough, but to penetrate beyond it is ticklish. Apart from Diodorus, we have parallel accounts in the form of *Lives* of Dion and Timoleon by both Plutarch and Nepos as well as a large amount of numismatic and archaeological evidence. Excavation and aerial surveys by Italian archaeologists since World War II have now made available a picture of settlement patterns in Sicily in the period of Timoleon which is far superior to that available for any other area of classical Greek culture. The picture, of reoccupation of sites, re-creation of industry and farming, and the rebuilding of city-walls (Plate 8a), temples and houses so completely confirms the literary record that Plutarch's figure of 60,000 for the total number of new settlers is now thought to be an underestimate, though he quoted it from a Syracusan historian contemporary with events, Athanis. Plainly we have to do not just with small-scale conflicts and power-grabbing but with a major social movement.

Yet the trouble is that the sources write above all in terms of individuals and their motivations. To do so obviously has explanatory value for the adventurers or for Dionysios II, whose evident inability to realign Syracusan public opinion round himself rather than his father was an important historical fact. It also has value for Dion, and not just because he was suspected of seeking tyranny himself. More pertinently, the portrait Plutarch gives us (one of his best) is of a man heavily influenced by Plato to the point both of being a missionary for Platonism in Dionysios II's court in 366 and of casting himself, after his return in 357, via the Syracusan position of 'general with full powers' as a Platonic ruler of distant and unbending rectitude backed by an oligarchic constitution: a role which left him quite unable to make the compromises needed to retain the support of public opinion.

However, such an approach fails with Timoleon, who was not an adventurer or would-be tyrant. The problems here are rather why the Sicilians approached Corinth, why the Corinthians agreed to help, why they chose Timoleon, and why he had such success. Plutarch offers us no serious answers in his *Timoleon*, instead so festooning the narrative with portents and divine assistance that it reads like a bad religious tract.

We therefore need more than an approach in terms of individuals in order to explain Sicilian affairs from the 360s till the 330s. It will not do to invoke the effect of mercenaries, precisely because all parties involved, including the Carthaginians, were using them and were meeting the same problems of paying them and keeping their loyalty. More important is the background of public opinion, influencing and limiting action in two ways. Firstly, it has been plausibly argued that the régime of Dionysios II collapsed so easily partly because the fear of Carthage had attenuated. Timoleon gained his strength, conversely, because that fear had revived by 344, and while he exploited it to create the necessary Greek unity he managed (as Dionysios II had not) to do so through constitutional means of alliance. Secondly, much of the apparent volatility of Syracusan politics in these decades has one focus, the office of 'general with full powers'. It was there in the constitution, it was needed, and it was used repeatedly: Dion held it twice, and though there is no explicit statement Timoleon's acts are intelligible only if he held it too. Yet a man who was felt to be abusing the office could lose public confidence very rapidly and might either be sacked (as happened to Dion) or murdered (as happened to Dion) or find his position totally eroded by the onset of even a minimum force (as happened twice to Dionysios II, to general Greek surprise). In other words, in spite of the achievement of Dionysios I, and unlike Maussollos' position as satrap, the Syracusan office of 'general with full powers' was not one on which a long-term principality could be securely built. Republicanism had too strong a hold.

We must now return to Greece proper, to a region of it – Macedon – where Republicanism had no hold, and to its king Philip, the 'unscrupulous and clever opportunist' (Demosthenes 1. 3) whose success transformed Greek politics. Just because of that success, to describe and interpret his career poses problems of method even more insistently than do the other dynasts described so far in this chapter. This is partly because though we have more evidence it is not easy to handle; partly because we are forced to pose, but have limited means of solving, the problem of whether the drive for expansion in Macedonian society lay with the sovereign or elsewhere; and partly because Philip has to be seen both as a regional dynast, like Iason or Maussollos, and as a national figure moving to occupy various roles in Greek political interaction.

No detailed narrative of Macedonian affairs is possible until Philip's own accession to the throne, at the age of 24, after his brother Perdikkas III had been killed in battle with the Illyrians along with 4000 men. The year was either 360 or 359. In the next year or so pretenders to the throne were dealt with by murder or bribery, the army was pulled into shape, an invasion threatened from Thrace was bought off, and invasions threatened from Illyrians and Paeonians in the north and west were met and smashed in battle. A first incursion into Thessaly probably followed, but the main push till 353 was to detach from Athens and to capture the Greek towns on the Macedonian and Thracian coasts as far as Amphipolis (probably winter 357–6) and Maronea (354). The next round was intervention in Thessaly at the request of the Aleuadai of Larisa against Phocian forces. After initial defeats, by late 352 Philip had *de facto* control of all of Thessaly. Badly documented and vaguely dated campaigns in Illyria, Epirus, Paeonia and Thrace were followed in 349–8 by the capture of Olynthus and the other towns on the Chalcidice peninsulas and their incorporation into Macedonia. Further expansion in eastern Thrace and Euboea, and an intensification of control of Thessaly, were only ineffectively countered by Athens (as at Olynthus), and his war with her since 357–6 ended in summer 346 with a peace and alliance (the so-called Peace of Philokrates) which in effect gav? him these objectives together with control of Phocis and of the Delphian Amphiktyony. For the next few years Macedonian military activity concentrated in the west and north and in eastern Thrace. Philip's bribery, threats of force, and local preferences had some effect in some cities of Peloponnese and western Greece, but the balance remained fluid till 341. However, from then on Macedonian pressure on the towns of Chersonese and Hellespont (hence a threat to Athens' corn supply) and on Euboea and Phocis (hence a threat to Thebes' control of Boeotia) threw many Aegean and mainland states (but not Sparta) into alliance with Athens against Macedon. The allies brought Philip to battle at Chaeronea in autumn 338, but encountered total defeat, leaving Greece at Philip's mercy. A general peace in winter 338–7 and the garrisoning of various strategic places in Greece were followed soon after by the incorporation of most Greek states willy-nilly into an alliance, known to historians as the league of Corinth after its meeting-place near Corinth at the Isthmian sanctuary of Poseidon. In 337 the alliance declared war on Persia and elected Philip as commander-in-chief. Spring 336 saw the first Macedonian forces cross into Asia Minor, but Philip's murder at Pella in July 336 halted the enterprise for two years until Alexander could reimpose Macedonian authority on a resentful but defeated Greece.

Thus a summary of salient events. It depends upon two extant narratives, one by Diodorus in Book 16 and the other in Books 7–9 of Justin; a handful of relevant inscriptions, mostly from Athens; a couple of speeches by Aeschines and a score or so either by Demosthenes or attributed to him; two biographies by Plutarch (of Demosthenes and of the Athenian general and politician Phokion); some pamphlets and letters by contemporary intellectuals; and some other minor biographical material in Polyaenus and elsewhere. As historical material this is all very raw indeed. One problem is chronology. Justin and the biographical and anecdotal tradition give no dates at all, and Diodorus' assignations can be very wayward. For example, he groups in one chapter (16. 8) under the year 358–7 a flashback to the Macedonian victory over Illyria and annexation of territory in (? spring ?) 358, the captures of Amphipolis (winter 357), Pydna (spring 356), and Potideaea (? autumn ? 356), the foundation of the colony of Philippoi north of Kavalla (summer 356), and some sentences of long-term anticipation:

> The gold-mines in the territory of Philippoi were thoroughly paltry and insignificant. By his improvements he expanded them so much that they could bring him a revenue of more than 1000 talents (annually). From these mines he soon amassed a fortune, and because of his supplies of money he soon raised the Macedonian kingdom to great prominence. He minted gold coins, which came to be known as Philippeioi after him, and with them he got together a considerable force of mercenaries and bribed many Greeks to betray their countries. (Diodorus 16. 8. 6–7)

Again, Demosthenes' speeches have proved to be very hard to date precisely, and in any case he was not concerned to narrate events but to instance them in order to persuade, bully, or cajole the Athenians. For instance, defending his whole career in 330 against prosecution by Aeschines, he said, 'I first proposed a delegation to the Peloponnese after Philip's surreptitious inroad there, then to Euboea when he got his hands on it, then the expedition to Oreos which was no longer a mere delegation, then to Eretria, when he established tyrants in the cities there. After this I was responsible for the sending of the forces which saved the Chersonese and Byzantium and our allies there' (18. 79–80). Later in the speech he says that he 'secured assistance for Athens from Euboea, Achaea, Corinth, Thebes, Megara, Leucas and Corcyra' (18. 237), and just afterwards claimed that 'never yet have I returned worsted by Philip's representatives from any delegation on which I have been sent by this country, from Thessaly or Ambracia or Illyria, from the Thracian princes or Byzantion or anywhere else, including the last occasion at Thebes' (18. 244). These passages are important because they give us a basis for tracing Demosthenes' creation in the late 340s of the alliance which fought Philip in 338. However, there were other missions of his which he does not mention; the only certain date comes from an inscription placing an Athenian treaty with one of the Peloponnesial states, Messene, in June 342 (*IG* ii², 225); and the dates, and degree of success of many of these missions, remain uncertain and controversial.

Still, Greek historians are used to living with chronological uncertainty. With accounts of Philip they also have to live with bias. That is obvious with Demosthenes, of course, for his speeches are not such that we can strip off the obloquy and discover straight reportage underneath. Some facts, for example, probably do underlie Demosthenes' comments in 349:

His second anxiety is Thessaly. It is by nature unreliable and it has proved so to everyone. Philip is no exception. Thessaly has passed a resolution to demand the return of Pagasae and prevented the fortification of Magnesia. I have even heard mentioned the proposal to deny him the benefit of open markets and ports, which should supply the general needs of Thessaly and not be appropriated to Macedon. And if he is to be kept from this source of supply, he will be in dire straits for the provisioning of his forces. One must indeed suppose that the peoples of Paeonia and Illyria and the rest would prefer autonomy and freedom to servitude. They are in no habit of submission, and Philip is a harsh master, it is understood. (1. 21–3)

Yet this assessment is fundamentally misguided. It need not have been wishful thinking, but rather a deliberate over-emphasis of reported unrest in order to support the view that Philip was after all vulnerable.

There is bias in the narrative accounts too. Here it is harder to neutralize, for our extant narratives give us not their own bias but that of their ultimate sources in contemporary writers. We know of three main contemporary sources: Ephoros, whose Books 26–30, completed by his son, covered Philip's reign till 341–40; Anaximenes, writing 9 books of *Histories about Philip*; and above all Theopompos, compiling no fewer than 58 books of *Philippika*. The trouble is that we have respectively about 11, about 11 again and about 300 fragments of their histories, and we do not know for certain if they all wrote independently, or influenced each other. Nor can we trace a sure line of descent from them to our extant accounts, though most scholars agree that Diodorus derives from Ephoros at least some of the time, while there is a case for making Theopompos a major source of Justin. To divine how the primary sources saw Philip and interpreted events has therefore to be done mainly from their extant fragments. Only from Theopompos are there enough fragments quoted to allow this, but he emerges (from fragments quoted for their *chiaroscuro*, admittedly) as an idiosyncratic, opinionated, discursive and vitriolic writer whom it would be naive to trust without corroboration.

A third weakness in the material is the concentration on Philip himself. An analysis of Philip in Thessaly runs:

Philip, wanting to get hold of Thessaly, did not make open war on the Thessalians. Since the Pelinnaeans were warring with Pharsalus and the Pheraeans with Larisa, the others taking sides with them, he always came to assist those who asked him in. After a victory he did not make the defeated stateless, did not take away their weapons, did not pull down walls, encouraged political cabals rather than broke them up, protected the weak, destroyed the powerful, was a friend to the common peoples, and cultivated the demagogues. By these means Philip controlled Thessaly, not by force. (Polyaenus 4. 2 19)

This has the great merit of concentrating on political techniques, but even so it is formulated in terms of Philip himself rather than in terms of Thessalian aims and fears, which are logically and chronologically primary to his exploitation of them. Even when the focus moves away from Philip it can be misleading.

Do not imagine for a moment that one and the same set of circumstances bring satisfaction both to Philip and to his subjects. His aim and ambition is glory. His way is the way of action and accepted risk, his goal the greatest renown in the history of the kings of Macedon. He prefers that to safety. But they do not share these ambitions. They are torn by marching from end to end of the country, and reduced to misery and continuous hardships. They are kept from their own pursuits, their personal affairs, and even what opportunities chance allows cannot be organized, because ports in the country are closed by the war. This affords a clear indication of the relation of most of Macedonia towards Philip. (Demosthenes 2. 15–17)

He goes on to be rude about Philip's mercenaries, but that was a game Theopompos could play much better:

If there was any man in Greece or among the barbarians who was perverted or shameless in habits they were all assembled before Philip in Macedon and called Companions of the King. Philip had no respect for men who were self-restrained in habits and cared for their private lives, but he honoured and promoted the extravagants, the alcoholics and the gamblers. So he not only made them like this, but even made them athletes in other wicked and loathsome behaviour. What shameful or frightful quality did they lack, what honourable and earnest quality did they possess? Some, though shaven and smoothed, went on being men, while others though bearded dared to have relations with each other. They would take round two or three male prostitutes, while they themselves performed for others the same services as these performed for them. Wherefore one might justly reckon them not Companions but Companionesses, call them not soldiers but strumpets: they were men-killers by nature but men-kissers by habit. What is more they preferred to be drunk rather than sober, and sought to snatch and kill rather than live decently. To tell the truth and to keep agreements was not for them, they thought, but assumed the right to perjure and cheat in the most sacred matters. They were careless of what they had, and for what they lacked – and that when they owned part of Europe. For I think that the Companions, who were not more than 800 in number at that time, enjoyed the produce of more land than 10,000 owners of the best and most extensive lands in Greece. (Theopompos, *FGH* 115 F 225)

These two passages are important because they miss the point. Only once, so far as we know, did Philip have unrest in his army, in 353 when he led them straight into a Phocian ambush. Otherwise, his supplies of money from Philippoi (p. 251 above), his booty from successful campaigns, or his conquests of territory and assignations of it to his followers, gave all concerned a very strong interest in his success. Drunkards they may well have been, but they were also tough and hardy:

Philip reduced to the ranks Dokimos of Tarentum, who was washing in warm water on campaign. Philip said, 'You don't seem to know Macedonian habits, among whom not even a woman in childbirth washes in warm water.' (Polyaenus 4. 2. 1)

Tough and hardy because they were poor, ruthlessly on the make once they had the necessary cohesion and leadership, Philip's soldiers, both rankers and noblemen, were themselves so much agents of violence and change that we should probably rate their push on Philip as being at least as important as his pull on them.

Here then we can already see Philip combining two roles, as successful mercenary commander and as king of his own nation. The first needs by now no additional commentary, but the second does. Macedon had had kings since about 650 BC, and though there is some evidence that the royal family were interlopers, more Greek than their subjects and themselves originally purely grabbers of land and power, they were accepted and integrated because regional leaders were needed to defend the fertile plain of Macedon against covetous invaders from the sea or from the mountains to the north, east and west. Virtually all the recorded activity of Macedonian kings till 360 – and indeed much of Philip's – consisted of coping with such potential invaders, by force, money, persuasion, marriage, guile, or submission. It was only exceptionally that they could exert real pressure on the Greek coastal towns, as Perdikkas II did in 430–29 (p. 72 above), or could wield effective influence in Thessaly in the way Archelaos was doing in 401 (p. 236 above). The fundamental interpretative problem which therefore arises is whether we can explain Philip's transformation from regional dynast to master of Greece purely in terms of his having been able to add a second role, as mercenary commander, to that of traditional King.

In terms of power the answer is probably yes. Firstly, as Demosthenes said in 349, 'his personal control of all activities, open or secret, his combined position in command of the army, state and exchequer, his invariable presence with his forces, give him a real superiority in military speed and efficiency' (1. 4). Again, just because he *was* the state, there was no such split between the position of constitutional authority and mercenary commander as had occurred in Syracuse or Heraclea. Thirdly, it was as King that he could call upon the military services of a population possibly larger than that of any single city-state (though what hints we have of Macedonian population provoke endless controversy), that he equipped the infantry much as Iphikrates had done (p. 186 above) so as to make them more of a hoplite army than anything Macedon had been able to field previously, and that he trained them in the latest professional techniques. Fourthly, *qua* mercenary commander he had a force available all the year round, while *qua* King he could naturalize his mercenaries by giving them baronies in the conquered territories (cf. what Theopompos said, p. 254 above). The army which Alexander used to cut through Persia was after all Philip's creation, and Philip only ever lost one large engagement.

All the same, power was not all that mattered, nor even

opportunity. Legitimacy mattered too, and we can describe its creation in two ways: by detecting currents of opinion running in his favour, and by identifying the roles available for him to fill. In Thessaly, for example, he became *Tagos* in fact if not in name, by the techniques Polyaenus described (p. 253 above), by helping Thessaly against Phocis, and even by becoming a husband:

> In the 22 years of his reign, as Satyros says in his life of him, he married Audata the Illyrian and had a daughter Kynna by her. He also married Phila the sister of Derdas and Machatas. Wishing to gain the allegiance of Thessaly, he engendered children from two Thessalian women; one was Nikesipolis of Pherae, who bore him Thettalonike, and the other Philinna of Larisa, who bore him Arrhidaios. He also obtained the kingdom of the Molossians by marrying Olympias, by whom he had Alexander and Kleopatra. When he captured Thrace, King Kothelas of Thrace came bringing his daughter Meda and many gifts. He married her too as a wife additional to Olympias. (Athanaeus 13. 556 b–d)

South of Thessaly he could exploit the opportunity offered by the Sacred War. That war had broken out in 356, when the Phocians had been prosecuted by their age-old enemies the Thebans before the council of the Delphic Amphiktyony on a charge of cultivating so-called 'sacred land' in the fertile plain below Delphi. Convicted and fined heavily, the Phocians had seized Delphi. When Thebes and her allies thereupon declared 'holy war', the Phocians intensified their offence by appropriating the treasures of the sanctuary and using the bullion to finance a formidable mercenary force. Since it was an Amphiktyonic affair, much of mainland Greece was involved, and alignments were naturally those current at the time. Against Phocis stood Thebes, most of Central Greece, and Thessaly: behind her stood therefore Sparta, Athens and some Peloponnesians. Neither Athens nor Sparta gave more than intermittent or token help, but for a few years the Phocians dominated the region. They more than held their own against Thebes, successfully invaded Thessaly, and twice in autumn 352 defeated the Macedonian army under Philip. All the same, their predominance rested only on able leadership and on a non-renewable source of money, and when in 346 the Athenians were on the point of leaving them in the lurch by making a separate peace with Philip, the Phocian commander thereupon betrayed his undefeated army to Philip. At that point, since Sparta and Athens had been caught hopelessly on the wrong foot, the weakness of Thebes allowed Philip to take over from Thebes a role as vindicator of the integrity of the Delphic oracle, which went back at least to the early sixth century in Greek religious politics. That role in turn gave Philip after 346 the central position in the Delphic Amphiktyony which Iason almost achieved in 370. Subsequently, it gave Philip considerable influence in various interstate quarrels which came before the Amphiktyonic Council.

Farther south again he could exploit a mood of general disgruntlement with the major powers. A fragment of Theopompos gives us part of a speech he attributed to the Athenian politician Philokrates during the peace negotiations of 346:

> Consider then that this is not the time for heroics and that the city's affairs are in poor shape. We are surrounded by many great dangers. We know that the Boeotians and Megarians are hostile to us, that some Peloponnesians are attracted by Thebes and others by Sparta, and that Chios and Rhodes and their allies are in a state of enmity with the city and are discussing friendships with Philip. (Theopompos, *FGH* 115 F 164)

The wording is no doubt Theopompos' rather than Philokrates', but reports by Demosthenes and Aeschines of what they and others said in 346 during the debates in Athens suggest much the same general drift. Specifically, in Peloponnese Philip could move into the role of guaranteeing local freedoms against Sparta, which Thebes had moved into in 370 but could no longer sustain. The classic statement of his attractiveness in this role comes from a historian writing 200 years after the events, Polybius of Megalopolis. After quoting Demosthenes' speech of 330, in which he had listed the leading pro-Philip politicians in each city and roundly called them all traitors, Polybius protests strongly:

> By bringing Philip into Peloponnese and humbling the

Spartans these men first of all allowed all the inhabitants of Peloponnese to draw breath and think of freedom, and secondly by getting back the lands and the cities which the Spartans during their fortunate times had filched from the Messenians, Megalopolitans, Tegeates and Argives, they strengthened their own countries unambiguously. In return for this it was not their duty to fight Philip and the Macedonians, but to do everything they could which redounded to his credit and honour. (Polybius 18. 14. 6–8)

No doubt Demosthenes was right, in that many Greek politicians were bribed, but Polybius' point is valid too: especially in Peloponnese, the overriding interests of the cities pointed Philip's way. Lastly there was the view, formulated in Athens by Isokrates and by Plato's nephew and successor Speusippos, and it seems widely shared, which saw in Philip a protection against radical pressure, a means of solving the social problem of mercenaries, and a means of realizing the Panhellenic dream of unity against Persia. In fact the surprising thing is that the opposition to Philip achieved the limited success it did. It poses the problem whether the creation of the coalition against him was due to the oratory of Demosthenes and his colleagues, and to a response to their appeals to a sense of justice and resistance to aggression in interstate relations, or whether it was due to a shift in perceived interests. Demosthenes has had much influence in persuading posterity of the former. Yet Athens only moved wholeheartedly against Philip when her corn-route was threatened, Thebes only when Philip's interference in Euboea and Phocis threatened what she regarded as traditional zones of influence. Structural reasons counted more than arguments about justice.

The same is true for Philip's destructive creation of a new political order. His abilities and ambitions and techniques of aggrandizement were exceptional but not unique, and since other men shared them we cannot invoke those qualities alone in explanation. What was unique was the deep-rootedness of his monarchical position in his own country. The nearest approach to it was the Spartan monarchy, and indeed Agesilaos in the 380s was nearly as much King of Greece as Philip was after 338. But Spartan society was built on repression in a way that Macedonian society was not, while, as we have seen throughout this book, for Sparta or Athens or Thebes to harness the military and political resources of their subordinate allies involved insuperable contradictions between the practice of power and the theory of the state. The only other possible role was that of 'general with full powers', but because fear of tyranny was so strong régimes built on that formula proved to be shallow-rooted. In contrast the Macedonian monarchy was strong enough to take the strain, just distant and outlandish enough to be acceptable, but just Greek enough for the monarch, as a Greek, to move into the various supra-polis roles which existed in Greek society. At the same time Philip's amalgamation of roles and resources owed much to his own drive, nerve and sense of opportunity. What he left was to be exploited by Alexander, the biggest opportunist of them all.

Date Chart

	Western Greece	Mainland Greece	Aegean and East Mediterranean
480	Sicilian Greeks defeat Carthaginians at battle of Himera	Greek–Persian war: battles of Artemision, Thermopylae, and Salamis	
479		Greeks defeat Persians at battle of Plataiai and Mykale	
Winter 478–7			Delian League founded
between 469 and 466			Greeks defeat Persians at Eurymedon River
466	Collapse of tyranny at Syracuse		
464		Earthquake in Sparta: helot revolt in Messenia	

	Western Greece	Mainland Greece	Aegean and East Mediterranean
461		Ostracism of Kimon and start of democratic revolution in Athens: First Peloponnesian War begins	
459			Athenian/League expedition to Egypt
458		Battles of Oinophyta and Tanagra: Athenian conquest of Boeotia	
454			Expedition to Egypt ends in disaster
451			Athenian/League expedition to Cyprus: death of Kimon
(?)449			Diplomatic understanding between Athens and Persia ('Peace of Kallias')
447		Parthenon begun in Athens	

	Western Greece	Mainland Greece	Aegean and East Mediterranean
446		Thirty Years' Peace between Sparta and Athens and their allies	
443	Thourioi founded		
441–39			Revolt of Samos
435–3	War between Corinth and Corcyra		
431		Second Peloponnesian War begins	
429		Death of Perikles	
428–7			Revolt of Lesbos
427	Athenian force in Sicily		
425		Athenian success at Pylos	
424	Peace conference at Gela	Boeotians defeat Athenians at Delion	

	Western Greece	Mainland Greece	Aegean and East Mediterranean
421		Peace of Nikias between Athens and Sparta and their allies	
418		Spartans defeat coalition at Mantinea	
415–13	Athenian expedition to Sicily		
412		War renewed: Spartan treaties with Persia	
411		Coup of Four Hundred at Athens	
409	Carthaginians invade Sicily		
405	Dionysios I becomes tyrant of Syracuse		Spartans destroy Athenian fleet at Aegospotami
404		Siege and capitulation of Athens	
404–3		Régime of Thirty Tyrants at Athens	
401–399			Expedition of Cyrus and the Ten Thousand against Persian King
399		Death of Sokrates	

	Western Greece	Mainland Greece	Aegean and East Mediterranean
396–4			Agesilaos' campaigns in Asia Minor
395		Corinthian War breaks out	
394			Persians defeat Spartan fleet at Knidos
387	Dionysios captures Rhegion		
386	Gauls capture Rome	Peace of Antialkidas ('King's Peace') between Persia and Greek states	
Winter 379–8		Liberation of Thebes	
378–7			Second Athenian League founded
375		Iason becomes *Tagos* of Thessaly	
371		Thebans defeat Spartans at Leuctra	
370		Death of Iason	

	Western Greece	Mainland Greece	Aegean and East Mediterranean
370–61		Theban invasions of Peloponnese	
367	Death of Dionysios I		
364		Thebans destroy Orchomenus	
362		Thebans defeat Spartans at Mantinea	
359		Philip II becomes King of Macedon	
357–6		War between Philip and Athens	Social War breaks out
356	Dion master of Syracuse	Sacred War breaks out	
355–4			Athens concedes defeat in Social War
354	Death of Dion		
348		Philip captures Olynthus	
346		Peace between Philip and Athens	

	Western Greece	Mainland Greece	Aegean and East Mediterranean
344	Timoleon reaches Sicily		
(?)341	Greeks defeat Carthaginians at R. Krimisos		
338		Philip defeats Thebans and Athenians at Chaeronea	
337		Corinthian League founded, and declares war on Persia	
336		Death of Philip	Invasion of Asia Minor

Primary Sources

Only the most frequently cited sources are listed here. Further details about them, and information about other sources, is most conveniently available in *The Oxford Classical Dictionary*, 2nd ed. (Clarendon Press, 1970). In the following notes LCL denotes Loeb Classical Library, LACTOR denotes the series *London Association of Classical Teachers: Original Records*. Asterisks (*) indicate titles useful mainly for those with a working knowledge of ancient Greek.

ARISTOPHANES (by 445–385 BC or later), the comic poet. Eleven of his plays survive, written for production at Athenian festivals between 425 and 388, classic for their combination of fantasy, burlesque, obscenity, farce, and real poetry. They contain much political and social information, invaluable even if transmuted by a detectable conservative bias. Translation in Penguin, LCL, and elsewhere, with many modern editions and commentaries. Surveys in V. Ehrenberg, *The people of Aristophanes* (Blackwell 1943, and reprints) and in Sir K. J. Dover, *Aristophanic comedy* (Batsford, 1972).

ARISTOTLE (384–322 BC), Greek philosopher and polymath, pupil of Plato. His directly historical works are lost save for the *Constitution of Athens* (q.v.), but his works on politics and ethics contain much historical information besides encapsulating and rationalizing current attitudes and value-systems. Translations in LCL or in the Clarendon Press series of translations: of the *Ethics* and *Politics* in Penguin and Everyman: of the *Politics* also by Sir E. Barker (O.U.P., 1958).

ATHENIAN CONSTITUTION. The only surviving example of the 158 Constitutions of Greek States compiled by Aristotle, or more likely under his direction. Chapters 1–41 of the extant text give a potted history of the constitution from mythical times till 403 BC; chapters 42–69 describes the constitutional structure of the 320s. Translation and commentary in J. M. Moore, *Aristotle and Xenophon on democracy and oligarchy* (Chatto and Windus, 1975), 139ff., or in P. J. Rhodes, *Aristotle: the Athenian Constitution* (Penguin, 1984), who has also published the major *Commentary on the text (Clarendon Press, 1981); translation also in LCL.

DEMOSTHENES (384–322 BC), Athenian orator and politician. 61 speeches and some letters survive under his name, though some speeches were certainly not written by him. Speeches 1–17, parts of Assembly debates, and 18–26, from political trials, are the most informative historically, but the other speeches illuminate Athenian life and society with vigour and venom. Translations of twelve speeches in Penguin (*Demosthenes and Aeschines and Greek Political Oratory*): of the public speeches in Everyman: of all in LCL.

DIODORUS (active 60–36 BC), a Greek from Sicily and writer of a universal history, books 11–20 of which provide a continuous narrative of Mediterranean history (mainly Greek) from 478 till 302 BC. For the period 362–336 BC his is the only extant account, and for other periods he preserves a tradition different from Thucydides or Xenophon, often garbled in transmission through compression and confusion but precious for its record of events. Translation in LCL.

EPHORUS, *c.* 405–330 BC: see FRAGMENTS below.

HERODOTUS (480s–420s BC), the historian of the Persian Wars. Though most of his subject matter precedes the period of this book, he reflected and was part of the intellectual atmosphere of Greece and Athens in the 440s and 430s, and has immense value for the historian of the fifth century on that account. Translations readily available in many editions. Recent studies of his work include J. Hart, *Herodotus and Greek history*

(Croom Helm, 1982); K. H. Waters, *Herodotus the historian; his problems, methods, and originality* (Croom Helm, 1985); J. P. A. Gould, *Herodotus* (Weidenfeld and Nicholson, 1989); D. Fehling, *Herodotus and his 'sources'; Citation, invention, and narrative art* (tr. J. G. Howie) (ARCA Francis Cairns, 1989); and J. A. S. Evans, *Herodotus explorer of the past* (Princeton U.P., 1991).

ISOKRATES (436–338 BC), speech-writer, pamphleteer and teacher of rhetoric at Athens. For the historian his most important writings are his political pamphlets, written in speech form from 380 onwards. They are valuable both for their romantic view of previous history and as evidence of contemporary conservative attitudes. Translations of two 'speeches' in *Greek Political Oratory* (Penguin); of all in LCL.

LYSIAS (by 436–after 380 BC), speech-writer at Athens, son of wealthy Syracusan immigrant. He took part in the resistance to the Thirty Tyrants in 404–03, but failed to become a citizen as a result. His 34 surviving speeches span the years 403–*c.* 380, and greatly add to our knowledge of Athenian society, politics, and law in those years. Translations of all in LCL, of one (xii *Against Eratosthenes*) in *Greek political oratory* (Penguin). The most detailed recent study is by Sir K. J. Dover, **Lysias and the Corpus Lysiacum* (U. of California P., 1968).

PLATO (427–347 BC) His voluminous philosophical writings are fundamental for the intellectual history both of his own time and of the fifth century, and also for their vignettes of social life in Athens in the circle of Sokrates and for his own powerful but idiosyncratic view of Greek history and Greek institutions. Translations in the Oxford series by Jowett and others, or in LCL, or elsewhere.

PLUTARCH (*c.* AD 46–120s), Greek philosopher, essayist and biographer. His *Lives* were written as studies of character, and form part of his ethical writings, but his interest in personality and his immense knowledge of historical and other source material make them an invaluable source for events, quotations and interpretations. Translations of many of his Greek *Lives* available in Penguin: of all in LCL. Guides to his approach in C. P. Jones, *Plutarch and Rome* (Clarendon Press, 1971) and D. A. Russell, *Plutarch* (Duckworth, 1972).

THEOPOMPOS (c. 379–after 323 BC): See FRAGMENTS below.

THUCYDIDES (by 454–390s BC), historian of the second 'Peloponnesian War'. Book 1 of his *Histories* is the basic source of information about Greek events between 478 and 432: Books 2–8 give a meticulously detailed account of military action between 431 and 411. Authoritative, objective as far as he can make them, intellectually ferocious and stylistically elaborate, his *Histories* are basic to any understanding of Greek history. The great 5-volume *Historical Commentary* on them (Clarendon Press, 1945–81) by A. W. Gomme, Sir K. J. Dover and A. Andrewes is already itself partially superseded by N. S. Hornblower, *A Commentary on Thucydides vol I: books I–III* (Clarendon Press, 1991). Hornblower's *Thucydides* (Duckworth, 1987) is the most accessible short analysis. Translations in Everyman, Penguin, LCL, etc.

XENOPHON (by 425–c. 355 BC), historian, philosopher and essayist: an archetypal Greek gentleman professional in war, amateur in history, and well enough up in cultural pursuits and public affairs to write as vividly and entertainingly about Athenian taxation as about Sokrates. His *Hellenika* narrate Greek affairs in 7 books from 411 till 362 in a mode similar to Thucydides, but much less precise or comprehensive. Translations of it and of his account of the Ten Thousand in Penguin: of all in LCL. An up-to-date Commentary on the *Hellenika* is badly needed, but J. K. Anderson, *Xenophon* (Duckworth, 1974) is some substitute.

* * *

FRAGMENTS All too much of what was once written by the Greeks in every genre is lost completely, or survives only via the odd word or phrase or paragraph quoted in later authors. Work on collecting these 'fragments' and on attempting to re-create some sort of sketch of the original is long established. The two collections quoted most in this book are *FGH* and *DK*. *FGH* – F. Jacoby, *Die Fragmente der griechischen Historiker* (Berlin, 1922–) (Greek text, German or English commentary, no translation) – collects the remnants of most (it is not yet complete) of the historians who wrote in Greek. The two lost historians of most importance for the classical period are Ephorus and Theopompos. Ephorus (*c.* 405–*c.* 330 BC) from Kyme in Asia Minor, a pupil of Isokrates (q.v.), narrated the whole of Greek history from the migration period till 341 BC in thirty books. His pious attitudes, use by Diodorus (q.v.), and general influence make him important, but a new study of his influence on Greek historiography is badly needed to replace G. L. Barber, *The historian Ephorus* (Cambridge U.P., 1935). Theopompos of Chios (*c.* 379–after 323 BC), like Xenophon, wrote *Hellenika* which continued from where Thucydides broke off, but then he moved on to write contemporary history under the significant title *Philippika*. Both works seem to have had a rhetorically abusive style calculated to depress the pretensions of the Great Powers (especially Athens) for which he had no sympathy; see W. R. Connor, *Theopompos and fifth century history* (Center for Hellenic Studies, 1968), and G. S. Shrimpton, *Theopompos the historian* (McGill-Queen's U.P., 1991).

Fragments of philosophers active till *c.* 400 BC are published in DK – H. Diels and W. Kranz, *Die Fragmente der Vorsokratiker* (6th ed., Berlin, 1951). [Greek text, German translation: English translation in K. Freeman, *Ancilla to the Pre-Socratic Philosophers* (Blackwell, 1947) or in Jonathan Barnes, *Early Greek Philosophy* (Penguin, 1987).]

INSCRIPTIONS The standard, in theory all-embracing edition is *Inscriptiones Graecae* (IG), published by the Berlin Academy from 1873 onwards and still in progress. However, many documents are normally cited from more modern editions and selections, especially

ML R. Meiggs and D. M. Lewis, *A selection of Greek Historical Inscriptions to the end of the fifth century BC* (Clarendon Press, 1969: revised addition with Addenda 1988).
SEG *Supplementum Epigraphicum Graecum*
TOD M. N. Tod, *A selection of Greek Historical Inscriptions, vol. II: From 403 to 323 BC* (Clarendon Press, 1948).

Translations of inscriptions, rare till recently, are now much more accessible. Most of ML is now available either in the series *Translated Documents of Greece and Rome* (eds. E. Badian and R. K. Sherk), vol. I: *Archaic times to the end of the Peloponnesian War,* by C. W. Fornara (Johns Hopkins U.P., 1977) or in LACTOR 1, *The Athenian Empire (*2nd ed., by R. W. J. Clayton, 1970). The fourth century is covered by LACTOR 9, *Greek Historical Inscriptions* 359–23 BC by P. J. Rhodes (1971), by J. Wickersham and G. Verbrugghe, *Greek Historical Documents: the fourth century BC* (Hakkert, 1973), and by *Translated documents . . .* vol. II: *From the end of the Peloponnesian War to the battle of Ipsus,* by P. Harding (Cambridge U.P., 1985).

Selected Documents in a wider sense, including portions of literary texts in prose and verse, are translated with explanations or linking narrative by M. H. Crawford and D. Whitehead, *Archaic and Classical Greece* (Cambridge U.P., 1983), or by P. J. Rhodes, *The Greek City States – a source book* (Croom Helm, 1986).

In the translation of inscriptions in the text, words or parts of words in square brackets represent Greek words missing on the stone but restored by modern editors with more or less certainty. Round brackets enclose words of explanation inserted by myself.

Further Reading

The main large-scale narrative and analysis of the period covered by this book is now provided by the new edition of the *Cambridge Ancient History*. Volume V (Cambridge U.P. 1992) covers the fifth century, Volume VI (forthcoming) the fourth century. Other surveys are J. B. Bury and R. Meiggs, *A history of Greece* (4th ed., Macmillan, 1975), N. G. L. Hammond. *A history of Greece to 322 BC* (Clarendon Press, 1959), with its companion volume *Studies in Greek History* (Clarendon Press, 1973), and R. Sealey, *A history of the Greek city states 700–338 BC* (California U.P., 1976).

On a smaller scale Simon Hornblower, *The Greek World 479–323 BC* (Methuen, 1983) covers the same ground as the present book in a very different but valuable because complementary style. Wider in scope are A. R. Burn, *The Pelican history of Greece* (Penguin, 1966) and J. Boardman, J. Griffin and O. Murray, *The Oxford history of Greece and the Hellenistic World* (Oxford U.P., 1991), the latter in particular being an excellent first introduction. Also valuable are Anton Powell, *Athens and Sparta: constructing Greek political and social history from 478 BC.* (Routledge, 1988), and R. Devlin, *Athenian officials 684–321 BC* (Cambridge U.P., 1989), a year-by-year listing of Athenian public officials and their acts.

In what follows, books and articles which require knowledge of Greek script and language are marked with an asterisk. Dates are those of original publication, not of subsequent reprints. Where possible, I have listed studies in English, but have also quoted some books in French or German or Italian if they are basic.

276   DEMOCRACY AND CLASSICAL GREECE

I. The Sources and their Limitations

For individual authors see *Primary Sources* above: titles listed here will concentrate on groups of authors or on genres of material.

Individual sites are usually best approached via local handbooks or the latest edition of the *Blue Guide: Greece* (4th ed. by S. Rossiter, Ernest Benn, 1981). Other perspectives are available from J. Travlos, *Pictorial dictionary of Ancient Athens* (Thames and Hudson/German Archaeological Institute, 1971), R. V. Schoder, SJ, *Ancient Greece from the Air* (Thames and Hudson, 1974), R. A. Tomlinson, *Greek sanctuaries* (Elek, 1976), and R. Stillwell with W. L. MacDonald and M. H. McAllister, *The Princeton Encyclopedia of classical sites* (Princeton U.P., 1976). An illustrated but broader-ranging counterpart of the latter is the *Enciclopedia dell' Arte Antica* (9 volumes with Supplement, 1958–1970).

Other artefact and environmental material, apart from what is seen as 'art', is less accessible. See however A. M. Snodgrass, 'Archaeology', in M. H. Crawford (ed), *Sources for ancient history* (Cambridge U.P., 1983), 137–84, and R. W. Wycherley, *How the Greeks built cities* (Macmillan, 1949; ²1962). The various chapters in C. Bérard et al, *A city of images: iconography and society in ancient Greece* (Princeton U.P., 1989) very valuably use vase paintings as windows into social activities and values rather than as 'art'.

For art and architecture see J. Boardman in Boardman-Griffin-Murray 1991, ch.12, the chapters by J. J. Pollitt (8a) and R. E. Wycherley (8b, 8c) in *Cambridge Ancient History V²* (1992), A. W. Lawrence, *Greek Architecture* (Penguin, 1957; ²1967; ³1973), M. Robertson, *A History of Greek Art I–II* (Cambridge U.P., 1975), and many other titles.

For inscriptions the principal survey remains that of A. G. Woodhead, *The study of Greek Inscriptions* (Cambridge U.P., 1959), but it is supplemented by F. G. B. Millar's 'Epigraphy' in Crawford 1983 (above): 80–136, and by B. F. Cook, *Reading the past: Greek inscriptions* (British Museum publications, 1987).

Greek historical writing in general is explored by A. D. Momigliano, *Studies in historiography* (Weidenfeld and

Nicholson, 1966) and *ibid.*, *The classical foundations of modern historiography* (U. of California P., 1990): see also C. W. Fornara, *The nature of history in ancient Greece and Rome* (U. of California P., 1983) and O. Murray's chapter 'Greek historians' in Boardman-Griffin-Murray 1991: 214–39. The local historians of Athens have been treated in detail by L. Pearson, *The local historians of Attica* (American Philological Association, 1942) and by F. Jacoby, *Atthis: the local chronicles of ancient Athens* (Clarendon Press, 1949). A. D. Momigliano also provides a masterly general survey of another genre in *The development of Greek biography* (Harvard U.P., 1971). The orators in general are sketched in G. A. Kennedy, *The art of persuasion in Greece* (Routledge and Kegan Paul, 1963).

Greek coins are now well served. The basic survey is C. M. Kraay, *Archaic and classical Greek coins* (Methuen, 1976), supplemented by the illustrations in C. M. Kraay and M. Hirmer, *Greek coins* (Thames and Hudson, 1966). See also C. M. Kraay, *Greek coins and history* (Methuen, 1969) and M. H. Crawford, 'Numismatics', in Crawford 1983: 185–233.

II. The Greek World in 478

Proper documentation for this chapter would be inappropriately out of scale. Fundamental surveys of Greek society are A. Andrewes, *The Greeks* (Hutchinson, 1967), republished as *Greek Society* (Penguin, 1971), Sir A. Zimmern, *The Greek Commonwealth* (Clarendon Press, 1911, and many reprints: still excellent for all its age), and E. Will, *Le monde grec et l'Orient, I: Le Ve Siècle* (P.U.F., 1972), 403ff.

Other titles may be roughly grouped by the order of topics in the chapter. The Greek language and its dialects are surveyed on *OCD*^{2} s.v. Dialects, Greek, and by J. B. Hainsworth in *Cambridge Ancient History* III^2 1, ch. 20*d*. Work on Greek religion has expanded vastly in recent years. W. Burkert, *Greek Religion* (trans. W. Raffan) (Blackwell, 1985) surveys the basic grammar of ritual and belief, as do the various articles in P. E. Easterling and J. V. Muir (eds), *Greek religion and society* (Cambridge U.P., 1985), or R. Parker's summary chapter (with valuable

further references) in Boardman-Griffin-Murray 1991: 306ff.
Other helpful books on particular topics in religion are H. W.
Parke and D. W. Wormell, *The Delphic Oracle I–II²* (Blackwell,
1956), H. W. Parke, *Greek oracles* (Hutchinson, 1967), R.
Flacelière, *Greek oracles* (Elek, 1965: ²1976), R. Parker,
Miasma; Pollution and purification in Early Greek religion
(Clarendon Press, 1983), and Chr. Sourvinou-Inwood, *'Reading'*
Greek culture: texts and images, rituals and myths (Clarendon
Press, 1991).

Rituals in a wider sense are surveyed by D. C. Kurtz and J.
Boardman, *Greek burial customs* (Thames and Hudson, 1971)
and by R. Garland's two complementary volumes, *The Greek
way of death* (Duckworth, 1985) and *The Greek way of life from
conception to old age* (Duckworth, 1990).

Works which place the Greek citizen-state in its social and
ecological setting are R. Osborne, *Classical landscape with
figures: the ancient Greek city and its countryside* (George Philip,
1987); O. Murray and S. Price (eds), *The Greek city from Homer
to Alexander* (Clarendon Press, 1990); R. Sallares, *The ecology of
the ancient Greek world* (Duckworth, 1991); J. Rich and
A. Wallace-Hadrill (eds), *City and country in the ancient world*
(Routledge, 1991); and E. J. Owens, *The city in the Greek and
Roman world* (Routledge, 1991).

Economic patterns have proved elusive. H. Mitchell, *The
economics of ancient Greece* (2nd ed., Heffer, 1957), and
G. Glotz, *Ancient Greece at Work* (Routledge and Kegan Paul,
1962), describe the patterns of getting a living, but motivations
and values are more complex: see A. Burford, *Craftsmen in Greek
and Roman Society* (Thames and Hudson, 1972), J. Hasebroek,
Trade and politics in ancient Greece (Bell, 1933, and reprints),
M. M. Austin and P. Vidal-Naquet, *Economic and Social history
of ancient Greece* (Batsford, 1977), and J. K. Davies in
Cambridge Ancient History V² ch. 8g. The social politics of food
supply are examined by P. D. A. Garnsey, *Famine and food
supply in the Graeco-Roman world: responses to risk and crisis*
(Cambridge U.P., 1988), Part III, and by the Greek-oriented
papers in C. R. Whittaker (ed), *Pastoral economies in classical
antiquity* (Cambridge Philological Society, 1988).

Wider-ranging work on social conditions includes L. Casson,

Travel in the ancient world (Allen and Unwin, 1974), ch. 4; A. Lintott, *Violence, civil strife and revolution in the classical city* (Croom Helm, 1982); and G. Herman, *Ritualized friendship and the Greek city* (Cambridge U.P., 1987). The most disadvantaged social condition, slavery, has been increasingly intensively studied. Salient titles are M. I. Finley, (ed)., *Slavery in Classical antiquity* (Heffer, 1960, and reprints); *ibid, Ancient slavery and modern ideology* (Chatto and Windus, 1980); T. E. J. Wiedemann, *Greek and Roman Slavery* (Croom Helm, 1981); M. I. Finley, *Economy and society in ancient Greece* (ed. B. D. Shaw and R. P. Saller) (Chatto and Windus, 1981; Penguin, 1983), Part II; T. E. Wiedemann, *Slavery (Greece and Rome,* New Surveys 19) (Clarendon Press for Classical Association, 1987); and Y. Garlan, *Slavery in ancient Greece* (tr. J. Lloyd) (Cornell U.P., 1988). Complementary thereto are several papers in P. D. A. Garnsey (ed), *Non-slave labour in the Greco-Roman world* (Cambridge Philological Society, 1980).

The study of family circumstances, and in particular of the role of women within and outside the household, has benefited from a similar concentration of attention. The following selective list conveys a general picture, since it is impossible fully to separate what concentrates on Athens from work on Greek conditions in general, or indeed from Greco-Roman Antiquity as a whole; W. K. Lacey, *The family in classical Greece* (Thames and Hudson, 1968); S. B. Pomeroy, *Goddesses, whores, wives and slaves* (Robert Hale, 1976); S. C. Humphreys, *Anthropology and the Greeks* (Routledge and Kegan Paul, 1978); D. M. Schaps, *Economic rights of women in classical Greece* (Edinburgh U.P., 1979); J. P. A. Gould, 'Law custom, and myth: some aspects of the social position of women in classical Athens', *Journal of Hellenic Studies* 100 (1980), 38–59; M. Lefkowitz and M. B. Fant, *Women's life in Greece and Rome* (Duckworth, 1982); S. C. Humphreys, *The family, women and death: comparative studies* (Routledge and Kegan Paul, 1983); M. Lefkowitz, *Women in Greek myth* (Duckworth, 1986); L. Foxhall, 'Household, gender and property in classical Athens', *Classical Quarterly,* 39 (1989), 22–44; G. Clark, *Women in the ancient world (Greece and Rome,* New Surveys 21) (Clarendon Press for Classical Association, 1989); R. Just, *Women in Athenian law and life* (Routledge, 1989).

For political forms see L. Whibley, *Greek Oligarchies: their character and organisation* (Methuen, 1986), V. Ehrenberg, *The Greek State* (2nd ed., Methuen, 1969), J. A. O. Larsen, *Greek Federal States* (Clarendon Press, 1968), but also H. Schaefer, *Staatsform und Politik* (Leipzig, 1932). Diplomatic forms and much else are surveyed by Sir F. A. Adcock and D. J. Mosley, *Diplomacy in ancient Greece* (Thames and Hudson, 1975), supplemented by M. Amit, *Great and small poleis: a study in the relations between the great powers and the small cities in ancient Greece* (Latomus, Bruxelles 1973). For attitudes expressed in the literary sources see C. M. Bowra, *Pindar* (Clarendon Press, 1964), H. Lloyd-Jones, *The Justice of Zeus* (California U.P., 1971), and Sir K. J. Dover, *Greek popular morality in the time of Plato and Aristotle* (Blackwell, 1974).

III. Regional Ambitions

Much of the subject-matter of this chapter is covered by G. E. M. de Ste Croix, *The Origins of the Peloponnesian War* (Duckworth, 1972), which covers much more than its title suggests. It is filled out still further by a large and growing series of studies of individual *poleis* or regions. The most important (in alphabetical order of place) are:–

Argos –   R. A. Tomlinson, *Argos and the Argolid* (Routledge and Kegan Paul, 1972)

Athens –   R. Meiggs, *The Athenian Empire* (Clarendon Press, 1972) chs. 3–5: and see 6 and 12 below.

Boeotia – R. J. Buck, *A history of Boeotia* (U. of Alberta P., 1979)

Corinth – A. J. Graham, *Colony and mother-city in ancient Greece* (Manchester U.P., 1964), 118ff; J. B. Salmon, *Wealthy Corinth* (Clarendon Press, 1984)

Cos –   S. M. Sherwin-White, *Ancient Cos* (Vandenhoeck & Ruprecht, 1978)

Crete –   R. F. Willetts, *Aristocratic Society in ancient Crete* (Routledge and Kegan Paul, 1955)

Epirus – N. G. L. Hammond, *Epirus* (Clarendon Press, 1967), Part 4

Macedon – N. G. L. Hammond and G. T. Griffith, *A history of Macedonia, II: 550–336 BC* (Clarendon Press, 1979); N. G. L. Hammond, *The Macedonian State. Origins, institutions and history* (Oxford, 1989); E. N. Borza, *In the shadow of Olympus: the Emergence of Macedon* (Princeton U.P., 1990)

Megara – R. P. Legon, *Megara* (Cornell U.P., 1981)

Samos – G. Shipley, *A history of Samos 800–188 BC* (Clarendon Press, 1987)

Sicyon – A. Griffin, *Sikyon* (Clarendon Press, 1982)

Sparta – W. G. Forrest, *A history of Sparta 950–192 BC* (Hutchinson, 1968); A. J. Toynbee, *Some problems of Greek history* (Oxford U.P., 1969), Part III – 'The rise and decline of Sparta'; M. I. Finley, *The use and abuse of history* (Chatto and Windus, 1975), ch. 10; P. Cartledge, *Sparta and Laconia: a regional history 1300–362 BC.* (Routledge and Kegan Paul, 1979); S. Hodkinson, 'Social order and the conflict of values in classical Sparta', *Chiron* 13 (1983), 239–81; D. M. MacDowell, *Spartan Law* (Scottish Academic Press, 1986); and A. Powell (ed), *Classical Sparta – the techniques behind her success* (Croom Helm, 1988)

Thebes – N. H. Demand, *Thebes in the fifth century: Heracles resurgent* (Routledge and Kegan Paul, 1982)

IV. The Athenian Revolution

C. Rodewald, *Democracy: ideas and realities* (Dent, 1974) is a selection of translated and annotated sources on the theme; P. J. Rhodes, **The Athenian Boule* (Clarendon Press, 1972), describes the workings of one of the central institutions, the Council; R. W. Wallace, *The Areopagus Council, to 307 BC* (Johns Hopkins U.P., 1985) does the same for another. W. G. Forrest, *The emergence of Greek democracy* (Weidenfeld and Nicolson, 1966), is a more general account, as is D. L. Stockton, *The classical Athenian democracy* (Oxford U.P., 1990), while

J. T. Roberts, *Accountability in Athenian government* (U. of Wisconsin P., 1982) concentrates on what is probably the main issue.

The complex relationships linking social circumstances, political action, and ancient political theory are traced in various ways by M. Ostwald, *From popular sovereignty to the sovereignty of law: law, society and politics in the fifth century Athens* (U. of California P., 1986); C. Farrar, *The origins of democratic thinking: the invention of politics in classical Athens* (Cambridge U.P., 1988); E. Meiksins Wood, *Peasant-citizen and slave: the foundations of Athenian democracy* (Verso, 1988); and J. Ober, *Mass and élite in democratic Athens* (Princeton U.P., 1989). The links between them and modern theory are treated by M. I. Finley, *Democracy ancient and modern* (Chatto and Windus, 1973) and *Politics in the ancient world* (Cambridge U.P., 1983).

V. The Athenian Empire

The literature is immense and controversies never-ending. The basic studies are B. D. Meritt, H. T. Wade-Gery and M. F. McGregor, **The Athenian Tribute Lists I—IV*, especially volume III (Princeton, 1950): Meiggs, *The Athenian Empire,* and Ste Croix, *Outbreak* (see III above): and J. de Romilly, *Thucydides and Athenian Imperialism* (Blackwell, 1963). Two more succinct guides and evaluations are by M. I. Finley, 'The fifth-century Athenian Empire: a balance sheet', in P. D. A. Garnsey and C. R. Whittaker (eds), *Imperialism in the ancient world* (Cambridge U.P., 1978), ch. 5, and by P. J. Rhodes, *The Athenian Empire (Greece and Rome,* New Surveys 17) (Clarendon Press for Classical Association, 1985). Fuller than either is M. F. McGregor, *The Athenians and their Empire* (U. of British Columbia P., 1987). Sources in English translation, with notes of guidance, in S. Hornblower and M. C. Greenstock (eds), The *Athenian Empire*[3] (LACTOR 1, 1984). T. J. Quinn, *Athens and Samos, Lesbos and Chios 478–404 BC)* (Manchester U.P., 1981), treats one important set of relationships.

VI. Athenian Society in the Fifth Century

Since the primary source material stems so overwhelmingly from the years 430–320 BC, only work which specifically relates to the fifth century is listed here: for the remainder see XII below. The fullest and most recent treatment is by various authors in ch. 8 of *Cambridge Ancient History* V^2 (1992), supplemented by the translated source material in LACTOR 2, *The Old Oligarch* (1968 and reprints), LACTOR 5, *Athenian Politics* (n.d.) and K. Freeman, *The murder of Herodes* (MacDonald, 1946). Other useful surveys are A. W. Gomme, *The population of ancient Athens* (Blackwell, 1933 and reprints); T. B. L. Webster, *Athenian Culture and Society* (Batsford, 1973); J. K. Davies, *Wealth and the power of wealth in classical Athens* (Arno Press, 1981); J. Roberts, *City of Sokrates: an introduction to classical Athens* (Routledge and Kegan Paul, 1984); and a Joint Association of Classical Teachers/Open University textbook, *The world of Athens: an introduction to Classical Athenian culture* (Cambridge U.P., 1984). Specifically on the politicians are A. R. Burn, *Pericles and Athens* (H.U.L., 1948), M. I. Finley, 'The Athenian demagogues', *Past and Present* 21 (1962) 3ff., and W. R. Connor, *The new politicians of fifth-century Athens* (Princeton U.P., 1971). Specifically on the buildings are essays by various scholars in *Parthenos and Parthenon (Greece and Rome,* Supplement 10 (1963)), or J. S. Boersma, *Athenian building policy from 561/0 to 405/4 BC* (Wolters-Noordhoff, 1970).

VII. The Peloponnesian War

A complete blow-by-blow account of the war is now provided in a four-volume series by D. Kagan: *The outbreak of the Peloponnesian War* (Cornell U.P., 1969, 2nd ed. 1981); *The Archidamian War* (Cornell U.P., 1974); *The Peace of Nicias and the Sicilian Expedition* (Cornell U.P., 1981); and *The fall of the Athenian Empire* (Cornell U.P., 1987).

Military technology and techniques are well covered in e.g. J. S. Morrison and R. T. Williams, *Greek Oared Ships* (Cambridge U.P., 1968) and L. Casson, *Ships and seamanship in the ancient world* (Princeton, 1971) for the sea, and A. M. Snodgrass, *Arms and armour of the Greeks* (Thames and Hudson, 1967) and W. K. Pritchett, *The Greek State at War* (California U.P., 1971–4) on land. What it meant to be a hoplite is brought out in three books by V. D. Hanson: *Warfare and agriculture in classical Greece* (Giardini, Pisa, 1983); *The Western way of war: infantry battle in classical Greece* (Hodder and Stoughton, 1989); and *Hoplites: the classical Greek battle experience* (Routledge, 1991).

Strategic tactics, and personalities, are discussed in various essays by H. D. Westlake, *Individuals in Thucydides* (Cambridge U.P., 1968), *Essays on the Greek Historians and Greek History* (Manchester U.P., 1969), and *Studies in Thucydides and Greek history* (Bristol Classical P., 1989). See also A. W. Gomme, *More Essays in Greek History and Literature* (Blackwell, 1962), P. A. Brunt, 'Spartan policy and strategy in the Archidamian war' *The Phoenix 19* (1965) 255ff., and J. Hatzfeld, *Alcibiade* (P.U.F., Paris, 1940, and reprints). The enigmatic personality of Alcibiades has stimulated two further books: E. F. Bloedow, *Alcibiades re-examined* (Steiner Verlag, 1973) and W. M. Ellis, *Alcibiades* (Routledge, 1989).

VIII. Spartan Supremacy

Studies of Spartan imperialism are A. Andrewes, 'Spartan Imperialism?' in Garnsey and Whittaker 1978: 91–102 (see V), C. D. Hamilton, *Sparta's bitter victories. Politics and diplomacy in the Corinthian War* (Cornell U.P., 1979), and P. Cartledge, *Agesilaos and the crisis of Sparta* (Duckworth, 1987). The Athenian revolutions of 411 and 404 are best explored in C. Hignett, *A history of the Athenian constitution* (Clarendon Press, 1952), P. Krentz, *The Thirty at Athens* (Cornell U.P., 1982), and T. C. Loening, *The reconciliation agreement of 403/ 402 BC. in Athens* (Steiner Verlag, 1987). Post-war Athens and her revanche of the 390s are surveyed by R. J. Seager, 'Thrasybulus, Conon, and Athenian Imperialism 396–86 BC', *Journal of Hellenic Studies* 77 (1967) 95ff., and by B. S. Strauss, *Athens after the Peloponnesian War: class, faction, and policy 403–386 BC*, (Croom Helm, 1986).

The Persian Empire itself is becoming more accessible than it once was. J. M. Cook, *The Persian Empire* (J. M. Dent, 1983), is a general account replacing older books, and is supplemented for the period of this chapter by D. M. Lewis, *Sparta and Persia* (Brill, 1977). The series *Achaemenid History (I–VII* so far) edited variously by H. Sancis-Weerdenburg, A. Kuhrt and J. W. Drijvers (Brill, 1987–) covers the whole period of the Empire, as does C. J. Tuplin, 'The administration of the Achaemenid Empire' and other papers in Ian Carradice (ed), *Coinage and administration in the Athenian and Persian Empires* (British Archaeological Reports, International Series 343, 1987).

IX. Social Change

Study may well begin from G. Murray, 'Reactions to the Peloponnesian War in Greek thought and practice', *Journal of Hellenic Studies 64* (1944) 1ff. The complexities of myth are explored by G. S. Kirk, *Myth: its meaning and functions in ancient and other cultures* (Cambridge and California U.P., 1970) and *The nature of Greek myths* (Penguin, 1974). New currents in art are documented in M. Robertson, *A history of Greek Art* (Cambridge U.P., 1970), chs. 6 and 7: in religion by M. Nilsson, *Geschichte der Griechischen Religion,* I[3] (Beck, 1967), 784ff., and E. R. Dodds, *The Greeks and the irrational* (California U.P., 1951) ch. 6: and in demography by P. McKechnie, *Outsiders in the Greek cities in the fourth century BC.* (Routledge, 1989).

X. Philosophers, Mercenaries, and Monarchs

Histories of Greek philosophy are numerous: monumental and fully documented is W. K. Guthrie, *A history of Greek philosophy, I–VI* (Cambridge U.P., 1971–), but a more manageable initial guide is provided by J. Annas' chapter 'Classical Greek philosophy' in Boardman-Griffin-Murray 1991. The educatonal aspect of the philosophers' activity is described in H. I. Marrou, *A history of education in antiquity* (Sheed and Ward, 1956), part I. Military changes and practices are documented in H. W. Parke, *Greek Mercenary Soldiers* (Clarendon Press, 1933, and reprints: fundamental), in J. K. Anderson, *Military theory and practice in the age of Xenophon* (California U.P., 1970), and in J. G. P. Best, *Thracian peltasts and their influence on Greek warfare* (Groningen, 1969). Mercenaries are also discussed in ch. 4 of McKechnie 1989 (IX above). For Sicily M. I. Finley, *History of Sicily* (Chatto and Windus, 1968), chs. 5–7, and B. H. Warmington, *Carthage* (Hale 1960: Penguin, 1964), are supplemented by the more detailed accounts in L. J. Sanders, *Dionysius I of Syracuse and Greek tyranny* (Croom Helm, 1987) and in B. Caven, *Dionysius I warlord of Sicily* (Yale U.P., 1990).

XI. Athens and Thebes after 380

Full-length separate studies of each are J. Buckler, *The Theban hegemony 371–362 BC.* (Harvard U.P., 1980) and J. Cargill, *The second Athenian League: Empire or free alliance?* (U. of California P., 1981), the latter usefully complemented by G. T. Griffith, 'Athens in the fourth century' in Garnsey and Whittaker 1978 (see V above), ch. 6. P. Cartledge, *Agesilaos* (ch. VIII above) is also helpful, while the diplomatic interchanges are explored by T. T. B. Ryder, *Koine Eirene* (Oxford U.P., 1965), and Sir F. Adcock and D. J. Mosley, *Diplomacy in Ancient Greece* (Thames and Hudson, 1975).

XII. Athenian Society in the Fourth Century

The most useful single portrait of fourth-century Athens remains that of N. R. E. Fisher, *Social values in classical Athens* (Dent, 1976), with annotated source material in translation preceded by a lengthy introduction.

Study of Athenian law has moved away from the static presentation in A. R. W. Harrison, *The Law of Athens, I: The family and property* (Clarendon Press, 1968) and II: *Procedure* (Clarendon Press, 1971). Other systematic accounts are by D. M. MacDowell, *Athenian homicide law in the age of the orators* (Manchester U.P., 1963) and *The law in classical Athens* (Thames and Hudson, 1978), by E. E. Cohen, *Ancient Athenian maritime courts* (Princeton U.P., 1973) and by D. Cohen, *Theft in Athenian Law* (München, 1983), but the tendency is now to see law not as an autonomous system but as one social mechanism among others. See R. Osborne, 'Law in action in classical Athens', *Journal of Hellenic Studies* 105 (1985), 40–58; S. C. Humphreys, 'Kinship patterns in the Athenian courts', *Greek Roman and Byzantine Studies* 27 (1986), 57–91; P. Cartledge, P. Millett, and S. Todd (eds), *Nomos: Essays in Athenian law, politics and society* (Cambridge U.P., 1991); and D. Cohen, *Law, sexuality and society: the enforcement of morals in classical Athens* (Cambridge U.P., 1991).

For cult and religious life, H. W. Parke, *Festivals of the Athenians* (Thames and Hudson, 1976) supplements the titles listed in II above.

The local communities of Attica are studied by R. Osborne, *Demos: the discovery of classical Attika* (Cambridge U.P., 1985) and D. Whitehead, *The demes of Attika 508/7–c. 259 BC.* (Princeton U.P., 1986). The non-local community of the resident alien is sketched in D. Whitehead, *The ideology of the Athenian metic* (Cambridge Philological Society, 1977).

Athenians' discovery – or creation – of their past is treated by N. Loraux, *The invention of Athens; The funeral oration in the classical city* (tr. A. Sheridan) (Harvard U.P., 1986), and R. Thomas, *Oral tradition and written record in classical Athens* (Cambridge U.P., 1989). The theme of literacy is also explored by E.A. Havelock, *The literate revolution in Greece and its cultural consequences* (Princeton U.P., 1962); F. D. Harvey, 'Literacy in the Athenian democracy', *Revue des études grecques* 79 (1966), 585–635; and W. V. Harris, *Ancient literacy* (Harvard U.P., 1989).

The debate about participation can be followed from A. H. M. Jones, *Athenian Democracy* (Blackwell, 1957) through M. H. Hansen, *The Athenian Ekklesia. A collection of articles 1976–1983* (Museum Tusculanum, 1983), and L. B. Carter,

The Quiet Athenian (Clarendon Press, 1986) to R. K. Sinclair, *Democracy and participation in Athens* (Cambridge U.P., 1988). Other forms of the distribution of power are discussed by J. K. Davies, *Wealth and the power of wealth in classical Athens* (Arno Press, 1981); P. J. Rhodes, 'Political activity in classical Athens', *Journal of Hellenic Studies* 106 (1986), 132–44; P. Millett, 'Patronage and its avoidance in classical Athens', in A. Wallace-Hadrill (ed), *Patronage in ancient society* (Routledge, 1989), 15–47; and R. Garland, 'Priest and power in classical Athens', in M. Beard and J. North (eds), *Pagan Priests* (Duckworth, 1990), 73–91.

Public and private financial structures are explored by M. I. Finley, *Studies in land and credit in Ancient Athens 500–200 BC*. (Rutgers U.P., 1952), by C. Mossé, *La fin de la démocratie athénienne* (P.U.F., Paris, 1962), by chapters in P. D. A. Garnsey, K. Hopkins and C. R. Whittaker (eds), *Trade in the ancient economy* (Chatto & Windus/Hogarth Press, 1983), and by P. Millett, *Lending and borrowing in ancient Athens* (Cambridge U.P., 1991).

The debate about the nature of the fourth-century democracy, broached in P. J. Rhodes, 'Athenian democracy after 403 BC', *Classical Journal* 75 (1979–80), 305–323, can be followed further in Ostwald 1986 and Ober 1989 (see IV above), in R. Sealey, *The Athenian Republic: democracy or the rule of law?* (Penn. State U.P., 1987), and in M. H. Hansen, *The Athenian democracy in the age of Demosthenes* (tr. J. A. Crook) (Blackwell, 1991), chs. 8 and 13.

XIII. The Opportunists

H. D. Westlake, *Thessaly in the fourth century BC* (Methuen, 1935) provides a further study of Iason, as does S. Hornblower, *Mausolus* (Clarendon Press, 1982) for Caria and S. M. Burstein, *Outpost of Hellenism; the emergence of Heraclea on the Black Sea*) (U. of California P., 1976) for Herakleia.

Sicily is well documented by H. D. Westlake, *Essays on the Greek historians and Greek history* (Manchester U.P., 1969), chs. 14–17: *ibid.*, *Timoleon and his relations with tyrants* (Manchester

U.P., 1952), and R. J. A. Talbert, *Timoleon and the revival of Greek Sicily 344–317 BC* (Cambridge U.P., 1974).

Two full accounts of Philip are J. R. Ellis, *Philip II and Macedonian Imperialism* (Thames and Hudson, 1976), and G. L. Cawkwell, *Philip of Macedon* (Faber and Faber, 1978), supplemented by the articles collected in S. Perlman (ed), *Philip and Athens* (Heffer, 1973), by M. B. Hatzopoulos and L. D. Loukopoulos (eds), *Philip of Macedon* (Heinemann, 1981), and by the more specialist study of J. Buckler, *Philip II and the Sacred War* (Brill, 1989).

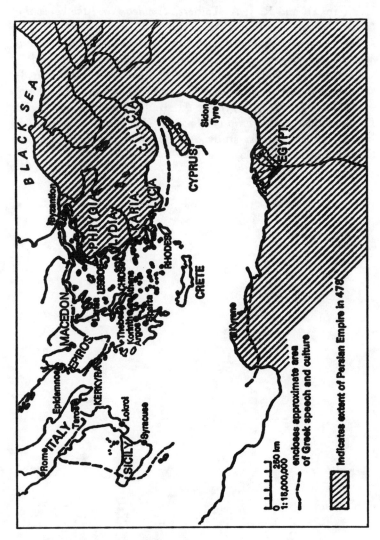

1. The Greek World and the Persian Empire

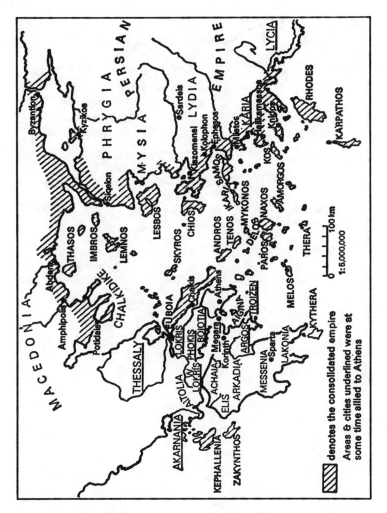

2. The Athenian Empire

3. Central Greece

4. Sicily and Southern Italy

5. Northern Greece and Macedonia

LESBOS

CHIOS

IKAROS

SAMOS

Smyrna

L Y D I A

Ephesos
Magnesia

Miletos

Iasos

Mylasa

Stratonikeia

Halikarnassos

C A R I A

P H R Y G I A

P I S I D I A

AMORGOS

KOS

Kaunos

P A M P H Y L I A

ASTYPALAIA

Knidos

Telmessos

Rhodes

L Y C I A

Kamiros

Ialysos

RHODES

KARPATHOS

KASOS

CRETE

0 20 40 60 80 100 120 140 km

1:4,000,000

6. South-Western Asia Minor

Index